STERLING
Test Prep

AP
Human Geography

Essential Review

3rd edition

www.Sterling–Prep.com

Copyright © 2021 Sterling Test Prep

3   2   1

ISBN-13: 978-1-9475563-6-2

Sterling Test Prep products are available at special quantity discounts for sales, promotions, academic counseling offices and other educational purposes.

Contact our sales department at: info@sterling–prep.com

Sterling Test Prep
6 Liberty Square #11
Boston, MA 02109

Congratulations on joining thousands of students using our study aids to achieve high test scores!

Scoring well on the AP exams is essential to earn placement credits and admission into a competitive college, which will position you for a successful future. This book prepares you to achieve a high score on the AP Human Geography exam by developing the ability to apply your knowledge and quickly choose the correct answer. Ability to apply reasoning skills to identify interconnected geographic concepts, interpret data, maps, and photographs, as well as an understanding of associated cultural, social, and economic outcomes are more effective skills than merely memorizing terms.

This book provides a thorough review of all topics tested on the AP Human Geography exam. The content covers the foundational principles and theories necessary to answer test questions. Instructors with years of teaching experience prepared this material by analyzing the AP Human Geography exam content and developing preparation material that builds your knowledge and skills crucial for success on the test. Our editorial team reviewed and systematized the content to ensure adherence to the current College Board AP Human Geography curriculum. Our editors are experts on preparing students for standardized tests and have coached thousands of undergraduate and graduate school applicants on test preparation and admission strategies.

The review content is clearly presented and systematically organized to provide you with a targeted preparation for AP Human Geography. You will learn the foundations and details of essential human geography topics needed to answer exam questions. By reading these review chapters thoroughly, you will learn important human geography concepts and the relationships between them. This will prepare you for the exam and significantly improve your AP score.

We wish you great success in your academics and look forward to being an important part of your successful test preparation!

Visit www.sterling-prep.com for more test prep resources.

201117gdx

Higher score money back guarantee!

Table of Contents

Table of Contents (*continued*)

We want to hear from you

Your feedback is important to us because we strive to provide the highest quality prep materials. Email us any comments or suggestions.

info@sterling–prep.com

Customer Satisfaction Guarantee

Contact us to resolve any issues to your satisfaction.

*We reply to all emails – **check your spam folder***

Thank you for choosing our products to achieve your educational goals!

AP Biology, Chemistry and Physics 1 & 2 online practice tests at
www.Sterling–Prep.com

Our advanced online testing platform allows you to take AP science practice questions on your computer to generate a Diagnostic Report for each test.

By using our online AP tests and Diagnostic Reports, you will:

- Assess your knowledge of topics tested on the AP exam

- Identify your areas of strength and weakness

- Learn important scientific topics and concepts

- Improve your test-taking skills

Book owners

Check the last page for special pricing access
to our online resources

AP prep books by Sterling Test Prep

- AP Chemistry Practice Questions
- AP Chemistry Review
- AP Physics 1 Practice Questions
- AP Physics 1 Review
- AP Physics 2 Practice Questions
- AP Physics 2 Review
- AP Biology Practice Questions
- AP Biology Review

- AP Psychology
- AP European History
- AP World History
- AP U.S. History
- AP U.S. Government and Politics
- AP Comparative Government and Politics
- AP Environmental Science

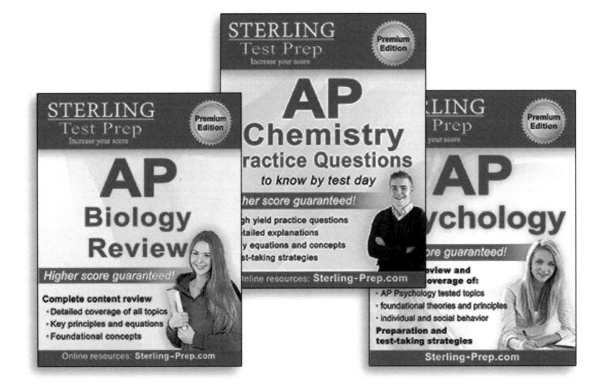

SAT Subject Test prep books by Sterling Test Prep

- SAT Chemistry Practice Questions

- SAT Chemistry Review

- SAT Biology Practice Questions

- SAT Biology Review

- SAT Physics Practice Questions

- SAT Physics Review

- SAT U.S. History

- SAT World History

AP Human Geography Preparation and Test-Taking Strategy

The AP Human Geography exam is designed to test analytical thinking skills; therefore, merely knowing the facts is not enough to succeed on the test. While knowing the facts and concepts is essential, critical thinking and the ability to link concepts together must be demonstrated to achieve a high score. Students must be competent in analyzing, applying, and evaluating information.

The exam challenges students to apply what they have learned to novel situations or combine concepts in nontraditional ways. In preparing for the AP Human Geography exam, several broad overarching strategies should be used, such as:

- extensively reading the course textbook(s);

- attending all class sessions;

- possessing a working knowledge of the geography, patterns, and migratory processes;

- familiarity with many of the historical events and significant developments that have shaped the world's populations;

- confidence in applying analytical skills and understanding the connections between concepts and ideas;

- appreciation of the founding principles that produce such knowledge; and

- commitment to least a few months of study time to prepare for the exam.

Multiple-Choice Questions Strategies

- Read all multiple-choice questions carefully. Do this before looking over the answer choices because it is essential to understand what the question asks.

- Rephrasing the question can help you understand what precisely the question asks. When rephrasing, make sure not to change the meaning of the question; assume it is direct and to the point.

- After selecting an answer, before marking the choice, quickly return to the question to ensure the selected choice answers the question.

- Be aware of the time and strive to spend no more than the average time required per question.

- Devote the allotted time first to questions you are more knowledgeable on and skip time-consuming questions on the first going through. This ensures that, if time runs out, you maximize the points for all the easy questions.

- If the correct answer is not immediately apparent, use the process of elimination. Eliminate as many choices as possible. Usually, there is at least one answer choice that is easily identified as wrong. Eliminating even one choice significantly increases the odds of selecting the correct one. After eliminating obviously incorrect choice(s), eliminate any answers that strike you as "almost right" or "half right." Consider "half right" as synonymous with "wrong" since these answers are purposely included.

- Leave no question unanswered as they lower your score since incorrect and skipped questions are weighed the same. Use guessing only as a last resort.

Free-Response Strategies

The free-response questions are representative of the varied content areas of the human geography and typically require students to process presented information into existing frameworks of understanding. There is a degree of personal choice in how to write the response.

Students might be required to present and discuss relevant examples, clarify or appraise geography principles, or perform a detailed analysis of social and cultural relationships and events. As with the multiple-choice section, the question may require to respond to stimulus materials (e.g., maps, charts, graphs).

- As with the multiple-choice section, it is crucial to understand what the question asks; any mental rephrasing should not add meaning. Assume the existing question, as it is written, is direct and to the point.

- You are not bound to answer the questions according to the order they are presented. Therefore, read all questions first and quickly decide which you are comfortable answering; answer all questions in the order of your comfort and competence level. This can avoid getting bogged down and frustrated, utilizing time more efficiently, and maximizing your points.

- Any additional work beyond the question's stated directives does not earn a higher score or result in extra credit. Therefore, for proper time management and keeping responses relevant, answer all questions in their entirety but avoid going further.

- Before writing, take a moment to brainstorm the questions' topics. Jot down notes or outline on scratch paper if this helps the composition process. This will help organize your thoughts, which leads to a more coherent response. Key definitions, ideas, examples, or names of significant individuals are often useful details to note.

- Keep track of your time and try to balance the brainstorming time and the time needed to write the response.

- If the reader cannot read your writing, it cannot be scored appropriately, so make an effort to write legibly. If you are a sloppy writer under pressure, practice essay writing under a time limit in advance of the test practice.

- A structured essay answer must contain complete sentences and paragraphs. Formal introduction and conclusion are not necessary, therefore go directly into answering the question.

- Write the sections of the essay in the order specified in the question. This ensures a grader-friendly structure, where they do not need to search for each criterion.

- It is important to answer questions in their entirety, not just partially. For example, some questions ask to both identify and explain. Performing only one of these steps is inadequate and will be graded accordingly. Listed below are the *task verbs* commonly used in the free-response questions – underline these directives as you see them. Refer to these required tasks and check them off when finished, so these are not overlooked when writing the response.

  Compare – provide a description or explanation of similarities or differences

  Define – provide a specific meaning for a word or concept

  Describe – provide the relevant characteristics of a specified concept

  Develop an argument – articulate a claim and support it with evidence

  Draw a conclusion – use available information to formulate an accurate statement that demonstrates understanding based on evidence

  Explain – provide information about how or why a relationship, process, pattern, position, situation, or outcome occurs, using evidence and reasoning. Explain "how" typically requires analyzing the relationship, process, pattern, position, situation, or outcome, whereas explaining "why" typically requires analysis of motivations or reasons for the relationship, process, pattern, position, situation, or outcome.

Identify – provide information about a specified topic without elaboration or explanation.

- Your written responses should include specific evidence and avoid unsubstantiated claims. Avoid long, meandering responses filled with loosely-related facts regarding specific concepts of phenomena, as well as contradictions, circular definitions, and question restatements.

- Present only relevant information that demonstrates the primary points of the argument clearly and concisely.

- All claims should be directly stated. You do not want the graders to infer or guess how something demonstrates a point. Regardless of whether they correctly guess your intentions or not, you will likely be graded more critically for ambiguities.

- As you proceed through the free-response section, if a mistake is made in the answer booklet, put a strikethrough through the error for the grader to disregard that portion.

- If all questions are completed and there is still time remaining, review each response. Assess if anything is needed to be added or requires correction. If content needs to be added, insert an asterisk (*) and refer the reader to the end of the essay. These thoughtful last-minute revisions can earn crucial points.

Chapter 1

Geography: Its Nature and Perspectives

Human geography is a discipline that emphasizes the importance of geography as a field of inquiry and engages the concept of spatial organization. Ascertaining the location of places, people and events can provide a rich understanding of complex environmental relationships and interconnections among places across landscapes.

In this chapter, geographic concepts such as location, space, place, the scale of analysis, pattern, regionalization, and globalization are parsed and analyzed in detail. Ways of understanding the basics of spatial interaction, spatial behavior, dynamics of human population growth and migration, patterns of culture, political control of territory, areas of agriculture production, changing the location of industry and economic strategies and evolving human settlement patterns are supplied. Through this, you will learn how map interpretation and use, as well as spatial data, applied mathematics and interpretation models, are deployed to gain a better spatial perspective and understanding of the world.

Consideration of the regional organization of various phenomena and encouraging graphic analysis to understand processes in an evolving world is also fostered. For example, geographic perspectives on the impact of human activities on the environment, from local to global scales, including effects on land, water, atmosphere, population, biodiversity and climate and explored. These human ecological examples are inherent, especially in topics dealing with population growth, agricultural and industrial practices, and rapid urbanization. This is intended to develop awareness of geographic methods and the relevance of geospatial technologies to a variety of situations (e.g., everyday life, planning, and public policy, professional decision making, problem-solving at scales from local to global).

Defining Geography

> **Geography, as a field of inquiry, looks at the world from a spatial perspective.**

Geography can be hard to define within the various families of academic disciplines; however, it is critical to understanding our world. Every event that has occurred has its history that has taken place in its own space; all history has a geographical element. Geography's contribution to science and society comes from the combined lenses through which geographers have perceived the settings surrounding them.

A small Anasazi dwelling lookout hole offers a view of the mountains of Colorado

Geographic information provides content for understanding spatial relationships and human-environment interaction.

To understand the outcomes of many events, geography works under the tenet "location matters," which ascribes an element to the equation that other disciplines might overlook. Geography hones in on the "real world" associations among events happening in a certain location and the relationships between different locations. For example, the influx of cultures, products, and people across areas creates distinctions, but it can also foster connections. There are "vertical" distinctions within an area, as well as "horizontal" connections between locations, both of which have their scale (in space and time) between them. This approach enables geographers to study the complexity of phenomena within and between areas that are usually assumed to be too theoretical by other disciplines.

Geography Concepts

Geography offers a set of concepts, skills and tools that facilitate critical thinking and problem solving.

The area in which a phenomenon takes place is in a sense a natural laboratory in which to study the processes within it. In this way, geographers can extract complex information that allows them to understand how a certain area relates to others, including how those relationships gave rise to the unique situation within the area in question.

Geographical concepts include location, place, scale, space, pattern, nature and society, networks, flows, regionalization, and globalization.

To understand the intricate, unique character of a location, the social, economic, political and environmental systems must be analyzed. Using this method, it has been shown that there are typical patterns of action individuals tend to follow in specific types of environments, and many of the distinguishing aspects of a location are the result of the cross-section of actions and the constraints that space imposes on those actions, helping to shape them. Such analysis is essential to both human and areal geography, and when it is applied to many locations, an understanding of geographic variability is fostered. To make a complete analysis of geographic variability, phenomena that occur between the boundaries of locations and connect them must be related, and scale must be taken into account as well.

A "place" is not only the measure of its internal distinctions but also the influx of individuals, materials (e.g., manufactured products, containment) and cultures from other areas. Such influxes create interdependencies among locations that are either reinforcing or diminishing diversity. For example, depending on how difficult it is to market and profit from crops, differing agricultural practices have emerged under similar environmental conditions. Macroscopically, the diversity of many cultures around the world has diminished slightly due to the influx of Western cultural values and economic systems. It is a central part of geography to understand such influxes and how they change places.

There are substantial difficulties in analyzing these influxes and what their impacts may be; these associations between places are nonlinear and complex, which is challenging to calculate and characterize. However, when it comes to science and decision making, they are becoming progressively more important.

There is a consensus amongst geographers that the scale with which an occurrence is observed at a place also matters. Geography encompasses both space and time with regard to scales. However, the lasting element of the geographic perspective is the importance of spatial scales, from a global perspective to a finely localized one.

For example, geographers understand that altering the spatial scale lends significant understanding of occurrences and provides insights into how those occurrences are connected at different scales. The "regionalization problem" (i.e., the issue of separating contiguous areas that share common physical features) has been an apprehension of geographers for some time. They understand that the demarcation and internal intricacy of geographic locations are dependent on the scale being used; therefore, they recognize that citing only a certain small group of regions is inherently partial and potentially an ambiguous illustration of geographical variation.

The geographic and temporal scope of a system can be best understood by identifying the scale at which a phenomenon demonstrates the greatest variation. For example, using temperature data that shows at which geographic scale there is the greatest variation in temperature can lead to an understanding about the relative impact of global circulation, microclimates and air masses on temperature patterns. A worldwide increase in average temperature could create many different alterations at local levels; it could even create a cooling effect in certain areas due to the interaction between global, regional and local patterns. Likewise, national and international political and economic processes can exhibit different effects with regard to the economic viability of cities and states. Using scale, geographers can study worldwide changes in local processes and vice versa.

Landscape analysis provides a context for understanding the location of people, places, regions and events; human-environment relationships; and interconnections between and among places and regions.

In geography, geomorphological research focuses on the study and forecast of Earth surface structure and processes. Due to both human and natural causes, the Earth's surface is in constant flux. This includes the movements of ice, waves, wind, and water and the changes brought about from volcanic and tectonic activity and even gravity.

Sea stacks, such as this Australian one, are the result of countless years of erosion.

Geomorphological research has emphasized the stability of landscapes and the balance between the forces of erosion and construction during most of the 20th century. However, in the past twenty years, the focus has shifted to distinguishing changes and the actions of surface systems. Either way, the method with which the research is done always incorporates the classification of mass and energy flows in a surface system and an analysis of the forces and resistances at play. It is a critical evaluation because, to foresee temporary changes (e.g., floods, landslides or coastal erosion from storms) or enduring changes (e.g., erosion from strip mining or land management), geomorphologists must understand the natural rates of change first.

Notes

Analysis in Geography

Geographic skills provide a foundation for analyzing world patterns and processes.

When seeking to comprehend the interconnected economic, political, social and cultural spheres, geographers focus on two kinds of questions: (a) how do those spheres contribute to the development of a certain area and (b) what are the special configurations and our comprehension of those spheres? In earlier geographical research, much of the focus was placed on localized decision making; spatial patterns and their development were understood regarding the cogent spatial decisions of individual participants.

Applications of spatial concepts to interpret and understand population and migration; cultural patterns and processes; political organization of space; agriculture, food production, and rural land use; industrialization and economic development; and cities and urban land use.

Starting with David Harvey, researchers began asking the question, "In what ways do social structures affect a person's behavior?" Recently, they began to wonder about the significance of cultural and political aspects about social change. This research culminated in the area of study known as a social theory, which posits working ideas to comprehend how space and place arbitrate the interconnections between individual behaviors and developing political, economic, cultural and social configurations, as well as how spatial arrangements are created through such interactions.

Both within and outside of geography, such research has earned a great deal of respect. Social research incorporates the concepts of space and place. Recent studies that involve both the development of places and the interdependencies among places showcase the impact of research that seeks to connect the ideas of space and place with social theory.

The scope of geographical research on the place is not bound only by modern events; researchers have focused on the development of places and regions for a long time. Those that have been involved with historical evolutions have aided the appreciation of past and present places, including explanations for the development of larger areas, studies of the shifting ethnic demographics of cities and identifying the role which capitalism has had in them. These analyses reach beyond traditional historical studies to show how the geographical circumstances and the qualities of places affect not only those areas but also the larger ideological and social structures.

Maps are used to represent and identify spatial patterns and processes at different scales.

Cartography, or the drawing of maps, has had a close connection to geography; it is one of the best examples of the importance of having a spatial dimension in geography's perspective. Following directly with the tenet that location matters, focusing on spatial representation complements and often compels research in other branches of geography. It is critical to society as a whole and geography itself that geographers analyze how to portray geographic space and understand how to define space in the context of advanced computers and telecommunications technology.

Geographers have some methods for spatial illustration to study space and place at many different scales. These methods for geographic spatial illustration are linked to a group of fundamental spatial concepts, including region, scale, change, location, distribution and spatial interaction, that determine how geographers illustrate the phenomena they perceive.

Before geography was an academic discipline, a visual representation of geographic space using maps was the key to solving many geographic questions. However, maps are not the only visual element used in geographic research.

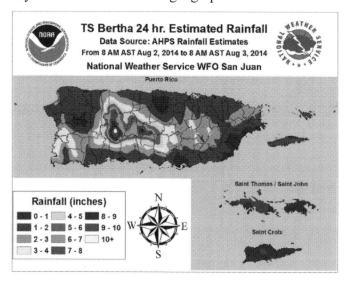

Precipitation map indicating the estimated rainfall in Puerto Rico and the U.S. Virgin Islands for an anticipated hurricane's passage

During the past thirty years, cartography has changed dramatically, primarily due to the proliferation of computers. Novel types of geographic visualization have been made possible by computers, such as animated or interactive maps and maps that are customized for a user's needs. These digitized maps have made new approaches for scientific visualization and spatial data study possible.

Types of Maps

Maps may be defined either as drawings or pictures of Earth's surface features (e.g., political or national boundaries, landforms, bodies of water and urban locations) or be thematic in nature to focus on specific questions (e.g., the distribution of a specific disease in a region or how much rainfall a certain area of a country has received). Thematic maps like these are becoming increasingly relevant with the growing use of Geographic Information Systems (GIS).

Geographers use a variety of maps, each with their topic and reason for consulting them. Below is a list of the major map types, what they are and an example of each.

Political Map: These maps focus on national and state boundaries. Depending on the level of detail with which the map was made, they may include the locations of major cities as well as smaller ones, but they do not showcase topographical information. A map of the United States that shows the boundaries of its 50 states and its international borders with Canada and Mexico is an example of a political map.

Physical Map: These maps focus on the physical features of an area (e.g., mountains, rivers, and lakes). Water is always printed in blue, whereas elevation fluctuations such as mountains are typically represented by different colors (usually green represents lower elevations, and higher elevations move from orange to dark brown). A map showing the state of Hawaii, with its various elevations, coastlines and rivers is an example of a physical map.

Topographical Map: These maps show physical features of an area, similar to a physical map. However, unlike a physical map (which uses colors), they differentiate between features by using contour lines. To show elevation fluctuations, contour lines are typically spaced at regular intervals (e.g., having each contour illustrate a 100-foot (30 meters) change in elevation, and where the terrain is highest, the lines will be closest together). For example, a map indicating the mountains of Mauna Loa and Kilauea on

Hawaii would possess tight contour lines to signify the high elevation of these areas and sparse contour lines for the lowlands beneath.

Climate Map: These maps display the particular climate of a region (e.g., climate zones based on temperature, snowfall of an area or the average number of rainy days). Differentiations are typically represented by using colors. A map showing the differences in the average temperature in the Victoria and Outback regions of Australia would be an example of a climate map.

Economic or Resource Map: These maps use symbols or colors to showcase differences in certain types of economic activity or natural resources available in a region. A map that used colors to represent the varied agricultural products of Brazil, letters to differentiate natural resources and symbols for different industries would be an example of an economic or resource map.

Road Map: These maps illustrate highways and roads and, depending upon the detail, can include the location of airports, cities, and landmarks like monuments and campsites. This type of map is one of the most popular. Typically, major highways are red in color and are often printed larger than other roads; lesser roads are generally a lighter color and printed using narrower lines. A map of San Francisco that shows its major highways in red, its minor routes in a lighter red and its city streets in grey would be an example of a road map.

Thematic Map: These maps focus on a certain topic or theme and do not usually contain features included in the abovementioned maps such as natural features, political divisions, elevations or highways. However, if they do show some of these characteristics, they are theme-specific (i.e., only meant as a reference point regarding the particular topic covered by the map). A map illustrating the population change of Canada in certain areas from 1996-2001 would be a thematic map, as it has a theme or special topic (note, however, that such an example would include a political map as its base, showing Canada's provincial borderlines to give it context).

There are three main purposes that thematic maps have:

1) To provide specific information about locations;
2) To provide general information about spatial patterns; and
3) To compare patterns on two or more maps.

All map projections inevitably distort spatial relationships.

Generally, the Earth is thought of as a sphere, but it is more accurate to think of it as a spheroid or ellipsoid. A scaled down model of the Earth is a globe, and while globes can illustrate the shape, distance, and size of many large features on the planet, they are not realistic for many purposes. For one, they are not easily transportable and are difficult to store (e.g., a student could not simply put a globe in their backpack). Another difficulty is that they are not practical at larger scales, such as when someone needs directions through his or her city. A third is that globes are expensive to make, particularly in varying scales. Lastly, the curved surface of a globe makes measuring a landscape very difficult, and it is not possible to see large areas of the Earth at once for comparison.

Because maps do not have the above limitations, they are generally more useful than globes. Cartographers have attempted to confront the difficulty in representing the Earth's spherical shape on a flat map; for this, they have developed map projections. A *map projection* uses mathematical equations to depict the curved surface of the Earth (or just a section of it) on a two-dimensional surface. To accomplish this, cartographers take the angular geographic coordinates that refer to specific locations on the curved Earth (longitude and latitude) and convert them into Cartesian coordinates that refer to the positions shown on a flat map (*x* and *y*).

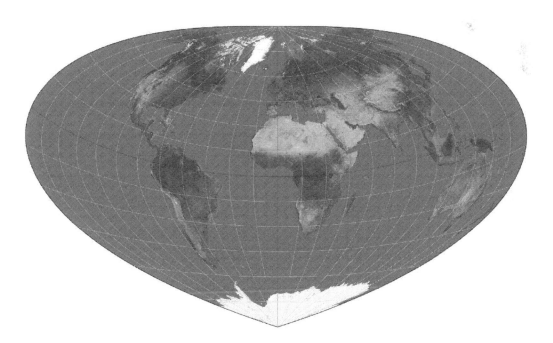

The Bottomley projection, created in 2003, is a less-commonly encountered map.

One method of categorizing map projections is by determining the kind of developable surface that the reference sphere is being projected onto. A *developable surface* is a geometric shape that can be spread out onto a flat surface without needing to stretch it or without it ripping. The developable surface provides three examples of how the flattening of a spherical object onto a plane is done: a cylinder, a cone, and a plane. Their corresponding projections are called *cylindrical*, *conical* and *planar*, respectively. It should be noted that while geometric processes are used for some projections, most utilize mathematical equations to convert coordinates to a flat surface from a globe. In most cases, the resultant map plane can be placed around a globe in the form of a cone, cylinder, or in the case of a plane, put to the side of a globe.

Spherical objects like globes can show shape, size, directions, and distance of Earth's features with practical precision. It is not possible to flatten out any spherical object (e.g., an onion layer) onto a two-dimensional surface without it tearing or stretching or having to trim some of it off. Likewise, if one tries to project a spherical object like the Earth onto a map (flat), its curved surface becomes distorted, making deformations of the shape (angle), direction, area or distance of the features. Therefore, all projections will cause a varying degree of deformation; there is no ideal way to ensure that all of the features of the spherical object (the Earth) will not be compromised. The solution is to use a projection that compromises the least regarding a certain purpose.

Projections can be made for varying purposes. With a particular purpose in mind, projections can be made to reduce deformities at the expense of the deformation of others. Factors such as what the map will be used for, what area is being studied and, because smaller scaled mapping increases distortion, what scale is needed are things to be considered when choosing a projection for a map.

Mathematical formulas and graphs are used to analyze rates of natural increase in population doubling time, the rank-size rule for cities and distance-decay functions.

Population geography is a subset of human geography and relies on the application of varying mathematical formulas and graphical representations to convey information. It analyzes how the nature of places is related to spatial fluctuations in the migration, growth, composition, and distribution of populations. It is demography (e.g., birth and death rates, income) from a geographical viewpoint and focuses on the features of population distributions that are altered in the context of space. Population density maps can showcase some examples of population geography.

Choropleth, isocline and dot maps are examples of maps that represent the spatial arrangement of a population. Population geography examines:

- demographic observations (e.g., mortality and growth rates, both spatially and temporally);
- population increases and decreases;
- the movements and mobility of populations;
- occupational structure; and
- how places respond to population changes (e.g., immigration).

Key formulas used in population geography to interpret population data and recognize trends are:

Rate of natural increase

The rate of natural increase (RNI), in demographics, is an equation used to arrive at the crude birth rate. High RNIs are usually present in developing countries, while developed countries usually show slightly negative, neutral or low RNIs. RNIs are expressed as a percentage.

Rate of Natural Increase (RNI) = [Birth Rate - Death Rate] × 100

Doubling time

Doubling time is the amount of time it takes for a given quantity to double in size or value at a constant growth rate. Researchers can find the doubling time for a population undergoing exponential growth by using the Rule of 70. To do this, they divide 70 by the growth rate (RNI).

Note: growth rate (RNI) must be entered as a whole number and not a decimal. For example, 5% must be entered as 5 instead of 0.05.

Doubling Time (DT) = 70 / RNI

For example, a population with a 2% annual growth would have a doubling time of 35 years:

Doubling Time = 70 / 2.0 = 35 years

Geographers use models as generalizations to think systematically about topics such as land use, industrial location and the distribution of settlements.

After WWII, many changes have occurred in geographic methodology, geographic thought and even how to define geography.

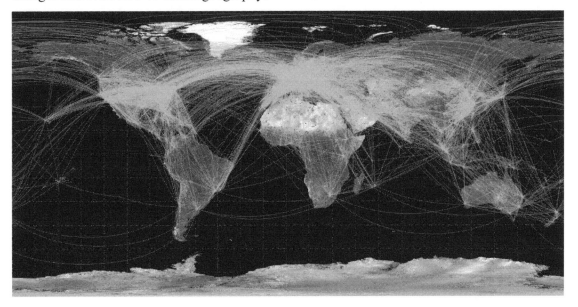

Map indicating scheduled airline traffic

In the past few decades, geographers have been more focused on the theme of geographic generalization (i.e., making models, general laws and theories) to have geography contend with other scientific disciplines. This sort of geographic generalization is also called "model-building."

Hypotheses, models, and theories are used to analyze the subject of geography (i.e., the complicated intermingling of humanity and the environment). It is a fundamental part of all models to simplify a complicated system to make it easier to comprehend and therefore study; they are the tools that facilitate the testing of theories. Models can also be thought of as extrapolative tools; however, that is a somewhat limiting viewpoint.

There are hard and fast laws and theories that exist in physical, biological and social science, and geographers have the desire to create such rules for their discipline as well. However, except in a general way, making a model for the incredibly intricate, interconnected system of all humanity and their environment is not feasible.

Therefore, making geographical models is done because:

1. When it comes to quantifying or finding an actual measurement of phenomena that usually cannot be seen or may be unobservable, using a model may be the only way to do so. This is because models assist in simulations, forecasts, approximations and the generation of information. The extent of cropping, utilization of land, projections of population growth, density and migration, urbanization, industrialization and the expansion of slums can be foreseen by referencing such models. Models are also helpful in predicting the weather, alterations in climate or sea levels, land formations, soil and forest reduction, and environmental pollution.

2. Geographical systems can be described, analyzed and simplified with the assistance of models. Models can be used to help comprehend and foresee the evolution of landmasses, patterns of migration, how agricultural land is zoned and used and to develop location-based theories of industries.

3. Much geographical information comes in, and it is becoming more and more difficult to comprehend. By filtering patterns and relationships, models can be used to help organize, analyze, explore and structure all that information.

4. Not all systems worth observing can be observed directly so that alternative models can be used as a substitute. These models can be used for creating evolution and endgame scenarios of a system in question and also for approximating the consequences of anticipated changes made to certain parts of a system.

5. Models assist in expanding the comprehension of causal mechanisms, the environment and the relationship between micro and macro features of systems.

6. Theoretical ideas can be represented and have their empirical legitimacy scrutinized by the frameworks provided by models.

7. By using models, geographers and social scientists can in a sense "speak the same language," as social scientists (and other disciplines) use them as well.

8. Models assist in developing theories and general and special laws.

The core features of a model are:

1. Humanity's relationship with the environment and the inherent geographical features of the Earth's surface are complicated. Therefore, models tend to pertain to a selective area or piece of information to be studied; they do not try to encompass all the cultural and physical aspects, both micro and macro, of an area.

2. Some features are distorted or obscured in a model, while some features are highlighted.

3. Within each model, there is an inherent method of simplification being used; forecasts of real-world events can be made with the assistance of models, as mentioned above.

4. Models are not the same as reality; they are analogous or corresponsive.

5. Hypotheses can be formed through models, and they can assist in generalization.

6. Conclusions can be made by the way in which models showcase real-world features in a more simplified, observable, accessible, familiar and easily-categorized or controlled way.

7. Data can be outlined by models, where they can then be classified, brought together and assembled.

8. Models assist in optimizing the amount of information that can be extracted from available data.

9. How certain phenomena occur can be clarified by models.

10. Models give the ability to compare certain uncommon phenomena with more common ones.

11. Certain groups of large or complicated phenomena can be imagined and understood with the help of models.

12. Models act as a vehicle towards the development of theories and laws.

The list of models that geographers have designed, adopted and applied are:

The *scale model* (also called "hardware model") is one of the easiest types of model to comprehend because it reproduces reality directly, albeit (usually) on a much smaller scale. Scale models can either be stationary (e.g., a land surface model with geological features) or dynamic (e.g., a wave tank). Of the two, the dynamic model is more useful in geological research because its operative processes can be manipulated, allowing variables to be studied individually.

Scale model of Paris

In *simulation models*, the operative process is replicated by way of creating an equivalent situation or operation, particularly for study or training purposes. In *stochastic models*, the operative process is not foreseen as precisely as in simulation models, but instead, phenomena are studied statistically by way of some random probability distribution or pattern.

Mathematical models are harder to construct, but they are thought to be more dependable. They do not rely on human standards, normative questions, and approaches but instead have symbolic representations of a verbal or arithmetical nature in rational terms.

Analogue models use an entirely different feature as an analogy for comparison. They use a more well-known or better-understood process to compare to (and parallel study) a less understood one. This differs from other models that attempt to emulate the reality of a subject as best they can. An analogue model's value is dependent on a researcher's ability to see a shared element between the two phenomena. The shared element is called the positive analogy. The element that is not common between the two is the negative analogy, and the irrelevant is called the neural analogy (both of which are ignored). Historically, reasoning from analogy has long been a part of geographical research. In his major work published in 1795, James Hutton saw the analogy between the circulation of blood in the body and a similar circulation of matter in both the growth and decomposition of landscapes.

Certain models are developed towards the study of certain concepts.

Johann Heinrich von Thünen was not a geographer but a German landowner. In the first volume of his essay "The Isolated State" (1826), Thünen came up with the first real management of spatial economics and economic geography and related it to the theory of rent. It is not the pattern of land use that is important here but his analytical approach.

Thünen came up with the basics of the theory of marginal productivity in a way that was mathematically rigorous, the formula for which follows:

$$R = Y(p - c) - Y\,Fm$$

where R = land rent; Y = yield per unit of land; c = production expenses per unit of commodity; p = market price per unit of commodity; F = freight rate (per agricultural unit, per mile); m = distance to market.

Thünen's model of farmland was developed before industrialization occurred in Germany, and it made the following simplifying postulations:

- the city is centrally located inside of an "Isolated State";
- the wilderness environs the Isolated State;
- there are no mountains or rivers, and the land is entirely flat;
- there are a constant climate and soil quality;
- farmers of the Isolated State move their products across the land via an oxcart, right to the central city to market since there aren't any roads; and
- to optimize profits, the framers behave rationally.

What use a section of land has is a factor of the expense to move the products to market and the rent a farmer can afford to pay for the land (figured by yield, which is constant in this example).

If a model were to be generated in four concentric rings of farming activity, dairying and intensive farming would sit closest to the city because fruit, vegetables, milk, and other dairy products have to get to the market quickest.

In the second ring would be firewood and timber for burning materials and fuel because it is very heavy (difficult to transport) and also because it is vital for cooking and heating.

Located in the third ring away from the city would be the large, expansive crops such as grain because they last longer in transport than fruits would and are lighter than wood.

In the final and most distant ring from the city would be land allocated for ranching because animals are self-transporting (i.e., they can be walked to the central city for butchering or sale as is).

After these four rings are the wilderness, which is much too far from the central city for any agricultural product to be transported.

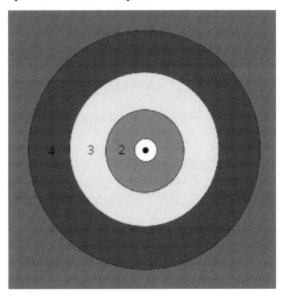

Thünen's land use model: the center black dot is a city; the central circle is land for dairy and market gardening; circle 2 - forest for fuel; circle 3 - grains and field crops; circle 4 - ranching; the area outside the circles represents wilderness where agriculture is not profitable.

In 1980, geographers Ernest Griffin and Larry Ford came up with a generalized model to explain the structure of cities in Latin America. This development came about after they concluded that particular patterns were being followed in the organization of many cities there. Their generalized model states that Latin American cities are established around a "core business district" (CBD). Surrounded by houses of the elite is a commercial spine that comes directly out of the CBD. This is then surrounded by three concentric areas of housing that decreases in value the farther one moves from the CBD.

During the colonial period, the structure of many developing Latin American cities was determined by a group of laws issued by Spain called the Laws of the Indies. These laws regulated the economic, political and social organization of Spain's colonies that were not in Europe; they "mandated everything from the treatment of the Indians to the width of the streets." According to the Laws of the Indies, colonial cities were directed to be built with a grid pattern around a central plaza.

Griffin and Ford, while studying these Latin American cities' organizational patterns, came up with a model to describe their arrangement that can also be used to understand nearly all large cities of Latin America. This model represents most cities having one privileged residential area, a centralized business area, and a commercial spine; these districts are then encircled by areas of lower and lower residential quality the farther one goes from the CBD.

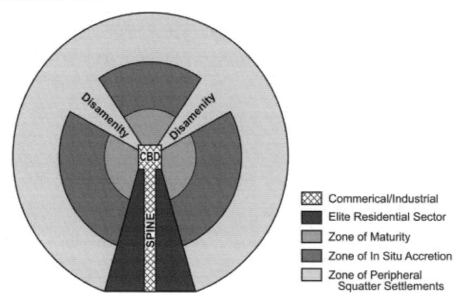

Latin American city structure model by Griffin and Ford

The foundations of modern location theories are said to have been established in Alfred Weber's work in 1909. A fundamental idea of his is that firms choose locations based on minimizing their costs. To calculate this requires a number of generalizations, including that location, is assumed to be within a region with no external influences (isolated) and has a singular market, the area has no real variance in transport costs other than those related to distance (isotropic) and the markets are within a specific number of centers. These conditions are comparable to Von Thünen's model of agricultural land use that was developed nearly one hundred years before Weber.

Within Weber's model, perfect competition is assumed, meaning that there would be many small firms to prevent monopolies and oligopolies and many customers for them. For both customers and suppliers, there would be a perfect understanding of market conditions. It is assumed that natural resources like water are readily available, and production necessities like fuel, labor, and materials would be at least available in specific areas. In Weber's theory, there are three main factors to take into account when determining an optimal industrial location: labor costs, transport costs, and agglomeration economies.

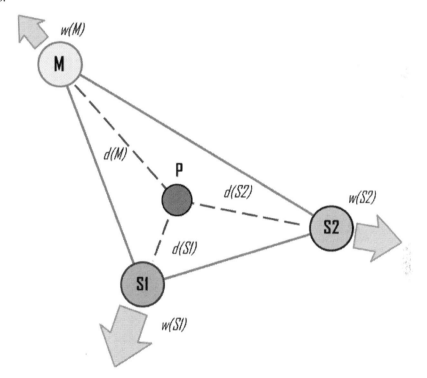

Weber uses the location triangle within which the optimal is located. The above figure illustrates the issue of minimizing transport costs. Considering a product of w(M) tons to be sold at market M, w(S1) and w(S2) tons of materials coming respectively from S1 and S2 are necessary. The problem resides in finding an optimal factory location P located at the respective distances of d(M), d(S1) and d(S2).

Geographical issues include problems related to human-environmental interactions; conflict and cooperation among countries; and planning and public-policy decision making.

As one of its themes, geography explores human-environment interactions, looking at the relationships between people and their environment, how populations adapt to their environment and how they change it.

When analyzing human-environment interaction, the community and the culture at large are studied, rather than the individuals. This means that human-environment interaction studies the relationship between social systems and the macro ecosystem. Within this interplay, geographers look at methods of sustainable agriculture.

The production of materials, animals, and food that uses conservationist farming methods for future use is called *sustainable agriculture*. Sustainable agriculture has become increasingly important as the human population has grown exponentially and resources have gotten scarcer. A food crisis would be possible without regard for the future of the environment. Up until industry was brought to the agricultural process, farming was comparatively sustainable. However, through industrialization, genetically modified foods, poisonous pesticides, poor animal treatment, and resource exploitation have become the norm, all of which have consequences for the environment.

The overuse of soil leaves it drained of minerals and unavailable for further use. Water is also overused and leaves reservoirs tapped, some of which even adds to runoff and enters the drinking supply. Animals are raised in unhealthy environments, which contribute to the unhealthiness of the people who eat them.

Sustainable agriculture practices are aimed at stopping these issues. Artificial growth hormones, fertilizers, and pesticides are taken out of the agricultural process. Where the norm is for a farm to raise one kind of crop, sustainable agricultural practices are to grow more than one crop per farm so that crop rotation is possible, which allows for one crop to restore nutrients that the other has depleted during its growing season. Water sustainability requires analyses of water sources so that they are not being used at a rate faster than they are being renewed. In sustainable agriculture, livestock is cage-free and graze on the land in which they live. The philosophy of sustainability goes beyond the production of food to include the fair treatment of farm workers and ensures that crop prices are such that farmers have an income they can live on.

Among the many critiques of sustainable agriculture, some claims are that it increases land use and results in small crop yield. It is also said that committing to sustainable agriculture is likely to result in food shortages for a growing world population (expected to be 8 billion by 2030). However, recent studies suggest that over time sustainably farmed land could produce just as much as conventional industrial farms.

Human geography also encompasses why certain populations unified, organized and divided up specific regions of the Earth. Both cooperation and destruction have been the result of the competition for land, which is a universal tendency among all societies. Earth's surface is separated into formal and informal political, economic and cultural interest groups (continuing conflicts over human migration, resettlement, trade, religions and ideologies and the exploitation of land and sea environments).

Patterns and processes at different scales reveal variations in and different interpretations of data.

Scales are necessary for human geography because certain phenomena that are traditionally studied in isolation need to be interrelated. These include, for example, global, national, regional and local economic operations and their political consequences. This need comes in part due to globalization.

The correct application of scale for a certain process is debated upon in geography, as it is in many other scientific disciplines. However, is it agreed that altering the scale which one uses changes the relevant variables. Also, the significance of a phenomenon in a certain area is typically motivated by causal processes that operate at different scales. Models that forecast migration patterns usually use regionally-gathered information or groups; often, variables related to labor demand, the business and investment climate and income are included in this data (i.e., group variables or "structural-contextual" variables). In intra-urban models, age, income, education, kinship, and other affinities are often included.

Distance and status can also be useful data to include in a model; however, at this scale most variables define individuals. When modeling and preparing water supply networks for developing countries, national-scale studies usually incorporate urban and regional demands for water. On the scale of the village, however, distances to a spigot and walking time are of the most concern. That is to say, measures about the individual or family will take the place of collective variables at the group and regional level.

There are apparent patterns in the defining characteristics of populations such as ethnicity, age, race, sex, and rural-urban allocations. What comprises a population provides insight into current conditions within it and also what the possibility is for change in the future. An investigation into the distribution of age and sex within a population, for example, illustrates a demographic narrative (past, present, future) about that location.

A population pyramid can be used to graphically represent the age and gender makeup of a population by showing the percentage of the total population that are in each age group and are of each sex. Pyramid graphs are often used to demonstrate how populations evolve at different demographic and economic stages. An example would be how the broad base of Ethiopia's pyramid represents the country's high fertility rate of 7.0, with 46% of the population being under the age of 15. From the economic conditions related to the high dependency ratio (i.e., the consequence of such a large population under the age of 15), inferences can be drawn about potential future growth. The near column-like pyramid of Spain is in contrast to this, and it represents the country's more stabilized demographic circumstances.

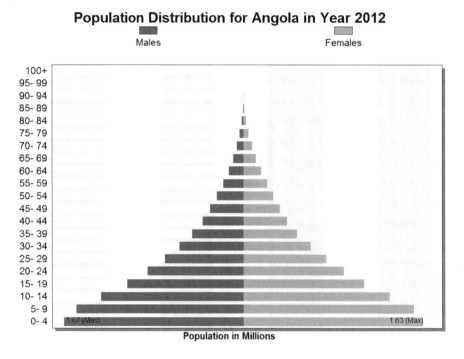

Pyramid graph indicating the 2012 age demographics of Angola

Pyramids may also represent the historical demographics of a country. A series of pyramids for the U.S. from the mid-1950s to the present day, for example, would reflect the baby-boom generation as it progressed to middle age and the "echo" generation that followed. A pyramid for Germany in the 20th century would reflect the two world wars and its post-war baby boom.

Using pyramids at smaller scales, one can compare various states; pyramid graphs for Florida and Utah, for example, could show how varied the U.S. population is. It could be shown with a pyramid that Florida has a median age of 37.6 years, while Utah's is only 26.8 years. The changing demographics from a metropolis to smaller towns to more rural areas can be studied by applying an even smaller scale to a pyramid graph. Population pyramids are important tools for demographic studies; however, geographers only use them for deduction, not as a direct answer to a question.

Population density is usually a measurement of living organisms; however, it can be used for anything physical. It is typically expressed as organisms or items per unit area.

According to this definition, however, population density is a figure contingent on the area measured and cannot be used as something constant to apply to an area over time. If the organisms or items measured are modeled as distinct points on a graph, the population density would change as the periphery of the area in question moved over individuals. There are problems with even modeling those individuals as spatially extended, as the scale of the area in question draws nearer to the scale of the object (e.g., if a home were to be considered the scale of a person, this could be a large area for some and a much smaller area for others).

To rectify some of these issues, population density can be viewed as a scale-dependent fractal quantity (like coastline distance). For human populations, population density is expressed as the number of persons per unit of area. The unit of area may include or exclude inland water (e.g., lakes), it may also only specifically reflect livable, inhabited, productive (or potentially productive) or cultivated land.

Human population density is often measured in persons/sq mile (or sq kilometer or hectare). This number is easily calculated by dividing the number of people by the land in question in square miles (or km or ha).

Human population density is often calculated for a country, county, city or even the entire world. For the country, the density is based on land area, not inland water. However, the list of countries in order of population density is based on total area, which includes inland water.

Macau, Monaco, Hong Kong, Singapore, and Gibraltar are the countries or territories with the highest population densities. This is due to these areas being comprised of a small stretch of land with a very high level of urbanization. They have economically specialized city populations that utilize rural resources outside of that area, revealing the distinction between high population density and overpopulation.

Bangladesh, where 134 million people live in a highly agricultural area, is the most densely populated larger state, with a population density more than 900 persons/km^2. The world population density currently averages 42 persons/km^2 overall.

The extent to which cities with high population densities are "overpopulated" depends on infrastructure, quality of housing and access to resources. While African Cairo and Lagos fall into the category of the largest densely-populated cities, most are located in southern and eastern Asia.

The definition of an urban area itself is important for interpreting city population. Technically, densities will be higher in cities that exclude recently-developed suburbs or are altered in the cases of agglomeration or "metropolitan area," where the latter often includes cities around a larger one.

Regions are defined by one or more unifying characteristics or patterns of activity.

Region is a human-created concept used to analyze and interpret the complexity of the Earth's surface. The meaning of regions, their physical and human characteristics and how geographers use and analyze regions to interpret and organize the Earth's surface is an important concept of human geography. Understanding this concept is essential to put environments, places, and people into their proper spatial contexts.

A region is defined as an area with distinct and cohesive features that set it apart from other (though possibly contiguous) areas. Boundaries of regions come from a set of criteria based on the presence or absence of certain physical and human characteristics, and they can vary in scale from global to local, be mutually exclusive or overlie, or be located within a hierarchy (e.g., counties, states, countries) and encompass the entire world or only certain parts of it.

There are three kinds of regions recognized by geographers. A *formal region* is characterized by shared human property (e.g., a common language, nationality, religion, culture or political identity) or a shared physical property such as a type of vegetation, climate or landform. Examples of formal regions are the Corn Belt, the Rocky Mountain region and Latin America.

The second type of region is a *functional region*. Functional regions are centralized around a node or focal point, with adjacent areas connected by communication or transport systems or other relationships such as retail and manufacturing trading. The focal point of the north-central region of the U.S. in Chicago, with its railways, highways, airport, telecommunications, and Great Lakes shipping.

The *perceptual region* is the third type of region that is based upon shared human attitudes and feelings about an area. It is the subjective view of people that defines a perceptual region, and so they may not have conventional regional features and names (or even strict borders). Examples of perceptual regions are Dixie, the Riviera, Southern California (SoCal) and the Australian Outback.

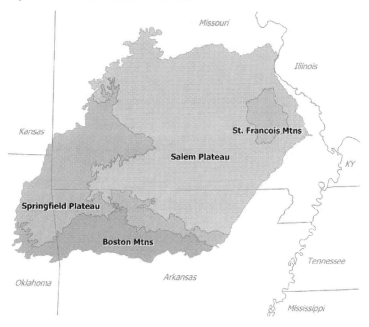

The Ozarks: a cultural, architectural, linguistic and geographic region of the U.S.

All regions, regardless of type, shift as the physical and human characteristics of the Earth's surface change. Therefore, with economic globalization, interactions between trading regions will change as people and capital move to benefit from the shifting prospects. With climate change, biome and ecosystem patterns will be altered as well.

World regions are defined by the maps in the course curriculum section of the AP Human Geography Course Description.

The following maps present world regions covered in AP Human Geography course. Some regions overlap and/or have transitional zones between them.

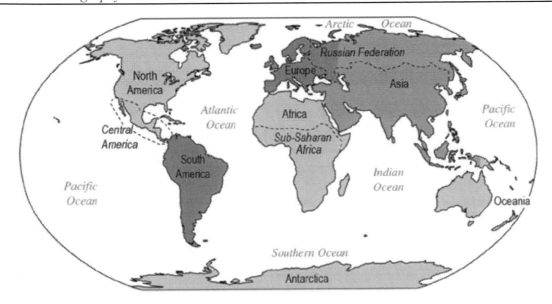

World regions: the big picture

World regions: a closer look

World regions may overlap and often have transitional boundaries.

Some regions are defined by their specific cultures, while others are based on the physical geography or physiographic features. Often there is no consensus among geographers as to where the boundaries of regions should be. For example, since both countries were once part of the Soviet Union, one geographer might place Armenia and Azerbaijan in Central Asia, while another might say they were more appropriately labeled as part of the Middle East. Another discrepancy is that some geographers label the same region as either Southwest Asia or the Middle East.

Regional thinking is applied at local, national and global scales.

Despite the conventionally-held belief that regions (and the terms used to signify them) were created and termed in the past, regionalization is an ever-occurring process and is malleable to current mental constructs. Regional thinking (i.e., regionalization) at the local, national and global scales is a constant act of interpreting and defining involving both geographers and non-geographers alike. For example, Hell's Kitchen, a Manhattan neighborhood less known as Clinton or Midtown West, carries varying accounts of how it received its name. Authoritative sources attribute the name to a variety of stories ranging from a derogatory comment made by Davy Crockett about Irish immigrants, incorrectly attributed to a neighborhood that he was not directly referencing, to community references made of a similarly named tenement building, local gang, and even a dive bar. Regardless of the true origins of the name, regional thinking processes shaped the identity and perceived borders of the neighborhood.

Regionalism refers to a group's perceived identification with a particular region on any scale.

It is people's life experiences and cultural upbringing that form the perceptions of places and regions; they are the foundation of how someone understands a place's importance, scope, characteristics and location with regard to the rest of the world. For example, if a child grew up in the Netherlands, they would have a very different understanding of the importance of water than would a contemporary that lived in the Sahara. The extreme difference in water availability between these two nearly opposing climates is reflected in their two cultures; one gives it a high priority, while the other emphasizes other issues. This creates a different global perception for these two hypothetical children.

A person's worldview and cultural identity will influence the way in which they perceive their corner of the globe as well as those parts outside of it. These include race, ethnicity, languages, ideologies, beliefs about gender and age, religions, politics, history and economic and social class. Many things reinforce a person's connection or sense of significance regarding a certain place, including their feelings of alienation or of belonging or their attachment to history and tradition. This means that certain places feel more significant to certain people, while other places might be perceived apathetically. Muslims, for example, typically feel a greater sense of significance towards the city of Mecca due to their religious beliefs, whereas non-Muslims might only be able to see Mecca regarding its cultural or historical importance.

Perceptions of a certain place may change over time. As neighborhoods grow and become more "developed," attitudes and perceptions about them shift as well. Another example would be the Great Plains in the U.S., the region once known as the "Great American Desert" or the "Dust Bowl," which is now more amiably called the "Breadbasket of America."

It is critical to examine the factors that influence the perception of places and regions; this especially includes personal and cultural worldviews that develop through an individual's maturation in a certain part of the world. Reflecting this way about perceptions of places and regions enables avoidance of the pitfalls of egocentric and ethnocentric stereotyping of the world and others.

Geospatial Technology

Geospatial technologies increase the capability for gathering and analyzing geographic information with applications to everyday life.

Geospatial technology is equipment deployed to aid in the analysis, measurement, and visualization of physical features. While much of geospatial technology use is unknown to the public at large, varying applications increasingly shape daily life in a visible way—from aiding tourists to navigate unfamiliar areas, to helping residents discover and locate new restaurants, to tagging place location data on digital photographs, to enabling a pregnant woman to see images of her unborn child.

A dashboard-mounted GPS device used for motor vehicle navigation

Geospatial technologies include geographic information systems (GIS), satellite navigation systems, remote sensing, and online mapping and visualization.

The three current types of geospatial technology systems include global positioning systems (GPS), geographical information systems (GIS) and remote sensing (RS). GPS has its origins in late 1970s U.S. Department of Defense research but has since then moved rapidly outside the scope of military affairs and into the civilian arena. Composed of an orbital satellite network, GPS provides a means of real-time navigation via a hand-held device (e.g., smartphones) or vehicles with the technology built in. This is accomplished by GPS receivers using trilateration through transmission exchange with at least three satellites to reveal the receiver's exact location that is then displayed on an electronic map. Speed, bearing, track, and trip distance are other types of information that can be determined.

GIS, as a term, can be traced back to 1968. It can be understood as a system used to store, integrate, analyze, manipulate, manage and present spatial or geographical data. GIS computer applications bolster usefulness by enabling rapid user-interactive queries to display the results of a variety of operations. For example, transportation infrastructure relies on GIS to support planning, design, construction, inventory, operations, and maintenance.

RS refers to gathering information on an object without committing physical contact with said object. Its technologies and usage are wide. For example, sonar is an RS technology that enables underwater topographical information to be gathered and used for mapping, navigation, and exploration by emitting pulses of sound and analyzing returning echoes to gain a visualization of the sea floor and also alerts ship crews to other vessels in the area. Other forms of RS technology include Doppler radar (commonly used by law enforcement to identify speeding motorists), ultrasound machines (used by medical practitioners to provide real-time visualization of fetuses) and seismographs (used to gain information of seismic activity such as earthquakes and volcanic eruptions).

Geospatial data is used at all scales for personal, business and governmental purposes.

Geospatial data, as research and technological innovations continue, becomes increasingly used in more and more sectors every year. A short list includes: agriculture, banks, city planning, education, emergency services, public health, retail, real estate, telecommunications, utility companies, waste management, and weather tracking. For instance, GIS data can be used by wood product companies to develop more sustainable forest management systems and it can also be used by newspaper delivery services to understand carrier route dynamics and demographics better to improve marketing and increase their bottom line. Geospatial data has also been employed to aid military, and intelligence organizations track down targets, to map floodplains, mark areas in need of ongoing environmental protection and even to track the spread of contagious diseases to develop containment strategies.

1854 London neighborhood cholera outbreak map

Notes

Field Experience

> **Field experiences continue to be important means of gathering geographic information and data.**

Field experience in gathering geospatial data can take on a range of forms and be sponsored by a variety of organizations. Census workers, land surveyors, election poll workers, and sonar operators, for example, all gather geographic data through field experience. While local or state governments typically direct census and election poll workers, land surveyors can be part of a larger company or be independent contractors.

Quantitative and qualitative geographic data are used in economic, environmental, political and social decision making.

Harvested quantitative and qualitative geospatial data can be used in a variety of areas. For example, in economics data can be used to identify struggling communities in need of support or investment; in politics, survey data can track the leanings of likely voters for political campaigns; and with concern to the environment, the patterns of pollution and environmental damage and can identified, tracked and better understood.

Notes

Chapter 2

Population and Migration

Interconnections between theories and concepts of cultural patterns, the political organization of space, food production issues, economic development concerns, natural resource use, and decisions and urban systems provide useful avenues toward understanding how human population is geographically organized. Themes of location, space, place, the scale of analysis and pattern directly relate with basic population issues, such as crude birth rate, crude death rate, total fertility rate, infant mortality rate, doubling time and natural increase rates.

Patterns and trends in fertility, mortality, and migration can often explain why populations are growing or declining in some locations. For example, analysis of fertility rates and age-sex structures can give critical insight into the relationships between place context and government policies. Likewise, analysis of refugee flows, immigration, and internal migration promotes understanding of the connections between population phenomena and other topics. This can be exampled by environmental degradation and natural hazards and disasters prompting population redistribution at various scales, which in turn creates new pressures on the environment, the culture, and political institutions.

Cumulatively, these analysis strategies enhance critical understanding of population trends across space and over time as consideration is given to models of population growth and decline. How this can then result in the evaluation of the roles, strengths, and weaknesses of major populations' policies attempting to either promote or restrict population growth is comprehensively detailed.

Populations and Geographic Patterns

Knowledge of the geographic patterns and characteristics of human populations facilitates understanding of cultural, political, economic and urban systems.

The study of human populations is called *demography*. Geographers use demographics to look for and study patterns of human populations to explain and understand cultural, political and urban systems. Studying demographics includes the spatial distribution of populations and how these populations are changing and moving over time. Analyzing the size, growth, and composition of a population of a country or region can help in understanding the well-being of a region or country. For example, in a country with high unemployment, the cause might be a demographic shift that has resulted in a large number of young people coming of working age all at the same time. The country's economy may not have been ready for such a demographic shift, meaning there were not enough jobs available to accommodate the changing population.

A crowd of Parisian concertgoers

Factors that explain patterns of population distribution vary according to the scale of analysis.

When geographers look at demographic patterns, such as age distribution, population growth or migration patterns, the explanation for these changes varies based on what scale of analysis is being used. If researchers look at the population distribution of a country, they will first attempt to explain why certain areas are less populated by looking at physical features. Mountains, deserts, and tundra tend to be less hospitable places to live, and it can be expected that these factors primarily determine lower population density in such places. By contrast, analyzing population density in a city, factors of physical geography will likely be less important. When looking at a city, factors such as the primary type of housing development, the crime rate and proximity to services will be much more important for explaining the density and distribution of populations within a city.

Methods for calculating population density are arithmetic, physiological and agricultural.

Arithmetic density is simply the total number of people divided by the land area. Arithmetic density is the most commonly used measure of population density. Any data on population density, unless otherwise specified, uses arithmetic density.

An example: The population of the state of Vermont is 626,042 people. The total land area of Vermont is 9,616 square miles. To get the arithmetic density, divide the population by land area, which is 646,042 / 9,616. This equals 67.18 people per square mile. This means that on average, there are 67 people for every square mile of land area in Vermont.

Physiological density calculates the average number of people per unit of arable land. It is calculated the same as arithmetic density except only arable land is used, not the total land area. Physiological density can be useful when comparing the density of people in countries with large uninhabited areas. Canada, for instance, is a large country with a low population. Its arithmetic density is only 4 people for every square kilometer. As an average, the arithmetic density can be misleading because it can make it seem like Canada's population is very spread out. In reality, Canada's population is heavily concentrated in the south because the majority of the country is too cold to grow crops. Canada's physiological density is 78 people per square kilometer, which demonstrates that in the places where people live in Canada, the population is fairly dense.

By comparing the physiological and arithmetic density, the population distribution can be determined. With Canada, the physiological density is 19.5 times higher than the arithmetic density, which shows that the country's population is not evenly distributed and that most of the country is relatively lightly populated. By comparison, the Czech Republic has an arithmetic density of 133 people per square kilometer and a physiological density of 244 people per square kilometer of arable land. The physiological density is only 1.8 times the arithmetic density, indicating that the population of the Czech Republic is fairly evenly spread across the country.

Agricultural density is the number of farmers per unit of arable land. This articulates how many people are working the land and can lead to some inferences. A very high agricultural density may mean that the arable land of a country is being put to good use and is not laying unused. At the same time, it could also indicate that a country's farming industry is very low-tech; requiring many farmers working the land may be an indication that there is a lack of mechanized farming equipment.

Population distribution and density influence political, economic and social processes.

It is important for political entities to understand the population distribution of the territories they govern. This knowledge usually comes through performing a census, which is a count of every person in the country that also gathers basic demographic data. By knowing how many people live in different areas, governments can respond appropriately. If there is a large amount of population growth in one area, for example, the government may respond by increasing the funding for health and education services in that area to keep up with growing demand. Governments and independent electoral bodies may also need to change the boundaries of districts to ensure that areas of surging population are represented in government. This is done by creating new electoral districts in countries with regional representation systems.

The knowledge of demography can also lead to *gerrymandering* in some countries, such as the United States. Governments who are in control of districts may use their knowledge of population distributions to create strange-looking boundaries for an electoral district to try to ensure their party can win the seat. Younger Americans and Black Americans tend to support the Democrats disproportionately, while older and richer Americans tend to support the Republicans disproportionately. Districts are often created to try to put as many people of one group as possible into the district to give one party an edge over the other. Gerrymandering relies on awareness of this demographic data. In most countries, however, electoral districts are determined by independent electoral commissions and not by governments, which makes gerrymandering less of an issue.

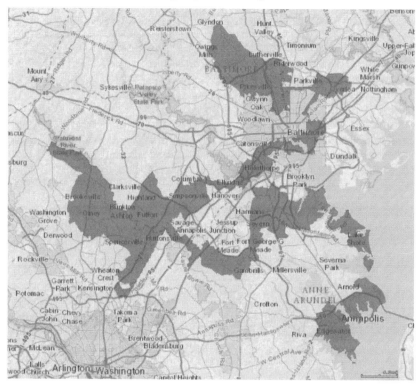

The shaded area represents the boundary of Maryland's 3ʳᵈ Congressional District, a prime example of gerrymandering.

Population distribution and density impact the environment and natural resources.

Human populations require the consumption of food and other natural resources to stay alive. Environments can be more or less suited to human habitation. The number of people an area can support is called the *carrying capacity*. Carrying capacity depends on some factors and changes due to technology, climate change, and political developments. A natural environment full of fertile land where crops can grow year-round will have a natural carrying capacity. At the same time, an area which does not have much natural carrying capacity may be changed through technology. Israel, for example, is mostly a desert and is generally not naturally habitable. The country has developed advanced irrigation methods to grow crops and vastly increase the carrying capacity through technology. Political and trade connections can increase carrying capacity as well. If an area can import much of what is needed, the natural environment will be less restrictive. If a country faces sanctions which limit international trade, then its carrying capacity may be reduced because it will have to rely on internal production.

Population distribution and density affect the need for infrastructure and urban services.

Demographic information such as population distribution and density allows policymakers to make informed decisions. In this manner, the population drives the need for services and infrastructure. A densely-populated area will have a much higher need for fire and rescue services than a sparsely-populated area. For this reason, fire departments in cities usually have full-time firefighters, whereas, in rural areas, firefighters are often volunteers who work other jobs and respond to calls as needed.

Densely-populated areas need more infrastructure and services than sparse areas, but a second issue is that infrastructure breaks down faster in dense areas because of heavier use. A bridge may have an engineering lifespan of 100 years on a road that sees light use because fewer people live in the area. A similar bridge may have a lifespan of only 50 years if it is in a dense area where many more cars roll over it. Population density and distribution are important factors not only to determine how much infrastructure and how many services need to be set up to maintain an area but also to understand when infrastructure will need to be replaced due to wear and tear.

Age, sex and ethnicity are elements of population composition that may be mapped and graphed at various scales.

Geographers often use Geographical Information Systems (GIS) to place data on a map. In doing so, they can create density maps that display not only the overall density of people but also other demographic information. Keeping track of ethnicity and then mapping it is important because it can allow geographers and urban planners to determine the characteristic of certain neighborhoods. By visualizing this data, urban planners can target services to certain ethnic groups or promote programs to foster better integration. Similar density maps using age can help target services as well. An area filled with senior citizens may need close proximity to health services and fewer schools, while an area filled with young adults will need commercial services, universities, and schools.

Businesses often look at density maps when determining where they should try to open new stores. A store that sells hearing aids will target locations near older people, while a Starbucks might aim to open stores in areas which have younger and more affluent people. A specialty Chinese grocery store will also look at ethnic density data to try to open their store where it is closest to the most people of Chinese origin.

Population pyramids are used to project population growth and decline and to predict markets for goods and services.

In addition to mapping information using GIS, another common visualization method is the creation of population pyramid graphs. A *population pyramid* is a horizontal bar graph which shows how many males and how many females there are for each age cohort. They are called population pyramids because traditionally populations have been distributed so that most people are younger and fewer people are older. This would create a pyramid effect as each age cohort would have fewer people than the one below it. Population distribution patterns have been changing in many Western countries as a result of the baby boom after World War II, and now many countries do not have pyramids because the biggest age cohort is now people in their 60s and 70s.

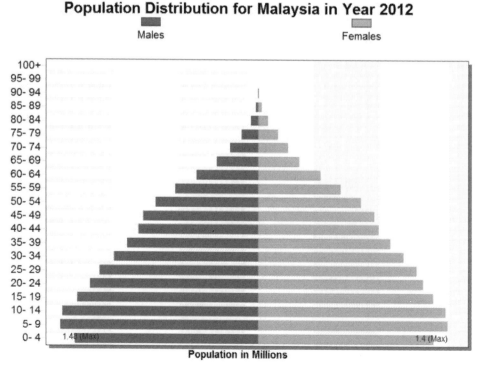

2012 population pyramid for Malaysia

By looking at a population pyramid, geographers can determine the age and sex distribution of a country. This is important information to know for public policy purposes. A country that is dominated by older people is going to have a need for a more robust and expansive healthcare system than a country where the biggest cohort is in their 20s. In countries with dominant younger cohorts, there are often unemployment issues. Many geographers pointed to the population pyramids of countries such as Egypt and Tunisia, which had very large cohorts of younger people, and argued that population distribution changes drove the revolutions in those countries in 2011 and 2012. Younger people wanted jobs that did not exist and were using technology that the older generations did not understand, leading to a generation gap that spurred political change. A similar thing occurred in the United States in the 1960s when the baby boomer generation was in their early 20s. This large generation of young people led to changing attitudes about sex, race and personal freedom.

A population pyramid can also help geographers predict what the population of a country will look like in the future. A country with larger cohorts of older people than younger people is going to experience an overall decline in population. The older people will die while the younger people will not have enough children to replace them. A pyramid with the younger cohorts being the biggest indicates that the population of a country will likely grow rapidly in the future as the younger cohort has children and very few older people die. Developing countries tend to have population pyramids with large bases because birth rates are high and life expectancy is low. By contrast, developed countries can often have population pyramids that are not a pyramid at all, as low birth rates and high life expectancy even out the cohorts.

Notes

Population Growth and Decline

> **Populations grow and decline over time and space.**

Part of human geography involves studying population changes. Geographers often analyze population trends over time and space. This would involve looking at events, policies and other factors that might explain these changes. In recent history, the population of Earth has increased dramatically. When population numbers grow exponentially, this is called a *population explosion*. A population explosion happens when reproduction rates and life expectancy both increase at the same time, leading to increasing numbers of people. An exponential explosion is different from linear growth because, with exponential growth, the rate of population increase grows each year. With linear growth, the population would always grow by the same amount each year. For example, in 1750, the Earth's population was estimated at just 700 million people, whereas it is now around 7 billion people. Human geographers seek to study the causes of population explosions as well as instances of population decline, which is now happening in countries like Japan.

Demographic factors that determine population growth and decline are fertility, mortality, and migration.

Geographers need to know certain basic statistics about population growth to determine whether or not a population is growing or declining. Fertility refers to birth rates. The birth rate of a country can be expressed in multiple ways. A *crude birth rate* is usually expressed as the number of births per 1,000 people. Mortality rates are measured similarly, with the *crude death rate* being the number of deaths per 1,000 people. These numbers can be compared over time and space to study how policies or events are changing the birth rate and the death rate.

In many developed countries, the death rate now exceeds the birth rate. A number of factors causes this. First is the fact that many developed countries in North America and Europe participated in World War II. After the war, there was a *baby boom* as soldiers returned home and started families all at once. The huge spike in birth rates between the 1940s and 1960s has created a large generation of people who are now beginning to reach retirement age, which has skewed the population older.

Parents pushing their young children in strollers

The healthcare systems of developed countries also tend to be better, which has increased life expectancy, allowing this larger cohort of older people to live longer than in developing countries. At the same time, birth control and sex education are more prominent in developed countries, which allows couples to plan for births. This sends the birth rate down as accidental and unwanted pregnancies are minimized.

While *birth rate* is an important statistic for measuring population replacement, the infant mortality rate can often be just as important, especially in developing countries. The *infant mortality rate* measures the number of infants who die before they reach their first year. In countries with poor healthcare systems, a high birth rate may be necessary when many infants typically die in their first year. The infant mortality rate is also a strong indicator of how advanced a country's health services are. This measure is often used to compare countries' healthcare systems and as a metric to measure improvements or declines in a country's healthcare system.

Life expectancy is another important measure of population demographics that is often factored in when considering birth and death rates. *Life expectancy* is how old the average person born today can expect to live. If the life expectancy number is going up at the same time that birth rates are going up, then the population will likely increase. At the same time, if the death rate exceeds the birth rate, but life expectancy is going up, then the population may not decrease as those who are born end up living longer. Life expectancy can be a misleading statistic at times though, so it should be interpreted carefully.

When looking at a country like Sierra Leone, which has the world's lowest life expectancy of 46 years old, it doesn't necessarily mean that most people will live to 46 and then die of natural causes or that there are very few people older than 46 in Sierra Leone. What it means is that the average age of death of 46 is skewed by the fact that the country recently went through a civil war where large numbers of people in their late teens and early twenties died. If a person in Sierra Leone was able to survive the war, there is a good chance they would live until old age. Since so many people died at a young age, it dramatically lowered the average age of death, which life expectancy is based on.

Fecundity is the range in ages where women can have children. The range is generally 15 to 45, but it can vary based on technology and social customs. This statistic is useful for explaining and predicting population growth. For a country that has a death rate that exceeds the birth rate, it might rightfully predict that the country's population will decline over time. However, looking at the population pyramid that shows a huge number of people in the 5-15 age cohort, it can be concluded that a large number of people will soon be approaching the age of fecundity and this could dramatically increase the birth rate and cause the country to grow in population.

Total fertility rate is the number of children a woman will have on average. *Replacement level fertility* is the number of children each woman needs to have to keep the population the same. In most developed countries, this number is close to exactly 2. Each couple needs to have two children to replace themselves. In some developing countries where more people in fecundity range die young, then the replacement rate may often be 3 or higher. Currently, the global replacement fertility rate is 2.3, which means if each woman in the world has an average of 2.3 children, the population will remain steady. It is important to note this is an average; many people will not have children at all, while others will have more than two.

As mentioned, in most developed countries the death rate exceeds the birth rate, and the average fertility rate tends to be below the replacement level. To maintain or grow the population, many developed countries take in immigrants to compensate for low natural birth rates. In a country like Canada, for example, the population has continued to grow linearly due to immigration, even though fertility rates are below replacement levels. In China, the government had determined that there were too many people and put in place the one-child policy, which stated that each woman was only allowed to have one child. This was done to purposely attempt to keep the country's population under control.

An Amazon Yanomami mother holding her child

Rates of natural increase and population-doubling times are used to explain population growth and decline.

By combining the birth rate and the death rate, researchers can arrive at the *Rate of Natural Increase* (RNI) for a population. The birth rate minus the death rate will show how much a population is growing or declining. For example, if the birth rate is 30 and the death rate is 10, then the population is increasing by 20 people for every 1,000. In a country with a population of one million people, this would mean that the population is naturally increasing by 20,000 people per year. The higher the RNI, the shorter the population's doubling time will be.

RNI is a helpful measure of the increase or decrease in a country's population. This statistic is often an important factor for driving immigration policy. If a country wants to maintain a steady population but has a high RNI, then it will likely allow very few immigrants. If a country has a negative RNI, then it will likely increase the number of immigrants to prevent the population from falling. So even if a country has a negative RNI, it does not mean the total population is declining because RNI can be offset by immigration.

RNI is also useful in looking at population changes across history. For example, the first agricultural revolution, when humans originally began to establish settlements based on farming approximately 12,000 years ago, led to a major increase in population growth. With less time spent looking for food due to having a consistent base of food from farming, human survivability increased and made it easier to have children. In the 1700s, the Industrial Revolution introduced new technologies that led to the second agricultural revolution. The second agricultural revolution improved crop yields and storage techniques, dramatically increasing the food supply and allowing the same amount of land to now support a larger number of people. As a result, the population of industrialized countries began to boom. Increased urbanization in this period also supported higher populations because concentrated populations are easier to service.

Social, cultural, political and economic factors influence fertility, mortality and migration rates.

The overall population growth or decline rate is not merely a natural effect of births and deaths; it is heavily related to social, cultural, political and economic factors. As seen with immigration policy, the government can directly increase the population regardless of birth and death rates by simply inviting more people to come to live in a country through immigration. Some countries that may be underdeveloped and cannot service a large population may encourage emigration.

Emigration is the opposite of immigration and is when people leave a country to live somewhere else. While a country like China sought to keep its rapidly rising population under control by restricting the number of children a woman could have, other countries such as the Philippines have encouraged people to emigrate. The goal with promoting emigration is that with fewer people to directly support government programs, the country might be able to spend more money on promoting economic development. The Philippines also promoted a policy that encouraged emigrants to send money back to their family members still in the Philippines through remittances.

A Filipino American stands next to his Californian produce stand, 1942

While migration policy is the most obvious factor affecting population growth, since the government directly controls it, other factors are less apparent. Increased fertility levels are associated with a large number of factors, which, depending on the country, may have more or less of an effect on the fertility level. No one factor can explain an increase or decline in fertility rates. Usually, the explanation is a combination of a number of the following factors.

Beginning with factors that tend to increase fertility and lead to higher birth rates, the factor of religion should be considered. Many religions tend to promote large families actively and having many children, and in this case, religion tends to increase the fertility rate. For example, the Catholic Church is officially opposed to the use of any form of birth control, including condoms and birth control pills. People who are devoutly Catholic and abide by these religious rules tend to have larger families since they do not use birth control. If someone is trying to determine why a country has a high fertility level, one thing to check would be whether or not people in that country identify as devout Catholics. If they do, then there is a good chance that religion is a major factor in higher fertility levels.

Another factor that correlates to high fertility levels is the number of children one's parents had. People who come from large families tend to have large families themselves. This is likely because large families are seen as normal, and the values of the parents are taught to the children. Studies have shown that the number of brothers and sisters someone has can be a strong predictor of the number of children that the same person will have. However, this factor only applies to developed countries where low fertility is the norm. In developing countries where large families are normal, this correlation has shown to be irrelevant.

Living in rural areas is strongly correlated with higher fertility rates in both developed and developing countries. There are multiple explanations for this factor. Some geographers point to the need for more children to help with farm chores when a family lives in a rural area. Some argue that living in a lower density area psychologically predisposes people to want to have more children. Others point out that jobs are less available in rural areas, and women are more likely to become stay-at-home mothers, as compared to women living in cities.

Another factor is the cultural attitude toward the importance of family. In some cultures, the family is positioned as much more important than friends, which leads to a cultural impetus to have more children and extend the family. In other cultures, friends are seen as more important, and there is less social pressure to have many children. This is called *familism* and also relates to levels of support. In a strong familist culture, a child might be raised not just by its parents but by aunts, uncles, cousins, and grandparents as well. This reduces the burden on the parents and makes having more children easier. Studies have shown that a strong state support system can supplement familism in cultures that do not prioritize family. Government-funded daycare, for example, can reduce the financial burden on parents who do not have family members to care for their children while they are at work, which can lead to higher fertility rates.

Patriarchal societies in which women have little political and social power and rights also tend to have higher fertility rates. In these societies, women are not given the option of how many children to have, but instead, have this decision made by their husbands. In the patriarchal societies of Middle Eastern countries, the lack of rights for women is a major factor which drives their higher-than-average birth rates.

Saudi women are often regarded as possessing the least rights and autonomy in the world

In addition to all these factors that can lead to more children, there are also some factors that tend to reduce fertility rates and lead couples to have fewer children. The biggest factor in this regard is income level. The more money people have, the fewer children they tend to have. This is a major factor which explains why the birth rate is significantly lower in wealthier countries than in poorer ones. It also operates within a country as well, as poorer people within a single country tend to have more children than wealthier people. There are numerous reasons to explain the income factor, many of which combine with other factors that will be listed below. One issue to consider might be an opportunity cost. Imagine a woman who is the CEO of a large company and earns millions of dollars a year. Assuming she would make but a very small portion of that amount while on maternity leave, having multiple children would dramatically decrease how much money she would make over her career. This factor is even more acute among working-class families in developed countries who now need two incomes to raise a family. Unlike in the 1960s when one income was enough to raise a family, taking time off to have more children can seriously harm the financial situation of a family.

Along with income, the other major factor is education. The higher the education level, the lower the fertility rates. In part, this relates to income, as higher education is correlated with higher income, but it is also explained by understanding how reproduction and birth control work. For example, in a very developing country the average child might drop out of school at a fairly young age and not receive any sex education. This can lead to a lot of accidental pregnancies that are easily prevented by more educated people who are knowledgeable about birth control. Higher education levels among females are very strongly correlated to lower birth rates. Therefore, a solution to exploding populations in developing countries is proper education for girls.

Related to income and education are birth and population control measures. While higher education and income levels lead to individuals being more likely to use birth control and have fewer children on an individual level, some countries have adopted population control policies. China's famous one child per family policy is an example of such a program meant to try to keep the population from exploding. In India, the country with the second largest population, the government has set up a ministry of family planning whose purpose is to try to encourage contraception and reduce fertility levels. This program has been seen as at least partially successful, as India's fertility rate has been cut in half since the 1960s, but the fertility rate is still well above replacement levels. As a result, India's very large population continues to grow.

Other factors have been shown to have no effect(s) but are varied and complicated. Many studies have shown that raw intelligence is not correlated to either higher or lower fertility rates. While those with more education and higher salaries have lower fertility rates, these are not necessarily the most intelligent people (as studies of IQ tests have shown). Another often-studied question is the quality of relationship status. It was long suspected that couples in happy relationships would have more children, but studies have shown that people in happy and unhappy relationships have the fewest children, and it is those people in medium-quality relationships who tend to have the most children.

Mortality rates are also affected by cultural, political and economic factors. A major factor is the quality of healthcare. Many infections and diseases that are easily curable in a developed country can lead to death in an underdeveloped country without the same level of healthcare. Healthcare systems also affect life expectancy dramatically. While AIDS is causing very large death rates in many countries in Africa, advances in healthcare and access to drugs in developed countries mean that AIDS is no longer an immediate death sentence. Despite the generally better healthcare systems in developed countries, the mortality rates in developed countries are beginning to increase due to the obesity epidemic. Heart disease and stroke (which are strongly linked to obesity) are now the biggest factors in early death in most developed countries; this factor is much less prominent in poorer countries.

Mall food court containing numerous fast food businesses

Infrastructure can also be a major factor in mortality. Lack of access to clean water causes many problems that lead to early death. Motor vehicle crashes can be a major factor in countries that are developed enough to have mass car ownership but not developed enough to invest in proper road infrastructure, driving licensing and regulation.

In some countries, violent conflict can be a major cause of mortality. Countries in the middle of wars, such as Afghanistan and Syria, have extremely high mortality rates associated with armed conflict. Gun violence and violent crime can also be a major factor, as the murder rate in countries such as Mexico and South Africa is high enough to affect overall mortality rates.

Some countries have unique cultural attributes that may lead to health problems. Russia has an extremely high mortality rate that compares to some of the poorest countries in the world, despite its relatively more advanced economic situation. Many researchers have cited alcoholism and depression as significant factors in Russia's higher-than-expected mortality rate.

The demographic transition model may be used to explain population change over time and space.

The *Demographic Transition Model* (DTM) can explain and predict population and demographic changes over time. It is mainly used to try to predict changes in the birth rate, death rate and rate of natural increase (RNI) as a country transitions through the phases of economic development. The model is based on the assumption that economic change is the key factor driving demographic change. The model also assumes that all countries will follow the same demographic path of passing through the four stages of demographic transition outlined in the model. It is important to keep these assumptions in mind, as they can help explain those instances where the model makes poor predictions.

The basic assumption of the DTM is that each country will pass through four different demographic stages as it develops economically. Stage One is the Low Growth-High Stationary phase. Birth rates and death rates are both extremely high in this stage and essentially cancel each other out, resulting in a very low RNI. This Low Growth phase is correlated with economic underdevelopment, and countries in this stage tend to be plagued by famine, disease, and war. Population tends to remain steady as the high birth rate is offset by the multiple causes of early death, resulting in population equilibrium. Most people in this stage are subsistence farmers, meaning that they grow enough food only to feed themselves. There is not enough excess food production to sustain people in non-farming occupations. Due to the spread of medical technologies and medicine around the world in the 20th century, almost no countries today remain in the first stage. Even the poorest countries today still have access to sufficiently developed medicine to ensure that famine, disease, and war do not kill enough people to keep the death rate as high as the birth rate. Most countries, if not all, are today considered to have moved beyond the first stage of the model because birth rates exceed death rates in even the poorest countries today.

Stage Two of the model is the High Growth-Early Expanding stage. In this stage, the birth rate remains as high as it was in the previous stage, but the death rate drops due to medical advances. Sustenance farming is still the dominant occupation, and as a result, the birth rate remains high. There is enough excess food production to sustain some industry, but the food supply is not evenly distributed. With the high birth rate and lowered death rate, the RNI increases dramatically, leading to a period in which the population grows dramatically. Many of the least-developed countries today, especially in Sub-Saharan

Africa, are in Stage Two of this model. For example, Kenya's birth rate is three times higher than its death rate, leading to a rapidly expanding population.

Stage Three is the Moderate Growth-Late Expanding stage. In this stage, the birth rate begins to fall as the state develops a better healthcare system and as people begin to move to cities to work in non-farming occupations. The shift from rural to urban dominance also leads to a culture change in which women often have a stronger role in the economy, leading to a decline in birth rates. Despite increasing urbanization and industry, the birth rate remains higher than the death rate. This means that the population is still growing, although not as much as it was in the previous stage. Much of Latin America is today in Stage Three of the model, as urbanization has become dominant, but populations are continuing to grow at a moderate pace.

Rural Chinese increasingly migrate to urban centers in hopes of securing jobs in more modern industries

Stage Four is the Low Growth-Low Stationary stage. In this stage, the birth rate now drops to almost the same level as the death rate, leading to close to zero natural population growth. Most developed European and North American countries are currently in this stage. Some geographers have proposed a Fifth Stage of the model in which the death rate exceeds the birth rate due to an aging population in combination with advanced life expectancy and high levels of education and individual income. The geographers who advocate for this Fifth Stage argue that Japan is today in this situation, as it has the highest life expectancy in the world (at 84 years) in combination with one of the lowest birth rates, leading to a declining population.

While this model is popular due to the fact it is fairly easy to understand, there are many criticisms. It was developed based on the demographic transitions in the United Kingdom and assumes that all countries' populations will change in the same way. This is a problematic assumption since countries today have dramatically different technological, social and political conditions than the United Kingdom had in the 19th and 20th centuries. This assumption is now considered ethnocentric, assuming as it does that the U.K. is the model for the world.

The model's focus on the population changes of the 19th century dealt with a world population in the millions, not in the billions like today. This can have serious consequences for the model, as it fails to take into account the effect of so many more people in an era of migration and globalization. The model also assumes that these transitions will be very gradual. England transitioned from stage 2 to stage 3 over the course of 100 years, while a country such as Malaysia or South Korea has experienced the same transition in a few decades. With such rapid changes, the stages tend to blur together, reducing the explanatory effectiveness of the model.

Malthusian theory is used to analyze population change and its consequences.

In 1798 Thomas Robert Malthus published an influential book titled *An Essay on the Principle of Population*. Malthus argued that because the population of the world at that time was growing exponentially while the food supply was only growing linearly, it would not be long before the population exceeded the carrying capacity of the Earth. Malthus warned that if the population were to continue to expand rapidly, the world would run out of food and experience mass starvation and famines. To avoid this doomsday scenario, Malthus argued in favor of controlling the overall population by purposely attempting to lower the birth rate by encouraging people not to have children and to use birth control. If people did not stop having so many children, the misery of famine would kill them off. Malthus argued that it was morally better not to have children in the first place, then to have large sections of the population die off from starvation.

Malthus' essay was extremely controversial at the time, in part because he called for celibacy and birth control, positions that were counter to the religious orthodoxy of the time. While Malthus was a cleric himself and made a moral argument about avoiding misery, the idea of limiting reproduction was divisive. Malthus' theory of population exceeding food supply remains controversial today. Many critics point out that Malthus failed to anticipate the agricultural revolution of the 1800s, which dramatically increased the food supply and allowed food to grow exponentially to match the population. Karl Marx argued that Malthus did not understand the economic situation and that starvation and famine were not a result of food shortages due to a lack of production but were caused by uneven distribution problems due to the nature of capitalism. Today some environmentalists use Malthus' population theory to argue that the Earth has a finite amount of resources (e.g., food, oil, minerals) and that there is a point where the population cannot continue expanding. These environmental thinkers often call for curbs on population just like Malthus did.

The epidemiologic transition explains the causes of changing death rates.

The *epidemiological transition model* (ETM) is like the demographic transition model, but the ETM focuses on changing death rates rather than focusing on changing birth rates like the DTM. The ETM has 4 or 5 stages with a focus on identifying and explaining the primary causes of death for a country in a given stage.

Stage One of the ETM is called the "Age of Pestilence and Famine." The primary cause of death for countries in this stage of the model is famine, drought, and pandemics. During the Middle Ages in the 14th century, most of Europe was in this first stage as a result of the bubonic plague. During this period, the plague killed almost one-third of the population of Europe. When pandemics such as the bubonic plague become the primary causes of death, a country is said to be in the first stage of the ETM. Keep in mind that a pandemic is a disease that rapidly spreads and affects a large geographical area. By contrast, an epidemic is a disease that only affects one relatively contained area.

Stage Two is called the "Age of Receding Pandemics." This is a period of rapid urbanization and poor sanitary conditions. The primary cause of death is now related to overcrowding in cities that lack a proper sewage system. Diseases such as cholera, which is spread by contact with human feces, become prominent causes of death due to a lack of sanitation infrastructure and inferior medical care. While cholera has a mortality rate of less than 1% if treated early, the mortality rate jumps to 50% to 60% if left untreated. Crowded cities with poor medical and sewage infrastructure in parts of Southeast Asia and the poorer countries in Africa are considered to be in stage two of the ETM since cholera, and related diseases are still major causes of death.

18th London cartoonists created the above satirical character Dirty Father Thames
to critique the hazardous pollution of the Thames River.

Stage Three of the ETM is called the "Age of Degenerative and Man-Made Diseases." Countries in this stage now have modern medical systems that make diseases such as cholera rare and easily cured when outbreaks do occur. The primary cause of death is now cancer, heart diseases, and HIV/AIDS. Stage Four, which is often lumped together with stage three, is the "Age of Delayed Degenerative Diseases." In Stage Four, the primary causes of death often remain as cancer and heart disease, but medical advances mean that these diseases are predominantly fatal for the elderly. The main difference between stages Three and Four is that a 60-year-old who has a heart attack in a Stage Three country will likely die, but if they are in a stage Four country, with more advanced medical systems, they would likely survive. An 80-year-old who has a heart attack, however, would likely die in both countries.

The classic ETM is only three stages, with some demographers adding the Stage Four mentioned above. Sometimes a fifth stage is added which hypothesizes that sufficiently advanced countries may become susceptible to stage one pandemics once again. While something like smallpox is nearly eliminated in most developed countries, if someone manages to contract it, it can lead to a pandemic if not properly contained because once a disease is considered to have been eliminated, people tend not to be as likely to receive vaccines for it. The fifth stage also responds to the fact of globalization by pointing out that people are now more interconnected and infectious diseases can now spread quickly over the world. An example of a possible Stage Five situation was the SARS outbreak in 2003, which spread from China to Canada and caused a major health scare. The Ebola virus and Zika virus are also possible pandemics whose ability to spread is enhanced by today's extensive air travel, tourism, and migration.

Types of population policies include those that promote or restrict population growth.

There are generally three approaches governments can take about population policy. They can encourage population growth through pronatalist policies; they can remain indifferent to population, or they can discourage population growth through antinatalist policies. *Pronatalist policies* are anything the government does to try to expand the population and encourage citizens to have more children. Examples of pronatalist policy include giving increasingly large tax breaks based on having more children, providing public services such as daycare and paid parental leave or sending baby bonus payments to new mothers.

Governments have engaged in pronatalist policies at various times in history. Between World War I and World War II, there was a major decline in population growth in Europe that spurred many governments to promote natalist policies to try to grow the population. In the 1930s and 1940s, Sweden put in place some natalist policies to provide government support for families that resulted in a boom in population. In 1946, Poland instituted an extra tax on couples who had no children to encourage population growth. In the 1960s in Romania, the government banned many forms of contraceptives and birth control and put in place penalties for childless women. This aggressive pronatalist policy in Romania backfired somewhat, as the surge in population stressed the healthcare system and led to revolts.

Today, countries like Japan and South Korea, which are experiencing population decline due to greying populations, are beginning to promote pronatalist policies. Japan has begun to offer financial incentives to people who have large families. Natalism is often promoted as an alternative to immigration by people who believe that countries should remain racially pure. Japan's focus on natalism is driven by latent racism, as the government wants to maintain the dominance of "native stock" people in the country. Natalism can also be used as a mechanism of demographic engineering. In Turkey, a country which is traditionally secular, the current government has been promoting pronatalist policies only among the country's Muslim population to ensure that the majority of the country will be Muslims and will continue to vote for the governing Islamic party.

The opposite of pronatalism is *antinatalism*, which is any set of policies meant to restrict the growth of the population. China's one-child policy is the most famous example of antinatalism, but many other policies fit antinatalism. Policies that provide free birth control or free vasectomies (male sterilization) are antinatalist as they help reduce population growth rates. Government support of family planning services is also considered antinatalist as it encouraged families only to have children when they are ready and prepared to do so. While pronatalist policies can often have racist elements, antinatalist policies can cause gender issues. In China, the one-child policy led to widespread female infanticide, since sons were more highly valued than daughters due to traditional cultural values. Today in China, there are many more men than women as a result of parents preferring to have only a son. Unbalanced sex ratios can spur a whole host of social problems as large cohorts of heterosexual young men without enough women to partner with can lead to aggression and violence that threatens social stability.

Chinese government sign translates "For a prosperous, powerful nation and a happy family, please practice family planning"

Changing social values and access to education, employment, healthcare, and contraception have reduced fertility rates in most parts of the world.

As outlined above, birth rates drop for some reasons, including changing social values, education, income, and healthcare. Currently, most developed countries have relatively low birth rates, while developing countries have higher birth rates. As countries develop socially, economically and politically, their birth rates tend to drop.

Changing social, economic and political roles for women have influenced the patterns of fertility, mortality, and migration.

Female empowerment is strongly correlated to higher life expectancy and lower birth rates. When women control their own lives, there is less pressure to be a mother and nothing else. Women with choices may delay having children and tend to have fewer children. A key aspect of reducing the exponential population growth in developing countries is to promote feminism, which empowers women with equal rights.

Population aging is influenced by birth and death rates and life expectancy.

As indicated above, populations are usually divided into age cohorts. When life expectancy increases at the same time birth and death rates decrease, then the population will become older on average. This is often called a "graying" population and is characteristic of countries such as Japan, with Europe and America likely to reach this point soon as most of the baby boomers enter retirement.

An aging population has social (e.g., retirement), economic (e.g., dependency ratio) and political (e.g., voting patterns) implications.

Aging populations tend to stress social services. Older people have more healthcare requirements and need to be paid old age security benefits. If there are not enough younger people paying into these programs, then governments can have trouble paying for the services needed to sustain an older population. Aging populations can also lead to generation gaps with political implications. When voting patterns become split based on age, this can lead to social turmoil. If young people feel that they have no voice in the political system because older people constitute a majority, problems can occur since it is the younger people whose taxes pay to support the retired generation. This situation can lead to resentment and major swings in the political system, as evidenced by the support for Bernie Sanders, who is outside of the traditional elite establishment.

Migration

Causes and consequences of migration are influenced by cultural, demographic, economic, environmental and political factors.

Migration, which involves immigration (coming into a country) and emigration (moving out of a country), has a myriad of causes. This section will look at factors that push people to emigrate and pull people to immigrate, as well as factors that force people to migrate against their wishes.

Push and pull factors can be cultural, demographic, economic, environmental or political.

Many factors push people to emigrate and pull people immigrate. Cultural factors can be both push and pull. An atheist living in a country that lacks religious freedom will feel a strong cultural push factor to leave that country due to oppression. Many atheists, religious minorities and LGBT people are persecuted in highly-religious countries, leading them to emigrate to maintain their freedom. On the other side, culture can be a pull factor as well. An artist may be pulled to a country with a strong appreciation for their work and art in general. Many actors and film-making professionals are pulled to the United States because of its thriving television and film industries.

An Alabama billboard reflects the presence of religious tensions and intolerance in the area

Demographic factors can be a major push and pull factors as well. Imagine being a young, heterosexual man in China where the unbalanced sex ratio means that finding a partner is less likely than in almost any other country. China is also very overpopulated, causing a strong push factor that would make someone want to immigrate to another country. Demographic pull factors often tie into cultural pull factors as well. India also has a massive population which drives emigration, but many people emigrating from India enjoy Indian culture, just not the overpopulation of their home country. They will be pulled toward countries with significant minority populations of Indians, especially if they have family members in that country. In that way, they can escape the overcrowding of their home country while moving somewhere that is not completely alien due to large émigré populations.

Economic factors are often the biggest push and pull migration causes. Mexican migrant workers who come to the United States are both pushed away from Mexico by its poor economic situation and lack of jobs and pulled to the United States with its relatively high-paying jobs. Economic factors operate among the working class, as globalization leads to jobs being constantly relocated, causing migrants to have to travel to find work. Economic factors can also push or pull the middle class. Someone with an advanced degree may have better opportunities in another country. When a country produces many people with advanced degrees who end up leaving the country due to a lack of opportunities, this is called a "brain drain," as the smartest people are leaving. A brain drain situation can cause a country's economy to become stagnant, as innovation suffers in a situation where all the most highly-skilled people leave the country. Most countries have immigration policies which seek to attract highly-skilled people with advanced degrees, making it easier for these people to migrate.

As climate change continues to be a problem, environmental issues are increasingly a push and pull factor. Climate change refugees are starting to become an immediate issue, especially in small island countries such as the Maldives and Kiribati, whose very existences are threatened by rising sea levels due to global warming. Droughts and floods are increasing in number and severity, which is causing people to move to escape these problems. Natural disasters are also major environmental push factors, as an earthquake or a tsunami can destroy people's houses and livelihood, causing them to flee the country for safety. The United Nations is increasingly moving towards recognizing climate refugees and encouraging countries to develop policies related to environmental migrants; this is expected to become an increasingly larger problem in the future.

Political push and pull migration factors are not as big an issue as they were during the Cold War, but they still retain some impact. During the Cold War, many people from Eastern Europe and Russia sought to move to the West to escape communism, and some people in America and Europe sought to move to Eastern Europe and Russia because they believed in communism. Defections were a major political issue, and it was considered international news when a prominent Russian or American would defect to the opposing side. Today in the globalized world, the concept of defecting is all but irrelevant, but many people still feel the push and pull factors due to politics. Many people continue to flee North Korea due to its totalitarian ideology, while many people are pulled to countries such as Norway, which is ranked as the best place to live in the world.

Push factors are often negative, while pull factors are often perceived as positive.

A *push factor* is something that causes people to want to emigrate. Push factors are usually something negative that a person is trying to get away from, such as a war or lack of job opportunities. When people migrate based on push factors, they tend not to be too picky about what country they move to, as their main concern is getting away from the country that they come from. *Pull factors*, on the other hand, are attractive qualities in another country that make people want to move there. Someone may enjoy life in his or her original country, but pull factors in another country may make it more desirable to move there. Pull factors may cause people to move to another country even if they are not unhappy with the situation in their current country.

Indefinite military conscription, starvation wages and state acts of violence against the civilian population push many Eritreans (such as these refugees) out of their rapidly-depopulating nation.

Forced migrations include those involving refugees, internally displaced persons and asylum seekers.

Push and pull factors that drive migration are often voluntary, but in some cases, migration is forced due to circumstances outside of an individual's control. One of the largest forced migrations in human history was the North Atlantic slave trade. Around 30 million Africans were captured and against their will transported to the Americas to work as slaves. Today, forced migrations are usually a result of war, natural disaster or political persecution.

Refugees are people who have been forced out of their home country and seek refuge in another country. Today, refugee crises, such as people fleeing the civil war in Syria, are met with various responses; however, the international community generally accepts that countries should share the responsibility for taking in refugees. This was not always the case, as many Jewish refugees in World War II were rendered stateless as a result of losing their German citizenship and having no other countries willing to adopt them. Refugees are usually classed as a special form of immigrant under the law, who are not subject to the same restrictions as voluntarily immigrants. Many countries are hesitant to take in many refugees because often these people flee situations of violence with nothing more than what they can carry and require many years of state support to get back on their feet. Despite the initial financial burden, refugees have tended to have a long-term beneficial impact on a country, as refugees tend to be very grateful to their new country and work hard to make it better.

Internally displaced persons (IDPs) are like refugees within a country. People often become internally displaced as a result of a major natural disaster within their country, which forces them to move to another part. After Hurricane Katrina, many residents of New Orleans became internally displaced, as their homes were destroyed. Internally displaced people need help from the government since usually almost all of their possessions are destroyed, but they can often stay in the country and sometimes even go back and rebuild after the disaster subsides. An *asylum seeker* is like a refugee but is fleeing a country because of individual persecution. Countries that disagree with the policies of another country often welcome dissidents by granting them political asylum and allowing them to immigrate to escape persecution in their home country.

There have been many major forced migration events that created many refugees in recent history. In the 1990s, the civil war in Congo and ethnic violence in Rwanda forced millions of people to flee their homes as refugees. Recently, Sudan has faced a multitude of forced migrations in Darfur and Southern Sudan as a result of religious violence. After the formation of Israel in 1948, millions of Palestinians were driven out of their homes and into temporary camps in Egypt, Syria, and Jordan. The civil war in the former Yugoslavia in the 1990s created seven million refugees, as people from Serbia, Croatia, and Bosnia fled to other parts of Europe and North America. In the 1960s and 1970s, the American invasion of Vietnam created a major refugee crisis, with two million people forced to flee their homes. Authoritarian governments in Cambodia and Myanmar also created refugee crises in the 1970s to 1990s, with tens of thousands of refugees either internally displaced by force or exiled from the country.

Voluntary migrations may be transnational, internal, chain, step or rural-to-urban.

There are a number of different types of migration patterns. *Transnational migrations* involve moving to another country, while *internal migrations* involve moving within a single country for the reasons outlined above in the push and pull factor section. *Chain migrations* begin when one person in a family moves somewhere else. After they became established, that person may bring their spouse and children to the new country, then eventually their parents, then down the chain as more and more family members migrate to be with the rest of their family. This pattern is called chain migration because it happens slowly over time.

Step migration is a series of shorter, less extreme migrations from a person's place of origin to their final destination. For example, moving from a farm to a village, then to a town and finally to a city. Some refugees have to engage in step migration while they wait for their destination country to take them. The refugees fleeing the civil war in Syria often first cross the border into Turkey and stay there for a while, before moving on to Greece. From Greece, they can end up in another mainland European country while they wait to cross to the U.K., Canada or the United States.

Syrian refugees in Slovenia largely endeavor to make their final destination Germany

Rural-to-urban migration is characteristic of an economy that is industrializing. More workers are needed in cities, and farms now produce more food through technology that requires fewer workers. The transformation of Europe from feudalism to capitalism was an example of a massive period of rural to urban migration. People were no longer tied to the land due to being owned by lords and were free to move to cities in search of work in factories. This led to a massive exodus from the rural countryside and a huge explosion in the urban population. Similar patterns are occurring in developing countries as people transition from subsistence farming to urban occupations.

Patterns of voluntary and forced migration may be affected by distance and physical features.

Physical geography plays a large part in determining migration flows. In the 18th and 19th centuries, to immigrate to America from Europe was a major undertaking involving crossing the ocean in a boat that could take weeks. Today, this same distance can be traveled in a plane in a few hours. Voluntary migration patterns have thus shifted dramatically as air travel enabled people to travel further and faster without concerns of physical geography.

In a forced migration, however, physical geography remains an extremely important aspect. In periods of war, internally displaced people often flee to the mountains for refuge. Rugged terrain can help protect people who are vulnerable to armed conflict. The ease of border crossings to neighboring countries that are land-based and not barred by impassable mountains, rivers, or lakes facilitate refugees fleeing a country. Syrian refugees have a relatively easy time getting into Turkey due to the long land border, but they face difficulties moving on to other countries due to the large size of Turkey and the necessity to cross bodies of water and mountains.

Major historical migrations include the forced migration of Africans to the Americas, immigration waves to the U.S. and emigration from Europe and Asia to colonies abroad.

The United States has experienced three major waves of immigration. Each of these waves involved people coming to America from different parts of the world. The first wave was during the colonial era (1600s-1776) and involved large numbers of Africans being forced to migrate to America as slaves and many Europeans voluntarily moving to America. During the 1800s, the second wave of immigration began. From 1776 until 1840, the vast majority of immigrants came from England, escaping the overcrowding of cities as England went through the industrial revolution. Many of these people had lost their livelihoods as farmers due to industrialization and sought out new farmlands in the U.S.A.

From 1840 to 1860, the source of immigrants shifted, with the majority now coming from Ireland and Germany. In the late 1840s and early 1850s, Ireland was experiencing the Great Potato Famine, and people left the country out of desperation to avoid starving to death in Ireland. Ireland's population was reduced by 25% during this period as many people emigrated to the United States and many others died of hunger. From 1848 to 1849, Germany experienced a revolution where a new class of liberal reformers who demanded a bill of rights and a democratic constitution were violently repressed by the autocratic governments of the German Confederation. Many of these liberal exiles fled to America to avoid persecution. The influence of these new German-Americans was so strong that the American government began to translate official documents into German to help the new immigrants assimilate. During this second wave of immigration to the United States, around 4.2 million people moved to the United States. By comparison, only 2 million people had immigrated to the United States during the colonial period.

During the Civil War, immigration to America dropped significantly, as obviously few people wanted to move to a country in the middle of a violent war. After the war ended, immigration picked up again dramatically from the late 1800s until 1929. This period saw not only continued immigration from England, Ireland, and Germany, but also huge influxes of people from Italy, Russia and the Austro-Hungarian Empire. Until 1882, there were no restrictions on immigration to the United States at all. Anyone who could afford the ticket on a steamship to cross the Atlantic or Pacific could move to the United States without worrying about borders, green cards or paperwork. In 1882 Congress passed the Chinese Exclusion Act, which prohibited all immigration by Chinese laborers. There had been a major wave of Chinese immigration to California during the gold rush of the 1840s. Many came seeking their fortune but ended up as cheap labor working on the transcontinental railroad. After their labor was no longer useful to exploit, racist attitudes turned against the Chinese and they were excluded from immigration, the first such restriction based on national origin.

In 1903, Congress passed a second act to restrict immigration called the Anarchist Exclusion Act. This act banned anyone with anarchist political views from entering the United States. This act came as a direct response to the Haymarket Affair of 1886, in which anarchists in Chicago had been organizing the working class to strike in favor of having an 8-hour workday. This was considered a radical reform at the time, as the standard workday was usually 12 hours. Some of the anarchists involved in organizing the Haymarket strike were put on trial in what many saw as simply political persecution. Many of these anarchists were German immigrants, and the calls to ban anarchists from immigrating were a combination of fear of political organizing and racism. American companies saw the reforms in labor conditions promoted by anarchists as an attack on their corporate interests and lobbied the government to ban anarchists from entering the country.

A Haymarket strike promotion written in both English and German

In 1917 Congress passed the Immigration Act, which restricted the immigration of people deemed to be socially undesirable and imposed English literacy tests on certain people. The bill was at first vetoed by President Woodrow Wilson who argued that it ran against the spirit of liberty that America stood for and that the open-door immigration policy had served America well. Congress overrode the veto, and the bill was passed. The main targets of the bill were the mentally ill, homosexuals, anarchists, "idiots" (actual language of the bill) and people from Asian countries.

In 1921 the U.S. government passed the Quota Act, which for the first time placed restrictions on the number total number of immigrants from every country. The law restricted immigration to 3% of the number of people from that country of origin then living in the United States. If there were 100 people from Greece currently living in the United States, three new Greek people could be admitted each year. The quota system allowed large amounts of immigrants from England, Ireland, Germany and other countries who had been the traditional sources of American immigration but severely restricted the number of immigrants from countries who had not previously participated in waves of immigration. Part of the reason for this was that xenophobic sentiment was running high during World War I when the bill was being discussed in Congress, and after the War, the U.S. was experiencing a wave of immigration from Austria and Hungary in the wake of the

Austro-Hungarian Empire falling apart. The act made an exception for people from Latin America, with no restrictions placed on immigration from those countries.

A possible fourth wave of immigration to the United States can be detected beginning in the late 1970s and 1980s, driven by Asian immigration in the 1970s and Latin American immigration in the 1980s. The 1980s are considered "the lost decade" in many Latin American countries, as civil wars and economic problems caused a severe economic downturn, leading many people to immigrate to the United States. Immigration policy continues to be a hot button issue in the United States, especially the issue of undocumented immigration, which is when people move to the U.S. to work without the proper documentation. This is a complicated issue because employers and taxpayers benefit from undocumented workers; employers can pay them less while at the same time those workers end up paying sales taxes on the items they buy, and also generally make no attempt to use social services for fear this could lead to deportation. Workers' advocates oppose undocumented immigration because it exploits the immigrants, while others oppose it because they are breaking the law and not following proper procedures. Xenophobia and racism also play a role in the debate on undocumented immigration in the U.S.

Governments institute policies to encourage or restrict migration.

As seen in the example of U.S. attitudes above, governments often put in place policies to restrict migration because of xenophobia and economic reasons. In some cases, countries put in place policies to actively encourage immigration. In the early-to-mid 1800s, Canada and the United States were trying to grow their population quickly and wanted to encourage westward settlement to expand their borders at the expense of the indigenous peoples who lived there. To encourage both immigration and western settlement, both countries adopted a Homestead policy, in which people who moved to the West to farm would be given free land. In both countries, a sizeable plot of land (160 acres) was given to an individual who was willing to settle and farm in the West. In the case of Canada, this policy attracted many immigrants from Ukraine and Hungary. In the United States, the Homestead Act of 1862 was significant because it even allowed women and blacks to receive free land. This leads to a relatively more empowered status in the "Wild West" for both groups who were then marginalized in both northern and southern American culture.

An ad promoting the sale of tribal lands likely illegally seized

In both cases, the policies led to an expansion of western settlement. In the case of Canada, a settler could double their land for $10 if they had the money. The increase in the western settlement did create a somewhat lawless situation in the United States and gave rise to the experience of the "Wild West." In Canada, no similar lawless situation occurred because of the North Western Mounted Police, which was a horse-based police force designed specifically to ensure that federal laws were applied in the new western expansions. While the governments of both countries saw these policies as a success in encouraging western expansion, the lands being settled were inhabited by indigenous groups who were often forcibly removed from their lands. The government of both countries essentially stole the land from the indigenous peoples and gave it away for free to immigrants.

Migration has consequences for areas that generate or receive migrants.

The consequences of migration can be broken into two parts: consequences for the receiving and the sending countries. The country that people emigrate from can often significantly benefit from emigration when people move to a richer country. These emigrants often send money back home to family members through remittances.

Remittances are economically beneficial for the origin country because people are receiving "free money," which they will then spend in the host country, improving its economic situation. In many cases, migrant workers will only stay in a country for a few years and then return home. This can have benefits because these workers may have often learned new skills and languages that can be applied at home to increase economic activity. Developing countries benefit from lower populations, as they tend to lack infrastructure, and thus emigration reduces the economic and social burden on the government.

Countries that receive immigrants and migrant workers receive many benefits as well. In many cases, migrant workers fill jobs that not many natives want to work. Migrant workers often staff difficult manual labor that pays minimum wage, such as working on large farms picking fruits and vegetables. The farms can then get their produce picked without having to raise wages. While this is somewhat of a benefit since it keeps prices of produce down and allows farmers to make more money, it also suppresses the number of jobs available. In a closed economy with no migration, the farmers would have to obey the logic of the market and raise wages to the level that the job would be attractive, thus increasing the well-being of domestic workers. The destination country also benefits since migrant workers pay taxes but rarely use social services. When a migrant worker retires, they return to their home country. This means that their home country must pay their retirement pension, leaving the taxes they paid in the destination country to be spent on something else.

Social impacts can involve the spread of religion. People in poorer countries tend to be less educated and more religious. When they move to wealthier countries, they can spread religion with them. An example is a spread of Roman Catholicism to the United States during the wave of Irish immigration in the 1840s. Before this time, very few Americans were Catholic, but with Irish immigration, Catholicism came to America and spread among the non-Irish population as well. For origin countries, emigration can often mean religious undesirables are leaving the country and no longer being a problem. When the Puritans left England for America, this was a relief to England where they were seen as religious fundamentalists who were harming English society.

Kansas City Irish immigrants, c. 1909

Immigration can benefit the destination country's cultural life as different practices are incorporated. Diverse cities such as Toronto allow residents to sample the cuisines of every country in the world, participate in cultural festivals and enjoy the music and art from around the world without having to travel. However, if these new practices do not become integrated into the wider society, the immigrants may become walled off, creating their cultural enclaves. People who live in these enclaves may feel very little attachment to their new country and may not participate in its social and political life. Such enclaves (e.g., suburbs of Paris that have come to be dominated by immigrants from Algeria) can become sites of racial tension and religious extremism.

Notes

Chapter 3

Cultural Patterns and Processes

Components and regional variations of cultural patterns and processes provide critical insights towards understanding human geography. This chapter endeavors to promote this learning objective by outlining the key concepts of culture and cultural traits as well as describing how geographers assess the spatial and place dimensions of cultural groups as defined by language, religion, ethnicity, and gender, in both the present and the past.

Cultural interaction at various scales, along with adaptations, changes, and conflict, are explored through the analysis of cultural patterns and processes. Pattern and process identification and analysis are charted to give insight into the geographies of language, religion, ethnicity, and gender. Tools are provided to confer the ability to distinguish between languages and dialects, ethnic religions and universalizing religions and folk and popular cultures, as well as between ethnic political movements. These distinctions offer vantage points toward understanding the forces that affect the geographic patterns of each cultural characteristic.

Also emphasized are how culture shapes relationships between humans and the environment. Culture is expressed in landscapes, and land use, in turn, represents cultural identity. Built environments enable geographers to interpret cultural values, tastes, symbolism, and beliefs. For instance, when analyzing Amish communities in the Western Hemisphere, it is important to understand how their unique values and practices (e.g., lack of power lines to buildings and the use of preindustrial forms of transportation) influence the cultural landscape.

Culture Concepts

Concepts of culture frame the shared behaviors of society.

Cultural geography studies the lifestyle patterns of groups of people and societies in relation to the natural and built environment. Cultural geography looks at how culture is expressed in different places and seeks to explain the relationship between different cultural practices and different geographies. Cultural geography can study both the material and immaterial practices of a culture. *Material culture* would be any cultural artifacts created by a society, such as a style of architecture, and *immaterial culture* would be any beliefs of people, such as their religious practices. Cultural geography is interested in how cultures diffuse over different lands, how cultural practices change over time and how cultures interact.

Culture is comprised of shared practices, technologies, attitudes and behaviors transmitted by a society.

Defining culture is not an easy task and is often a matter of complex philosophical debate. In the broadest sense, culture can be thought of as any set of shared practices, attitudes, technologies and behaviors that are common to a group of people. A broad definition like this introduces many problems when trying to study cultural differences. For instance, people in the United States and Canada both predominantly speak the same language with a similar accent, both enjoy the same television shows, and movies and both have a similar level of technology. Are the United States and Canada part of the same culture? This is a difficult question to answer, as many would argue that both of these countries contain many cultures inside their borders, and any wider similarities are too broad to link the two countries.

One major point of dispute in the debate about what a cultural group consists of depends on whether the set of practices and beliefs are considered exclusive or inclusive. In this definition, a *culture* is defined by the fact that its members engage in exclusive practices and beliefs that are not to be shared with outsiders. By contrast, practices and beliefs that are considered open for all are what define a civilization rather than a culture. The word culture has its root in the word cult, which involves an exclusive membership not open to outsiders. Cult also links to cultivation, which has to do with living on a farm where one does not encounter many different cultural practices. Civilization, by contrast, comes from the Latin word *civitas*, which means "city." *Civilization* is defined by an open set of practices, beliefs, and activities that are available to anyone, as cities tend to be much more culturally diverse. Under this division between "culture" and "civilization," culture consists of sets of exclusive practices and beliefs that are meant only for those within a culture, whereas civilizations consist of sets of inclusive practices and beliefs meant for anyone who wishes to partake.

This means that exclusionary practices such as religion and ethnicity are cultural, whereas inclusionary practices such as cuisine, art and literature would be civilizational practices. Many adherents of a specific culture get upset when their practices are stripped of their religious meanings and become enjoyed by everyone. The practice of yoga is today enjoyed by many people around the world as a way to become more flexible and exercise. This attitude toward yoga makes it a civilizational practice that India contributed to global civilization. However, yoga began as a specific aspect of Hinduism, and some Hindus get angry when they see people practice yoga divorced from its Hindu religious element. This would be a cultural attitude toward yoga.

Indian practicing yoga on the banks of the Ganges River

In this sense, when geographers talk about the cultural landscape of shared practices, they often lump civilizational and cultural practices together. Since no one can agree on whether a practice should be limited to a specific culture or open to anyone, this is a further complication of trying to define what exactly differentiates one culture from another. There are also issues with subcultures, as the dominant practices of one region may not be practiced at all by a significant minority who otherwise do not differ from the dominant group. For example, in Iran, the dominant culture is a conservative form of Islam, but many people in the largest city, Tehran, are not religious and feel that this form of culture is being oppressively imposed on them. These cultural dissidents are not a different religion, ethnicity or nationality; they do not agree with the dominant cultural practices. Geographers need to be careful to keep such practices in mind, lest they end up making inaccurate assumptions about the practices and beliefs of people in different regions.

To get around these problematic questions about culture, cultural geographers often focus their studies on issues that are much more specific. For example, a cultural geographer may study the fans of football clubs and compare Argentina and England, looking for differences in fandom and trying to explain how these differences might be explained by differing political, economic or geographical conditions. In this sense, most contemporary cultural geographers are less concerned about culture in the broad sense and tend to narrow the focus to something very specific, so they do not get bogged down trying to define who exactly is part of a "culture."

Cultural traits are individual elements of culture and include such things as food preferences, architecture, and land use.

As mentioned above, the main focus of cultural geography is the study of specific cultural traits. These traits can involve any practice, ranging from the type of cuisine, architecture, land use or social habits. For example, a cultural geographer might be interested in the Japanese cultural custom of bowing to show respect in contrast to the American custom of shaking hands. The cultural geographer would then seek out the origins of these practices and analyze how they have spread to different regions or how they have independently popped up in other cultures. Cultural geography tends to be very comparative in nature and is concerned with explaining how traits differ over space.

One of the major questions for cultural geographers is trying to determine whether where someone lives determine their cultural traits. One way to consider this question would be to ask if living near rivers led to different societies of people ending up with similar cultural traits. One of the earliest approaches to answer the question was *environmental determinism*. This position argues that the physical landscape entirely determines human cultural traits. This idea was popular in ancient times, with ancient Chinese thinkers believing that people who lived near winding, fast-moving rivers are more likely to be greedy and war-like. The ancient Greeks also believed that landscape determined the nature of peoples. The idea became popular again in Europe during the colonial period, in which it was argued that the physical geography of the New World determined the cultural and political orientation of the indigenous peoples.

Another theory relating cultural traits to geography is *possibilism*. According to possibilism, cultural traits are largely determined by human social patterns rather than only by geography. Possibilism does point out that cultural traits can often be limited by geography. For example, it is unlikely that a culture that lives in the tropics would develop cultural practices for dealing with snow. In languages that developed in cultures with colder temperatures, there are often many different words to describe different types of snow and ice that would not be distinguishable in a language that developed in a tropical climate. Possibilism would argue that this is an example of a geographical constraint on culture, but it would also point to the fact that almost every other word in the language cannot be simply traced back to geographical constraints. In this sense, possibilism argues that environmental determinism is generally wrong.

In contrast to both environmental determinism and possibilism, there is *cultural determinism*, which argues that physical geography does not affect whatsoever on the development of different cultural traits. Cultural determinists argue that cultural practices are only limited by human imagination. They often point to the popularity of golf courses in desert countries such as the United Arab Emirates. Both possibilists and environmental determinists would expect that golfing would not be something people from a desert country would adopt as a popular cultural practice because golf courses require grass and much water, two things that are very scarce in deserts. However, human ingenuity has developed systems of irrigation and water pumps to make golf courses viable in the UAE, allowing the unlikely sport of golf to become quite popular. Cultural determinists point to examples like this to argue that physical terrain has no effect on cultural practices, especially in the modern world.

A golf course and resort being constructed on the Arabian Peninsula

A fourth approach is *political ecology*, which reverses the traditional question of how the environment affects cultural practice. Political ecologists are interested instead in how human practices affect and change the natural environment. Political ecologists argue that the other three approaches are old-fashioned because they see humans at the mercy of natural forces when the reality is that today humans are the ones in control. According to political ecology, one needs to consider how our cultural practices are changing the physical environment, especially about issues such as climate change, deforestation, over-fishing and the pollution of rivers. Political ecology seeks to push people to understand how their practices affect the environment and why our cultural beliefs might need to change to preserve the natural world.

Geographers use maps and the spatial perspective to analyze and assess language, religion, ethnicity, and gender.

A common technique for keeping track of various patterns of culture is to map them. A map of languages and language groups can visually demonstrate patterns of culture and various cultural boundaries. By combining language groups, religion and ethnicity on a map, geographers can visualize patterns of cultural cohesion that do not necessarily follow the political boundaries of a map. For example, the Kurdish people are a large ethnic group that is based on a somewhat mythological origin in the Medes people who conquered the

Assyrian city of Nineveh in 612 B.C. The Kurds share a common language, which is generally what is used to mark them as different from other ethnic groups. By mapping areas where the Kurdish language is commonly spoken, one can see that Kurds are a group that cut across Turkey, Iran, Iraq, and Syria. By maintaining their language, Kurds have been able to sustain a separate cultural identity even though they do not have their own country. Given that the borders of that part of the Middle East were arbitrarily assigned after World War I by the British and French, the Kurds have long felt that they deserved their own country whose borders should have been determined by mapping the use of the Kurdish language.

Communication technologies are reshaping and accelerating interactions among people and places and changing cultural practices.

The internet is leading to both massive amounts of cultural sharing while at the same time promoting cultural enclaves. With the internet, one can access and communicate with people from around the world and learn and share their unique cultural practices. While this is inevitably a positive, as it allows interesting music, art, and practices to become globally accessible, it can also lead to the loss of these practices. One example of this dual nature of the internet is indigenous languages in the western hemisphere. Now that English, French, and Spanish have become the dominant languages of North America, most Native Americans must learn these languages to function in society. This can mean a possible loss of their traditional languages as fewer and fewer people know how to speak the traditional languages. The loss of these languages is a problem because it means different ways of thinking are lost. Language shapes how one experiences the world, and a language becoming extinct means a specific experience of the world can become extinct.

Global interconnection accelerates this process of language extinction, but it can also help remedy it. Many small languages at risk of becoming extinct are now being cataloged online, and people who still speak these traditional languages are putting their knowledge into databases to help preserve these languages and allow future generations to learn them. It also helps historians and anthropologists seeking to study these cultures. It would be a problem if there were written stories that no one could read, but if the technology is used to store the meaning of these languages, researchers will be able to interpret newly found documents. The internet can also facilitate communication among speakers of dying languages to allow them to find others whom they can talk to and practice the language. In this sense, the internet has been useful at connecting people from cultural groups who may have moved far away from their traditional home, allowing them to continue to practice their traditional customs in a foreign land.

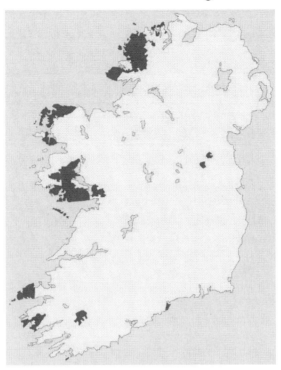

Shaded, scattered areas of the Republic of Ireland where Gaelic remains the predominantly-spoken language can benefit from the internets' ability to promote community cohesion

Globalization, which is driven by communication technologies, has affected cultures in ways that were not initially anticipated. At first, many people thought that the world would all become Americanized, consuming only American culture, speaking English and wearing American clothes. It turns out that consumer products from around the world are now readily available almost anywhere, not just those produced in the U.S. At the same time, globalization has led to a reassertion of traditional cultural values, especially religion. The spread of American consumer products and economic values to countries such as Turkey and India has been endorsed by religious fundamentalists in both those countries, who combine American-style neoliberal economic openness with a reassertion of traditional Islamic values in Turkey and traditional Hinduism in India.

The debate about the impact of globalization and the internet on culture was prominent in the early 1990s and was characterized by the disagreement between two American political theorists, Francis Fukuyama, and Samuel P. Huntington. Fukuyama argued that with the end of the Cold War and the onset of economic globalization, society had reached "the end of history." By this, he meant that there would be no more wars or violent conflict because everyone in the world would adopt American culture. By contrast, Huntington argued that this new period of globalization would cause a "clash of civilizations" and increase tension between groups of countries with different cultural values. Huntington argued that the increased connection, communication and trade would only accentuate cultural differences.

After the 9/11 terrorist attacks and the rise of Al Qaida and other religious and cultural terrorist groups, Fukuyama admitted that his theory was not quite as successful at explaining the new state of the world as Huntington's was. At the same time, however, Huntington does overplay the clash of cultures, as many countries, such as the United States, Canada, and Brazil, have many different cultural traditions that coexist together, rather than leading to armed conflict.

Variations in Culture

Culture varies by place and region.

While sociology and anthropology are more concerned with studying cultural traits on their own, cultural geography is more interested in the link between culture and space. Cultural geographers investigate how cultural traits spread across the land and try to explain why similar regions may have different cultures.

Regional patterns of language, religion, and ethnicity contribute to a sense of place, enhance placemaking and shape the global cultural landscape.

Each region of the world has different language and religion patterns that can shape a sense of place and make different regions feel different from the people who live there. This feeling of difference is not merely a result of living in a different place but is the result of different cultural practices. Such differences can vary in scale, as in two completely different languages or a slightly different accent in the same language. Many people feel more "at home" when they remain in an area with the same culture, while many others find this stifling and boring. The latter group tends to seek out new cultures and experiences and find traveling enjoyable. The first group is often resistant to change and difference and tends to find traveling and experiencing new cultures a frightening experience.

Language patterns and distributions can be represented on maps, charts and language trees.

Geographers will always say that the best way to represent data is on a map. Language distribution patterns are interesting to map because they can show subtle connections between different areas. One interesting example is a map of the most commonly spoken, non-dominant languages in a country. Such a map can show which regions have large cultural minorities and can also shed light on immigration patterns. Such a map for the United States is particularly interesting.

Consider this map of the most commonly spoken languages other than English or Spanish in the United States. By mapping this, a lot can be inferred about various settlement patterns. One can see that Native Americans continue to have a strong cultural presence in South Dakota, Alaska, Arizona, and New Mexico. One can see that states in the Northeast near the border with Quebec have a significant number of French speakers, along with Louisiana which was originally settled by France. It also demonstrates immigration patterns, as there is a strong presence of Vietnamese in Texas and Washington, Arabs in Michigan and Chinese in New York.

A language map can also demonstrate patterns of diffusion and demonstrate how languages from a similar family tend to diffuse to neighboring areas. Consider the map below showing the language families of Europe.

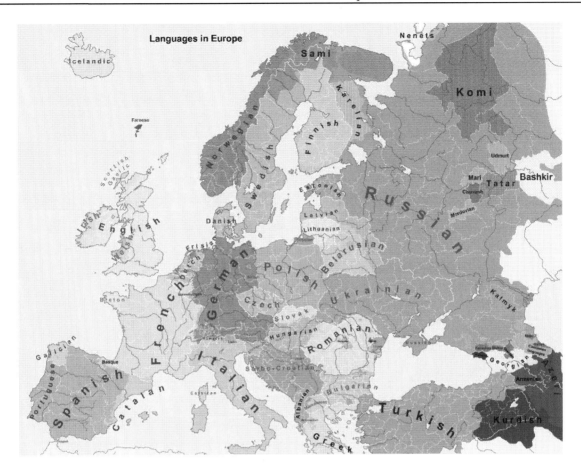

Germanic Languages	Altaic Languages	Slavic Languages	Celtic Languages
• English	• Turkish	• Russian	• Welsh
• German	• Azeri	• Polish	• Irish
• Swedish	• Kalmyk	• Ukrainian	• Scottish Gaelic
• Danish	• Gagauz	• Czech	• Breton
• Norwegian	• Bashkir	• Belarusian	• Manx
• Dutch		• Serbo Croatian	
• Frisian	Celtic Languages	• Slovak	Romance Languages
• Icelandic	• Welsh	• Slovenian	• French
• Faroese	• Irish	• Bulgarian	• Italian
• Luxembourgish	• Scottish Gaelic	• Macedonian	• Spanish
	• Breton	• Sorbian	• Portuguese
Baltic Languages	• Manx		• Catlan
• Lithuanian			• Galician
• Latvian			

Here one can see on the left a chart of language families and how they map onto Europe. One can see the proximity between the Romance languages of Spanish, French and Italian, as well as how the Germanic languages spread from Scandinavia to Germany, Austria, Switzerland, and the Low Countries and then on to England. England and France have the lightest shades of their language group, indicating that both these languages were influenced by each other. The map also has political implications, as today Russia attempts to claim a sphere of influence over the Slavic countries whose languages are closely related to Russian. The map can also point out outliers like Romanian, which is a Romance language derived from Latin surrounded by Slavic and Uralic languages. The map also visualizes the hard difference between the Asian languages of Turkey and Azerbaijan with the rest of the European languages.

Languages of a similar family tend to diffuse into neighboring countries, as is the case with the Romance languages in France, Spain, and Italy, as well as the Germanic languages diffusing from Scandinavia (Sweden, Norway and Denmark) into Germany, Switzerland, Austria, the Netherlands, Belgium and England. Language families can also be influenced by each other, as was the case between France and England. Separate from the rest of Europe is the Asian-influenced Altaic languages of Turkey and Azerbaijan. The diffusion of languages also has political implications; Russia attempts to claim a sphere of influence of the countries that speak the Slavic languages, all of which are closely related to Russian.

Religious patterns and distributions can be represented on maps and charts.

As with language, religion can be mapped. This can not only help show what parts of the world are affiliated with which religion but also helps in understanding patterns of diffusion.

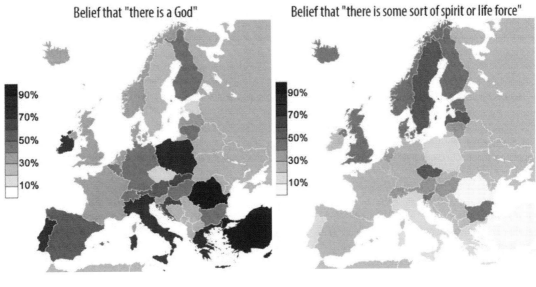

Consider these maps and charts of religiosity in Europe. In the top left map, one can immediately see a pattern that southern Europe (including Turkey) is much more religious than northern Europe, with the notable exception of Ireland. It can be noted that Southern Europe is more Catholic and Northern Europe is mostly Protestant, with Ireland's increased belief in God being explained by the fact that it is a rare Catholic country in the North. The bottom left map shows that France, Sweden, Estonia, and the Czech Republic have the most atheists, which is to be expected since those countries have very secular governments.

The top right map shows how the Scandinavian countries stand out for believing in "spirits or life forces." This is interesting to cultural geographers because these countries had strong pagan religions and were among the last countries in Europe to be converted to Christianity. So even though these countries may not be strong believers in the Christian God, they seem to retain a pagan attitude that there are spirits and other supernatural forces in the world.

Specifically, in Estonia only 16% of people believe in God, making it the least traditionally religious country in Europe. Slovenia has the most atheists with 33% rejecting both God and supernatural spirits. On the other end, Islamic Turkey has 95% of its people believing in God.

Ethnicity and gender reflect cultural attitudes that shape the use of space.

Uses of space are often culturally enforced. If a culture has strong attitudes about maintaining a connection to others of the same culture, then the tendency for ethnic/cultural neighborhoods to appear will be much larger. Cultural attitudes, usually stemming from religion, often shape various social attitudes. Traditional gender roles are enforced by religious cultures that are stubbornly resistant to change and modernization. An area with a strong presence of religion will likely have a stronger power to enforce and reproduce conservative attitudes toward gender. These areas will often have fewer women in the workforce and less female leaders in politics and community life.

One can imagine the difference in two small towns, one of which is strongly religious while the other has a strong sense of civic attachment. These cultural attitudes may entirely determine the spatial arrangement of these two towns. The religious town will have a church as the town center, and residential patterns will emanate out from the church. The civic-minded town might have a public square and a town hall at the center of town, which arranges the social space of the town toward political and community life rather than religion. By studying the spatial arrangements of cities, geographers can figure out the cultural attitudes that shaped the early settlement patterns of these towns.

These spatial arrangements can also indicate historical changes in culture. For example, in many Scandinavian cities, a church was originally the town center. As attitudes changed to become less religious, cities expanded and created new downtown areas focused on public squares. Churches are now positioned outside of the downtown core and have often been converted into private residences or public spaces as the churches lost their congregations due to changing cultural attitudes. Geographers are keen to study the layout of cities in this manner, so they can see how cultural attitudes have changed over time and how those attitudes have affected the spatial development of cities. Today, one of the major concerns of urban geographers is the loss of public space as cities become increasingly privatized.

Language, religion, ethnicity, and gender are essential to understanding landscapes symbolic of cultural identity.

Landscapes devoid of human development are often viewed as wild, untouched or natural. Those areas containing evidence of human history, habitation or activity, however, should be viewed as landscapes symbolic of cultural identity. For example, culturally symbolic landscapes can be evidenced in the seemingly mundane form of street signage or by the presence of sacred sites. To understand these symbolic landscapes better, language, religion, ethnicity, and gender specifically should be brought into the frame.

Language, and the human drive to name locations they interact with offers unique inferences of cultural identity. Language can reveal some things about a place: who lives or lived there, what they value or valued, events that transpired, etc. For example, take place-naming practices in the United States. Being a nation founded through European colonialism, place names in the U.S. are inherently diverse. They reflect both indigenous and immigrant origins, bringing issues of ethnicity into consideration. In the northern borderlands of New England, French place names (e.g., Montpelier, Vermont, Ouellette, Maine) reflect a region historically contested between England and France during the colonial era. In the Midwest and West, German place names (Germantown, Tennessee; Heidecke Lake, Illinois; New Berlin, Wisconsin) signify the immigrant communities who settled there. In the West, the high prevalence of indigenous names (e.g., Spokane, Washington; Flathead Lake, Montana; Chiloquin, Oregon) reflects the enduring presence of indigenous communities and their lasting influence in the region. Place names can also signify the current or historical value attached to the area, as can be discerned in Mechanicsburg, Pennsylvania or Beaverton, Oregon, one community marked by a bygone prevalence of mechanics, the other by the previous fur trade in beaver pelts. Other place names ignore broad ethnic or industry references altogether and instead signify individuals highly regarded by the community (e.g., Hershey, Pennsylvania, named after chocolatier Milton Hershey; Houston, Texas, named after politician Sam Houston; Seattle, Washington, named after Chief Seattle).

As with language, religion can mark a landscape through names (e.g., Moses Lake, Washington) or physical markers, such as sacred sites. For example, abandoned Hindu temples throughout Southeast Asia (e.g., Angkor Wat) evidence not only the faith's previous historic range that has since receded (and been replaced by Buddhism), but also signify the lasting influence of Indian civilization on the region. Mecca in Saudi Arabia, through its high-capacity design and opulent architecture, can easily be seen as a city intended as the yearly destination of millions of Muslims on their Hajj pilgrimage. In Europe, cathedrals, and churches, being in past centuries the unquestioned center of spiritual life for communities, typically occupy locations in the center of town with subsequent buildings radiating out from them.

Finally, a factor as basic as gender itself can exert influence on landscapes. Take, for example, gendered spaces. These spaces are areas implicitly or explicitly intended for a particular gender. They vary greatly from culture to culture, meaning that in some cultures these spaces are strictly regulated while others are much more flexible and tolerant. Examples can include separate bathrooms, nail salons, Turkish baths, gay and lesbian bars and clubs, gendered sections in places of worship, etc.

Types of diffusion include expansion (contagious, hierarchical, stimulus) and relocation.

Culture is transmitted across space through time and migrations of people, being passed down by each generation. Both factors can change cultural patterns. Someone moving to a new area may bring cultural traits that become melded with the traits of the new area, creating a new form of culture. Younger generations may practice cultural traits differently, leading these cultural practices to evolve. One of the ways geographers study this is through the concept of *cultural diffusion*, which is the spread of culture over space and time. Geographers are primarily concerned with space and break cultural diffusion down into two categories: cultural expansion and cultural relocation.

Cultural expansion diffusion is when culture spreads outwards from its origin point in such a way in that its origin point continues to remain the strongest point for the culture. This strong origin point is called a "cultural hearth." Islam for example, spread through expansion diffusion from its origin point in the cities of Mecca and Medina in what is now Saudi Arabia. Mecca remains the central hearth of Islam, and many Muslims travel there each year in pilgrimage. Expansion diffusion can be further broken down into three subtypes: contagious, hierarchical and stimulus expansion.

Spam musubi, a popular local Hawaii dish that

evidence the American and Japanese cultural blending

Stimulus expansion diffusion occurs when a cultural practice is spread from its hearth outwards, but the new adherents alter the practice to fit their customs. An example would be the spread of iced tea around the world. Many cultures have their adaptations of the drink based on local culture in customs. In the southern United States, iced tea became sweet tea because people preferred to drink it with much sugar. In Brazil and other parts of South America, it is often served with lime instead of lemon. In India, it is often flavored with ginger; in Japan, green tea is used instead of black tea. While regular iced tea continues to exist as a globally ubiquitous beverage, there are also many regional adaptations of the drink that provide an example of stimulus expansion diffusion.

Hierarchical expansion diffusion occurs when a culture spreads from a central position of power or influence to places of lesser influence and importance. This method can stem from the influence of an important person, such as a ruler or influential artist, or a culturally important city. One example of hierarchical expansion diffusion is the spread of hip-hop across the United States and then the world. Hip-hop originated in New York City in the 1970s and spread to other major American cities due to the influence of New York as a cultural hub. As hip-hop became popular in the early 1990s, it spread out to suburbs and eventually around the world. One can see a hierarchical pattern; New York City was the influential central point, which then spread hip-hop culture to other larger cities such as Los Angeles, eventually diffusing to the suburbs and the rest of the world. Hip-hop followed a fairly hierarchical pattern of spread — urban first, then suburban before it is globalized and became popular everywhere.

Contagious expansion diffusion is when those connected to an origin all adopt the culture and spread it evenly from the center. This type of expansion is modeled after diseases, where there is a patient zero who spreads a contagious disease through contact. In this model, the culture slowly spreads from person to person based on proximity first. In contrast to hierarchical diffusion, which jumps to large, influential areas and then spreads to less influential areas, contagious expansion slowly creeps out from the center and does not involve large jumps across space. Mormonism is an example of contagious expansion diffusion from its cultural hearth in Salk Lake City, Utah.

Cultural relocation diffusion is when the cultural originators pick up and move to another area, bringing their culture with them. This is different from expansion diffusion because the culture does not remain at its original hearth, but the hearth itself is essentially moved along with the people. In expansion diffusion, what travels across the land is the culture itself, whereas with relocation diffusion, what travels are the people who practice a specific culture. Major migration events, such as in a war or natural disaster, often cause relocation diffusion events.

In the United States, there is the American "Bible Belt," which got its name from the majority of Protestant Christians found across the middle and southeast of the country. Other notable concentrations of religion are the prominence of Roman Catholicism along the Mexican border (due to Mexican immigration), in southern Louisiana (from its French settlements) and around Boston and New York (due to Irish Catholic immigration). The Canadian province of British Columbia and the territory of Yukon have a lot of atheists (partly because the Vancouver area has high immigration rates from China, where most people are atheists).

If all the people associated with a cultural practice are forced to move, the culture may no longer exist in its origin point but will still be practiced in the many new places the migrants settled. Over time, the origin of a culture that has experienced relocation diffusion can become lost. The more people move around, the harder it is to track an origin.

St. Louis Cathedral in New Orleans, the oldest cathedral in the United States

All these various diffusion patterns can also mix. What begins as relocation diffusion may then change to adapt regional customs and become a stimulus expansion diffusion, which may then be adopted by locals living nearby causing contagious expansion diffusion. Mixed patterns are more common in the era of globalization, as migration and global communications technology make it easier for culture to spread and people to move. It also makes it harder to track origins as increasingly cultural traits have their origin in online culture itself, which then spread into other aspects of culture.

Language families, languages, dialects, world religions, ethnic cultures, and gender roles diffuse from cultural hearths, resulting in interactions between local and global forces that lead to new forms of cultural expression.

The interplay between culture and civilization is a constant force. Civilizational forces blend cultures to create new, open and accessible practices, while cultural defenders work to try to keep their practices walled off from outsiders. As a result, the spread of cultural practices involves cultural convergence and divergence. *Convergence* is a civilizational pattern, as it incorporates multiple different cultural traits into the whole. For example, English has spread across the world as the international language of business. As a result, in many countries, students learn English as a second language from a young age to prepare them for dealing with a globalized world. This is an example of civilizational convergence.

Divergence occurs when a cultural group explicitly tries to differentiate and keep itself separate from other cultural groups to prevent their practices from becoming a part of a larger civilizational whole. Many religious groups are today attempting to practice divergence by returning to abandoned practices as a means of differentiation. The followers of Islam are now much more likely to adopt older traditions, such as women observing hijab and wearing coverings over their hair, then they were 50 years ago. In most countries with a majority Muslim population, observing hijab was considered an old-fashioned ritual inappropriate for the modern world as recently as the 1950s and 1960s. After globalization, many Muslims returned to this old tradition as a way to mark themselves as different and attempt to practice cultural divergence.

Colonialism, imperialism, and trade helped to shape patterns and practices of the culture.

Three major factors in cultural diffusion are colonialism, imperialism, and trade. One of the most famous historical examples of culture spreading through trade routes is the Silk Road, which connected the Mediterranean with India and China in the ancient era. Traders seeking riches from other civilizations would come into contact with people from other cultures and have access to the material products of their culture. This meant that economic exchange led to cultural exchange as well. The Silk Road was instrumental in spreading Buddhism from India to the east, and when Arab merchants controlled the core of the Silk Road, Islam was spread by these traders. In many cases, these economic exchanges led to cultural blending. Some Chinese coins from around 600-400 B.C. have been found that incorporated Greek-style art. Today globalization influences culture, as material cultural products such as film, television and video games from around the world are easily accessible through the internet.

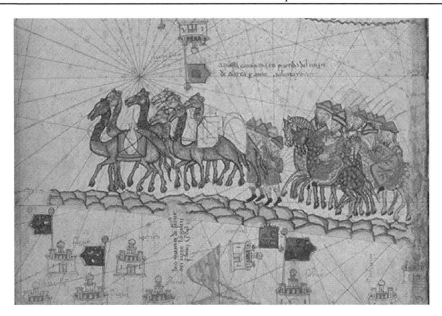

Silk Road caravan traders

Imperial conquests often had significant effects on the culture of not just the region that was conquered but sometimes on the conqueror as well. The spread of Islam was largely driven through military conquest because Mohammed was a military leader of extraordinary talent, able to conquer various pagan tribes and convert them to Islam. Later Islamic dynasties would continue to use imperial conquest as a way to spread their religion. In some cases, imperial conquest can affect the culture of the winners as well. When Alexander the Great conquered the massive Persian Empire, he incorporated many Persian cultural practices into his lifestyle and encouraged Greeks to emulate the Persians in many ways. In part, Alexander found many of the Persian customs interesting and worth adopting, but he also believed that by intermixing the two cultures he could try to blend Persia and Greece, two traditional enemies, into a single culture and secure the power of his empire.

Acculturation, assimilation, and multiculturalism are shaped by the diffusion of culture.

Acculturation occurs when two cultures come into contact, and the smaller culture begins to adopt aspects of the larger culture. An example of acculturation would be when the various groups of Plains Native Americans, including the Apache, Blackfoot, and Sioux, traded with Europeans to gain access to horses. Horses were not a native species to North America, and these cultural groups had never seen horses before. They did, however, quickly realize how useful horses were by observing Europeans and quickly adapted horses into their cultural practice. The use of horses was so quickly and strongly acculturated by these groups that today they are often depicted as riding horses, even though this was a cultural trait picked up very late in their history.

Assimilation differs from acculturation because it involves the complete absorption of a smaller culture. So while the Blackfoot, for instance, became acculturated with aspects of European culture, they did not become assimilated because they kept their cultural uniqueness. In some cases, acculturation can lead to full-on assimilation as a smaller group becomes indistinguishable from a larger cultural group. Assimilation often occurs with groups that are either very small in population compared to the larger culture or very weak in political power. One example of cultural assimilation was in Europe in the 1700s and 1800s. During this time, in most countries, Jews were not considered citizens of a country and were not given political or civil rights. To gain these basic rights, Jews would have to assimilate culturally. Many Jews in this period converted to Christianity, stopped teaching their children Hebrew and gave up other Jewish cultural practices to assimilate with mainstream Christian culture and obtain political and civil rights.

Multiculturalism occurs when various cultural groups live in close proximity with minimal acculturation and no assimilation. A multicultural society is one where the cultural practices and beliefs of different groups operate independently of each other with no overlap. Sometimes the government of a multicultural region will enable this situation by allowing different groups to have different laws apply to them based on their different culture. Multiculturalism is often confused with *pluralism* (sometimes called "transculturalism"), which is when people from various cultures live nearby but all mix. Multiculturalism maintains rigid cultural boundaries whereas pluralism tears down these boundaries and cultural practices become inclusive rather than exclusive. Pluralism is also different from assimilation because instead of a smaller cultural group being absorbed into a larger group, everyone is sharing and adapting the cultural traits of one another. In this sense, pluralism is like a horizontal version of acculturation. In regular acculturation, the smaller group adapts traits from the larger group. In a pluralist society, every group adapts traits from every other group to create a more cosmopolitan society.

Ethnic religions are generally found near the hearth or spread through relocation diffusion.

There are two main types of religions, universalizing and ethnic religions. An *ethnic religion* is one that is tied to a specific group of people. Ethnic religions do not try to convert outsiders to their religion but instead, try to maintain the power of the religion for a specific group. Since these religions are associated with specific cultural groups, they tend to originate near a cultural hearth and only spread through the movement of people. Examples of ethnic religions today are Judaism and Hinduism. Examples of ethnic religions in history include Norse, Greek, Germanic, and Roman paganism. Ethnic religions can be either monotheistic or polytheistic.

The depiction of the Norse god Odin meeting with a vǫlva (female shaman)

The belief systems of an ethnic religion tend to be tied to the experiences of a specific group of people and their circumstances. Judaism involves the exodus of the Jewish people from Egypt, and it involves themes of keeping the cultural group intact and positing its superiority to other cultures. These beliefs were tied to the experience of early Jews fleeing persecution and trying to maintain cultural cohesion. Early European paganism also involved beliefs tied to the circumstances of specific cultural groups of people. In ancient Greek polytheism, different cities often focused on worshipping different gods whom they felt a stronger attachment to. In Athens, where philosophy and science originated, they focused much of their worship on Athena, the goddess of wisdom. By contrast, in the militarily-oriented Sparta, their favorite gods were Ares and Apollo, the gods of war and healing.

The largest surviving ethnic religion today is Hinduism, which has around one billion adherents, making it the third largest religion in the world. Hinduism is also the oldest surviving religion, with origins dating back to the earliest human settlements in the Indus Valley in 1750 B.C. Hindu beliefs are a combination of various traditional cultural beliefs of ancient India. Because Hinduism is so tied to the cultural practices of ancient Indians, it is considered an ethnic religion. Beyond the major beliefs in karma, samsara and dharma, it focuses on practices that are varied and tend to relate to a person's cultural heritage and position in the caste system. As such, it is mainly concerned about keeping alive ancestral practices rather than trying to win new converts. A new convert to Hinduism is a concept that is somewhat alien to the religion, as a new convert would have no ancestral and cultural heritage within Hinduism, which dictates the types of religious practices they should engage in.

Since the concept of a new convert is foreign to Hinduism, the religion has spread through relocation diffusion. Due to its ancient origins, it spread across India with the spread of human civilization throughout the fertile Indus River Valley. As early human settlers expanded, the religion spread to the island of Sri Lanka and regions bordering what is today India. Since India has maintained a very large population, the religion has been able to persevere against many threats. Buddhism was an early rival which sought to replace Hinduism, but it eventually died out in India due to the strength of the caste of Hindu priests called Brahmins in the 12th century. In the 16th century, much of India was invaded by Muslim peoples, and the Mughal Empire was established in much of India and survived until the 19th century. Despite the government taking on Islam as the official religion for India and many instances of persecution of Hindus, the vast majority of the population resisted conversion, allowing Hinduism to survive.

Hinduism is very closely associated with the cultural landscape of India, which is a large and diverse country with many different languages and regional practices. As mentioned above, Hinduism accommodates these regional practices, and it is aided by the fact that it does not have a singular holy book, but a collection of scriptures called "Vedas." The basic beliefs of Hinduism are "karma," which is the idea that good and bad deeds are rewarded and punished after one dies. "Samsara" is the belief that humans are continually reincarnated, with their karma determining the quality of life their next reincarnation will lead to. "Dharma" is a set of duties that one should follow to maintain a high level of karma. "Moksha" is the ultimate goal of Hinduism, and it involves obtaining a higher level of being as a result of many samsara cycles, which allows an individual to become one with God and become liberated from the cycle of death and rebirth.

Hinduism greatly affects how space and people are organized. Traditionally, India has been governed by a strict caste system set out by Hinduism. A caste system is a social and economic hierarchy in which one's birth affects their position in life. Being born to parents of a high caste means one will be of high caste and being born to parents of a low caste means a person will be of low caste. This system of rigid social hierarchy that prevents upward mobility is justified by the belief that people born into the lower castes are being punished for having bad karma in their past life. One can also see how Hinduism was a useful political ideology for the ruling elites, who could claim that their superior position was backed by religious truth. Hindus also hold the Ganges River in India to be a sacred place, further tying the religion to its geographical origins. Many Hindus seek to bathe and cremate their dead in the Ganges River, believing it to be holy.

Illustrations from the manuscript Seventy-Two Specimens of Castes in India

Judaism is also considered an ethnic religion, primarily because it is generally believed that one must be born a Jew to be a Jew. Some sects allow conversion, but due to the association with a specific ethnic-cultural group of people, conversion is generally a limited exception rather than something that is actively promoted. Today there are three main branches of Judaism plus one special case. Orthodox Judaism seeks to retain the original practices of Judaism, and it is fiercely traditional, fundamentalist and seeks to reject the modern world in favor of ancient practices. Orthodox Jews consider all non-Orthodox Jews not to be Jewish and believe the religion is passed down by the mother. They follow the Torah (holy book) literally and are in many ways like the Amish of Judaism, with many rejecting modern practices in favor of ancient laws and codes of behavior.

Reform Judaism is the most liberal of the branches, and it seeks to modernize Judaism. It emerged in the late 1700s among the mass conversion of Jews to Christianity to win political rights in Europe. It promoted modernizing Jewish practices to make them seem less alien to mainstream European Christianity in the hopes that Jews could win political rights as Jews and not have to convert to Christianity. This version of Judaism argues that religions need to evolve to keep up with the times. As a reaction against Reform Judaism, Conservative Judaism arose around the same period and sought to reaffirm traditional practices, albeit in a less extreme way than Orthodox Jews. In the United States, Conservative and Reform Jews have about the same number of adherents, with a much smaller number of Orthodox Jews. The special case, which is about 10% of Jews in the United States, are people who identify as Jewish culturally and ethnically but are atheists and do not believe in the religious aspects of Judaism. They treat the religion purely as a folk culture and deny there is any higher meaning to it.

Jewish groups have affected the cultural landscape in many ways throughout history. After various Jewish rebellions against the Roman Empire were crushed, many Jews based in Palestine began to settle on the outskirts of the Empire in Europe and unconquered areas, such as Germany. These Jews spread through relocation diffusion and brought with them their cultural practices. In the Middle Ages, Jews formed the basis of the urban merchant class as strict Christian laws prevented Christians from loaning money. Jewish culture became associated with urban living, and after the Enlightenment, many Jews were at the forefront of science and philosophy owing to their unique position as non-Christians, which made them much more receptive to the radical new ideas of the Enlightenment. Today, synagogues can be found across Europe and North America, along with the characteristic six-pointed star that symbolizes Judaism. Orthodox Hasidic Jewish communities, such as in Brooklyn, New York, have brought unique cultural practices that have shaped the landscape of the area.

Other ethnic religions include Shintoism and Confucianism. Shintoism is a syncretic combination of Buddhism blended with traditional Japanese folk religion that became the state religion of Japan from the 1800s until after World War II. Shintoism is folk religion, and it involves the worship of one's Japanese ancestors and thus is tied specifically to Japan. Shintoism often becomes a political issue in China-Japan relations. There are Shinto Shrines dedicated to generals and soldiers of the Japanese Imperial Army that committed war crimes against the Chinese. When the Japanese Prime Minister visits or decides not to visit such shrines, it is a big deal in China, where visiting such a shrine is considered an insult to the Chinese people.

Religion is often a source of conflict, regardless of whether it is ethnic or universalizing, polytheistic or monotheistic. One reason geographers are interested in ethnic and universalizing religions is in how they interact on the boundaries of other religions. It may seem like an ethnic religion might be prone to less conflict since it would not be trying to spread to other areas like a universalizing religion, but ethnic religions can have an almost racist element that universalizing religions lack. An ethnic religion usually promotes one cultural or ethnic group as "the chosen people," as in Judaism, with all other people considered inferior. This can cause border tensions.

Some of the major religious boundaries that geographers today are interested in are often called *cultural fault lines*. Just like a physical fault in which two continents rub together, causing tension and often earthquakes, cultural/religious fault lines are often areas of violence and war. Nigeria is a site of a major religious fault; the northern half of the country is Islamic, and the southern half is Christian, which leads to persistent violence. India is a site of multiple faults, owing to its popularity as an origin place of religion. There is a major boundary between Hinduism and Islam along the India-Pakistan border and again between Hinduism and Sikhism in the Punjab region.

Darunaman Mosque in Chiang Rai province

In Eastern Europe, the boundary between Muslim Bosnia and Christian Serbia and Croatia was the site of a major war in the 1990s. Palestine and Israel is a continued source of conflict between Jews and Muslims. Today Iraq has become a major religious fault line,

---

as part of the country follows Sunni Islam, while another (bigger) part follows Shia Islam. In Thailand, there has been violence carried out by the Buddhist majority upon the people of the southern peninsula who are mostly Muslims and vice versa. Sri Lanka is also marked by a persistent conflict between the Buddhist majority continually oppressing the Hindu Tamil minority. Religious boundaries are today one of the major causes of violence and war, and they are an increasingly important field of study for cultural geographers.

Universalizing religions are spread through expansion and relocation diffusion.

In contrast to an ethnic religion, a *universalizing religion* tends to be less connected to a specific cultural group, and its practices are more attractive to converts. Universalizing religions see their religion as the truth for all people and seek to convert people from all cultures to their religion. Naturally, this means that these religions spread very fast, as they rely on diffusing ideas rather than people. With a universalizing religion, the beliefs are often specifically designed to appeal to people of different cultural backgrounds. Christianity and Islam are major universalizing religions and encompass people from different cultures around the world.

Christianity is an interesting example of a universalizing religion because it began as an ethnic religion. The teachings of Jesus were originally meant for Jews, as Jesus positioned himself as the Jewish Messiah. In the early years of Christianity, its followers were exclusively Jews who largely saw themselves as Jews who had recognized that Jesus fulfilled the Jewish prophecy of the Messiah. Christianity in its earliest form was an ethnic religion that did not spread very far from its cultural hearth of Jerusalem. However, once the teachings of Paul were incorporated into Christianity, it became a universalizing religion. Paul was a Roman citizen and originally a pagan, and as such he was an outsider to the primarily Jewish-based early Christian teachings. Paul taught that Jesus' teachings applied to everyone, not just Jews, and started a movement to convert Romans to Christianity. Paul's key teaching was that Jesus did not care if one was a Roman or a Jew and all that mattered was believing in Jesus and God.

By universalizing the belief system so that anyone could feel that he or she could follow Christian teachings, Paul affected the radical transformation of Christianity from an ethnic to a universalizing religion. When the Roman Emperor Constantine converted to Christianity in the fourth century, decriminalizing Christianity and setting it up to become the new religion of the Roman Empire, he commissioned the composition of an official Christian Bible out of the variously fragmented bibles floating around at the time.

Constantine also incorporated Roman pagan practices and rituals into Christianity, creating a second universalizing revolution. Pagans could now convert to Christianity while still being able to celebrate their traditional festivals, which were simply renamed to correspond to Christian beliefs. Early Christianity was a very syncretic religion, taking many themes and beliefs from Roman paganism, such as virgin births, halos around saints, the holy blood of a savior and the eating of the symbolic body of the savior. Such pagan practices incorporated into Christianity made conversion easier. Today, Christianity retains this syncretic element in parts of Africa and Latin America where folk religions have been incorporated into mainstream Christian practice.

Islam is also a major universalizing religion, with the second most adherents in the world today. Islamic monotheism originally spread through the military genius of Mohammed, who was able to conquer various pagan tribes in the Arabian Peninsula and unite them under Islam. As with Christianity, early Islam was syncretic in that it incorporated many of the practices of the pagan tribes to make the new universal religion more appealing. The concept of "jinn," fire beings that can be either positive spirits serving Allah or demons serving Shaytan, has its basis in Arabic paganism and was incorporated into Islam by the early spreaders of the religion. Since Islam is insistently monotheistic, unlike Christianity in which there is a tripartite God and Judaism in which pagan gods are recognized (though the Jewish god Yahweh is superior), these pagan syncretic elements are often hard for Islamic theologians to explain. The Black Stone, which sits as the cornerstone to the Kaaba in the Grand Mosque in Mecca, is considered one of Islam's holiest sites. Originally, this black rock was worshipped by Arab pagans; it was subsequently incorporated into Islam so that pagans could adopt the new religion while maintaining their historical, cultural practices.

Like Christianity, Islam directly affects the cultural landscape through the construction of holy buildings that tend to have common features. Most people can recognize a mosque, a Roman Catholic Church and an Orthodox Christian church based on the common architectural patterns they follow. Islamic mosques, like many Christian churches, were often the center of a town and had bells which were rung to call people to attend religious services. Many mosques are designed with ornate geometrical patterns because of the Islamic prohibition of depicting human forms in art.

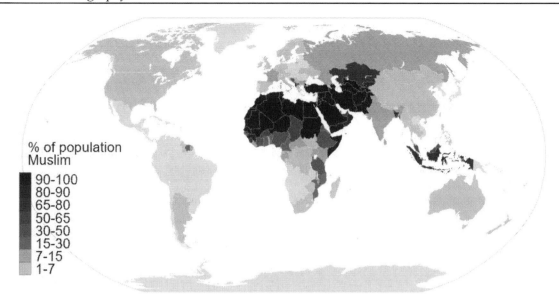

World Muslim population by percentage

By contrast, many Catholic churches are characterized by their stained-glass windows depicting the various saints of Christian mythology. Due to the Islamic requirement to participate in the hajj at least once, hundreds of thousands of Muslims travel to Mecca every year. As a result, the cultural landscape of Mecca has adapted to facilitate large-scale religious tourism. In recent years, the government of Saudi Arabia has been criticized for not providing proper safety measures for the large numbers of people and for building shopping malls in very close proximity to the Grand Mosque.

Cultural landscapes incorporating religion can also become highly contested sites of conflict. The city of Jerusalem in Israel is considered a holy city by Judaism, Christianity, and Islam, with each religion at one time having control over the city. Due to this historical situation, there are very important holy sites for each of the three big monotheistic religions all practically right beside each other. This creates conflict, as sometimes followers of the different religions can be intolerant and indeed hostile of the others. It also creates political issues for the government of Israel, as Christians and Muslims often claim they have a right to visit their religion's holy sites, while Israel is worried about tourists disrespecting the Jewish sites and increasing conflict in an already volatile region.

In addition to Christianity and Islam, the other major universalizing religions today are Buddhism and Sikhism. Buddhism originated as a Hindu deviation created by Siddhartha Gautama in the 5th century B.C. Buddhism and Hinduism share a common belief in karma, reincarnation and the quest to achieve liberation from the rebirth cycle.

Buddhism differs because it is not interested in the pantheon of local and cultural gods that are embraced by Hinduism. Buddhism focuses on achieving a state of existence free of desire rather than seeking a form of selfless unity with the creator god as in Hinduism. By divorcing some of these Hindu practices and beliefs from the concept of god, Buddhism moved away from being an ethnic religion. Having a traditional god that one's village is associated with, which dictated the type of religious practices they would engage in, no longer mattered in Buddhism because the elimination of desire is more of a personal quest. This opened Buddhism up to people of many different cultures. Buddhism also openly attacked the Hindu caste system that was deeply ingrained in Indian society, further liberating it from concerns specific to India.

As Buddhism divorced itself from specific cultural concerns unique to India, it spread through active attempts to convert people. By contrast, most Hindus believe that to be a Hindu one must be born a Hindu because the cycle of rebirth links one back to traditional Indian culture. For Buddhists, evangelical attempts to convert people become a priority because the Buddhist focus on rejecting desire means a rejection of specific cultures or ethnic practices. Buddhism primarily spread to the east from its hearth in India, winning many converts in Tibet, Burma, Thailand, and Indonesia before spreading to China, Mongolia and Japan.

Buddhist monks gather in front of Angkor Wat in Cambodia

Eventually, Buddhism was all but eliminated in India, but it remained strong in other countries. This is an interesting example of expansion diffusion where the religion spread rapidly to other places but was lost in its original location. Like other religions, Buddhism changes the cultural landscape through a form of common architecture among its pagodas. Buddhism is also strongly associated with the Bodhi tree, which is a type of fig tree that is often planted widely in Buddhist-dominated areas.

Sikhism is a smaller and relatively more recent religion, with its origins in the late 15th century. Guru Nanak created Sikhism and spread from its origin in Pakistan to the Punjab region of Northern India. Much of Sikhism borrows elements from Hinduism and Islam, the two predominant religions during the time of its creation. Sikhism incorporates the Islamic idea that anyone can be a Sikh and specifically repudiates the idea of a caste system found in Hinduism. Sikhism is monotheistic but also teaches that, like in Hinduism, the goal of each believer is to become one with God. Sikhs believe in reincarnation and karma, but they also incorporate elements of Islamic theology in that they believe that God's grace can forgive people and determine their actions. While Buddhism can be simply summed up as Hinduism without gods, Sikhism can be summed up as Hinduism with only one god.

Sikhism initially spread among the poor in the Punjab region because it rejected the rigid caste system of Hinduism without eliminating common beliefs like the government's preferred religion of Islam did. After persecution by the Islamic Mughal rulers of India throughout the 1600s, the Sikhs began to organize politically and militarily and formed the Khalsa as a quasi-political entity with the intent to form a military and overthrow the Mughal rulers. By 1799, the Sikhs had carved out their empire in what are now parts of Afghanistan, Pakistan, and Northern India, with its capital in Lahore, Pakistan. The Sikh empire did not last long, as British colonization in 1839 led to the disintegration of the empire and its reincorporation into British India. After British decolonization, when India and Pakistan were separated into two countries, one being Hindu and the other Muslim, Sikhs became the target of violence on both sides as the minority religion in both countries. This led to a wave of emigration, and many Sikhs fled to the U.K. and Canada to avoid the violence.

The Sikhs who remained in India and Pakistan continued to agitate for their own country and were met with repression. In 1984, the Indian government launched Operation Blue Star to remove the pacifist Sikh leader from a temple he was protesting at, which resulted in the military killing many Sikhs. Two Sikhs then assassinated the Indian Prime Minister Indira Gandhi, and increasingly Sikh separatists resorted to terrorist attacks, including the bombing of Air India Flight 182 from Montreal to Delhi. This terrorist attack killed all 329 people on the plane and was carried out by Sikh extremists based in the

Canadian diaspora. Outside of India, Canada has the largest population of Sikhs, who make up 1.4% of the population. Sikhs in Canada have risen to major political positions as well, including four cabinet positions. By contrast, only two Sikhs hold cabinet positions in India. In this manner, Sikhism has changed the cultural landscape of Canada through its political engagement both in a representative democracy and in its association with the largest terrorist attack ever committed against Canada.

Cultural landscapes are amalgamations of physical features, agricultural and industrial practices, religious and linguistic characteristics and other expressions of culture.

A *cultural landscape* is the combination of physical terrain and human-created changes to that landscape. The idea of a cultural landscape captures the interaction between human culture and physical geography. One can think of the physical terrain as a canvas on which human cultural groups paint their art. The geographer Carl Sauer, who popularized the term cultural landscape, describes culture as an agent that acts on the physical landscape, creating a cultural landscape. The United Nations World Heritage Committee has identified some important cultural landscapes that are of universal value to the human species.

Batad Rice Terraces

An example of a cultural landscape recognized by the World Heritage Committee is the Batad Rice Terraces in the Philippines. It involves a series of rice fields that follow the contours of the nearby mountains, demonstrating human culture interacting with the physical environment. The landscape also has elements in the wooden buildings, which are unique to Southeast Asia. The people who live here can trace rice cultivation on the hillsides back 1,000 to 2,000 years, which also demonstrates how changing irrigation technologies have led to expansions of the rice farms to different areas and previously inhospitable terrain. This cultural landscape has also affected the local culture and folk beliefs, which have managed to remain partially alive as the unique terrain has made it difficult for outsiders to conquer or assimilate the people who live there.

Folk culture origins are usually anonymous, rooted in tradition and found in rural or isolated indigenous communities.

The Batad Rice Terraces are an example of folk culture, as the people have a set of cultural practices dating back to a now extinct ancient civilization. These practices have remained intact due to the isolated and rugged terrain. *Folk culture* by definition is generally limited to small groups of people, often isolated or separate from larger cultural groups. The origins of folk culture are often anonymous and sometimes survive today as superstitions or other practices of which no one knows the origins. For example, the idea that a black cat crossing one's path will give that person bad luck is an example of a folk culture belief.

Sometimes folk culture is purposely preserved in reaction against the dominant popular culture followed by most people. For example, Amish communities in the United States only use technology from the late 1800s and earlier, while the rest of the country continues to use newer technologies. Amish people ride around in horse and buggy while most Americans now use a car, train or plane.

Folk culture often spreads through relocation diffusion, and the Amish are an example. They originated in Switzerland in 1693 after a religious dispute among subsects of Anabaptists. Eventually, the Amish decided to emigrate from Switzerland and come to America, where they settled in the 18th and 19th centuries, bringing their version of Christian culture with them and resisting assimilation and acculturation with the other immigrants to America. Today folk culture is generally used to refer to any traditionally-bound cultural practices that are no longer in fashion.

Popular culture origins are often urban, changeable and influenced by media.

Popular culture is the opposite of folk culture, in that it diffuses through expansion and is generally mainstream. The difference between popular culture and folk culture can be demonstrated through the types of music that people listen to. The difference between a pop singer like Taylor Swift, who is popular among all sectors of the American population and sells millions of albums, and an Alaskan Inuit throat singer who is only popular in her small cultural group is a good example of the difference between pop culture and folk culture. Folk culture is often seen as old-fashioned, while many see pop culture as superficial. Pop culture is predominant in urban areas and is spread through media such as radio, television and the internet. Folk culture is largely isolated to traditional and rural communities and tends to stay alive through oral transmission rather than mass media and technological reproduction.

In many cases, popular culture begins as folk culture but undergoes a series of minor changes to make it accessible to everyone. For example, the Hawaiian tradition of giving all visitors to the islands a lei (a garland usually strung with flower blossoms) was once a part of folk culture integral to the religious practice of Hawaiians. However, it has become a part of popular culture, along with wearing Hawaiian shirts and saying "Aloha." Many forms of music also began as folk songs but were incorporated into popular culture. Rock and roll music was originally folk music of African Americans that incorporated elements of rhythm and blues, gospel music and boogie-woogie genres. Interestingly enough, rock and roll entered popular culture through the radio, which blurred the race of the performers. Since there were cultural taboos and racist stereotypes at the time associated with white people listening to "black music," the fact that the music was being heard over the radio allowed rock and roll to enter the pop culture.

The first rock and roll concert, which happened in Cleveland in 1952, ended up being shut down by police who were concerned about a large gathering of racially-mixed youth. The political spectacle of black and white kids all enjoying dancing to the same music (whose lyrics were full of sexual innuendo) caused the white authorities to fear that this was a potential revolution in the making and shut down the concert after one song. From this point on, what was once marginalized as African American folk culture exploded to become the dominant form of mainstream popular music for the next 60 years. Many music historians today credit the popularization of rock and roll music with helping to break down some of the racial prejudices dominant in early 1950s America, showing how changes to the cultural landscape can lead to changes in the political landscape as well.

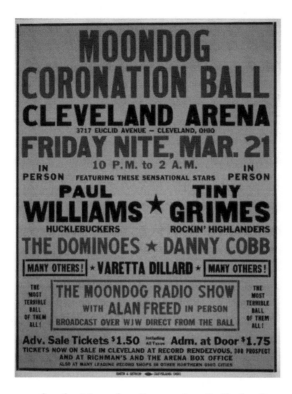

Promotional poster for the Moondog Coronation Ball, the first rock and roll concert

Popular culture is also much more dynamic than folk culture. What is popular is always changing, and new material is always coming out. By contrast, in folk culture newness is looked down upon. The attitude is generally along the lines of "We already have the songs that we've sung for two hundred years, why write new ones?" Folk culture is inherently conservative because it tries to conserve the traditions of the past, while popular culture is inherently innovative because it is always trying to come up with "the next big thing."

Chapter 4

Political Organization of Space

The nature and significance of the political organization of territory are often discussed regarding scale: local, national and global. In contemporary times, the world map is shaped by many different contributing forces. Ideas of territoriality are frequently reflected in political patterns. How the Earth is organized affects how power over space and boundaries are exercised. To a significant degree, the modern state's political geography and international relationships are major themes. Also, the advent of European nation-states transformed the spatial organization. Likewise, the influence of colonialism, imperialism, supranational organizations, and devolution states have been powerful agents of change.

Political maps and how to read them involves navigating important inconsistencies, such as between maps of political boundaries and maps of ethnic, cultural, economic and environmental patterns. Understanding the forces that are altering the modern world roles of individual countries is gained through analysis of ethnic separatism, terrorism, economic globalization and (cross-border) social and environmental problems. Complete understanding of subnational and supranational political units (e.g., state level and regional alliances) is also requisite. Also affecting political, social and economic processes are the functions and interactions of the sub-state level, such as electoral districts, municipalities, indigenous areas, provinces, and autonomous lands.

World Political Map

The contemporary political map has been shaped by events of the past.

Looking at a map today, the borders between countries appear somewhat static. Countries rarely change their borders over one person's lifespan, and it can seem like a map of political boundaries is as natural and fixed as a map of physical terrain. However, the borders of countries are human creations and have been shaped by history. A map of the world from 1988 would look very different from a current map, as the fall of the Soviet Union led to a major rearrangement of the borders within Europe and northern Asia.

Modern-day Russian Federation (in black) with regions in white indicating lost territory after the fall of the Soviet Union; Crimea (striped) is currently contested between Russia and Ukraine.

Independent states are the primary building blocks of the world political map.

Political geography often deals with different scales. Scale is usually broken into three levels: global, country and local. World maps are concerned with the country-level scale and depict the borders between independent states. The focus on the borders between states reflects a predominant view that the current era is dominated by relations between states and the idea that states are the most powerful political entities today. This situation was not always the case. For example, in the colonial era maps would focus not on differentiating states, but on grouping colonial possessions. A map of the British Empire would contrast itself with the colonial possessions of Spain and France, for example, but be unconcerned with differentiating between Canada and the thirteen colonies in New England. In the future, if suprastate entities such as the European Union become more dominant, maps may not be concerned with visualizing the individual countries of Europe and paint the entire EU in the same color. In this sense, how a map of the world is depicted is a reflection of how the world is imagined, rather than any objective reality which a terrain map depicts.

Types of political entities include nations, states, nation-states, stateless nations, multinational states, multistate nations, and autonomous regions.

In addition to standard global maps that focus on political boundaries between countries, political maps can depict other scales and entities which are not independent states. A map of nationality is often interesting to superimpose on a map of states to see how well nations match to states. In much of Europe, where the idea of a nation having a one-to-one correspondence with a state originated, many states line up with nations. A notable exception is the United Kingdom, named as such because it encompasses not just the nation of England but Wales, Scotland and Northern Ireland as well. Northern Ireland is interesting because most people who live there are Irish by nationality but do not live in the state of Ireland. It is important to remember that a nation refers to the people, usually with a common culture and language, and state refers to the control of a territory by a centralized political authority.

In areas where nations which have a state overlap into the territory of other states, such as with Northern Ireland, there is often tension. Throughout much of the 20th century, the Irish Republican Army operated in Northern Ireland as a paramilitary group which aimed to make Northern Ireland part of the independent state of Ireland. They argued Northern Ireland was Irish by nationality and it was unjust that the United Kingdom politically controlled it. Sometimes nations exist without a state, such as Scotland within the United Kingdom. Scotland has a unique culture, and a significant minority of people in the nation of Scotland believe that it should become an independent state. The United

Kingdom is a good example of a multinational state, as it encompasses England, Scotland, Wales, and Northern Ireland. While some multinational states can be a site of tension between the nations, such as in the U.K., as the world becomes more globalized and super-state entities become more common, the idea of a nation having its state becomes less and less relevant.

In addition to the idea of nations, states, nations without states, and states with multiple nations, there are "multi-state nations." These are nations which stretch across multiple states. The Irish are a good example; they stretch across Ireland and Northern Ireland as well as having a significant presence in the United States. The Kurdish nation stretches across parts of Northern Iraq, Syria and Southern Turkey. The Kurds have often fought for an independent state but given that they cross so many different existing states, this has been a tough task. It is much easier for a nation which is wholly contained within a state to break away and become independent, as when South Sudan became independent of the rest of Sudan.

After the U.S. invasion of Iraq in 2003, the Kurds of Northern Iraq have been able to form their government and operate as an autonomous region. This means that they are still formally part of the independent state of Iraq, but they largely are in control of their territory and are somewhat independent of the Iraqi government. The Kurds in Northern Syria have also formed their autonomous government in Rojava, which operates free of both the Syrian government of Bashir al-Assad and the Islamic State movement to its south. Despite both of these autonomous Kurdish regions neighboring each other, they are not allied and not necessarily even on the same side in the Syrian civil war. The Rojava autonomous region has a decentralized political ideology that promotes radical democracy, while the Iraqi Kurds prefer to have a very centralized and more authoritarian political system. So even groups of people with the same nationality and same wish to be autonomous can be divided by differing political views.

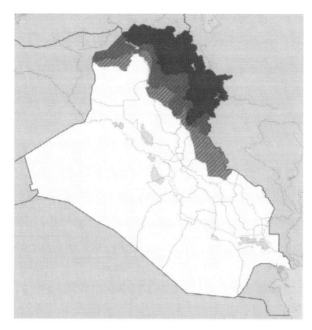

Iraqi Kurdistan (in black) in May 2015, with territory controlled (dark and striped) and claimed (light striped) indicated

The manner in which autonomous regions and areas of contested control of territory are shaped may depend on the political views of the map maker. In this sense, maps can become a propaganda tool. In the civil war in Syria, those loyal to the Syrian government forces often depict Syria as it was before the civil war, as a single state all under the control of the central government. Those sympathetic to the Kurds often make a point of demarcating Rojava as an autonomous region that governs itself. Maps are a reflection of political ideology and are never merely neutral instruments, as the way they depict contested regions is meant to shape how people view the world. Another example is that in maps made by the Chinese government, Taiwan is usually depicted as part of China, when in reality it is an independent country. This is meant to project the idea that Taiwan is rightfully Chinese territory in the minds of people.

The concept of the modern nation-state began in Europe.

Although states are dominant today, they are a relatively recent concept in world history. The earliest unit of human organization was the family and then the tribe, which settled into villages and cities. The ancient Athenians invented the concept of the city as a political unit which was governed by the people democratically, rather than by a tyrant who took power through force or by a king who ruled through family and tribal connections. Empires also preceded the state, as they were often ruled by a king who expanded territory outward, subjugating all the people he could conquer. Much of the ancient world was dominated by a combination of empires which controlled vast tracts of land and subjugated many different cultures and peoples, and independent cities who would often form alliances with like-minded cities. The idea of a nation-state was an alien concept in this era; either cities were the highest political entity, or great empires, which spanned multiple nations, were the highest form of authority. There was no concept for instance, of the various Greek cities forming a national government for Greece. When Alexander the Great brought the various Greek cities under his control, his first plan was to conquer the foreign Persian Empire.

In the Middle Ages in Europe, as the Roman Empire disintegrated, a new system of feudal territorial organization sprang up. Political organization was replaced with a religious organization, and people saw themselves as Christians rather than as French or German or English. While there were monarchs who eventually controlled large swaths of territory, they were seen as having a divine right to rule and mainly controlled their territory through the allegiance of feudal lords. The monarchs eventually increased their power and began to centralize authority and adopt the idea of ruling a common nation of people, such as the French or the English, in the name of religion. By 1517, there was growing discontent with the religious-based kingdoms, and the German Theologian Martin Luther began a rebellion which led to the Protestant Reformation. The Protestant Reformation had sweeping political consequences, as it helped stir nationalism and led a massive war in Europe called the Thirty Years' War.

Germany at the time of the Reformation was under control of the Holy Roman Empire, which was then ruled out of Spain. Many German princes who had begun to feel a sense of German nationalism saw the Reformation as a way to oppose the Catholic Empire and win independence for Germany. As a result, many of the German princes converted to Protestantism, and the core of the Holy Roman Empire became deeply divided along religious lines. Eventually, these religious tensions led to an outbreak of war as Protestant rebels seeking independence in the Netherlands led the Spanish King of the Holy Roman Empire to attack the Netherlands and attempt to put down Protestant revolts in Germany. The war eventually ended when the Catholic King of France, seeing the opportunity to weaken the Habsburg control of the Holy Roman Empire and take control of it for himself, intervened on the side of the Protestants.

The resulting Peace of Westphalia of 1648 was a monumental occasion in the history of Europe. It set out the concept of national self-determination and state sovereignty and ushered in a major shift from religion to nation-states as the most powerful political entity in Europe. Religious entities such as the Pope and the Holy Roman Empire were not to interfere in the national affairs of any nation-state, and a system of diplomacy was created so that states could discuss issues directly with each other. Out of the Peace of Westphalia came the idea that each nation should have its state and should be free to control its internal policies, including what religion it adhered to. This concept, known as sovereignty, has been the basis of the international state system.

A painting portraying the ratification of the Treaty of Münster, the primary agreement of the Peace of Westphalia ending the Thirty Years' War.

Colonialism and imperialism led to the spread of nationalism and influenced contemporary political boundaries.

Many of today's political borders can be traced back to the era of imperialism and colonialism. Colonization occurs when one state takes over another region by imposing political and economic control over it. In most cases the colonized territory was not organized as a state or was relatively weak compared to the colonizer, allowing foreigners to settle in the colonized region and control its government. A major wave of colonization in recent history began in the 16th century, as European powers began to colonize the Western Hemisphere and Southern Asia, eventually culminating in what was known as "the Scramble for Africa." Seafaring empires had a major advantage during the colonial era, as England, France, and Spain colonized the Americas. The Netherlands, although small, used its naval power to colonize Indonesia. Portugal and Belgium were able to colonize parts of Africa, expanding their controlled territory by many orders of magnitude.

In addition to the desire to grow political power by expanding from a nation-state into an empire, the other major motivations for colonialism were religion and economics. Especially among the Catholic colonizers such as Spain, the desire to spread Christianity to native populations was often used as a righteous justification for colonization. The Protestant colonizers, such as England, were more overtly concerned with economic gain. Regardless of the motives and justifications behind colonization, the colonizers treated the native populations as less-than-human nuisances to eliminate and a workforce to brutalize. At the time of colonization, mercantilism was the dominant economic system, and colonization was a form of economic extraction. Natural resources, especially gold, were extracted from the colonies and sent back to the "mother country." Mercantilist economic theory is based on the idea that there is only so much wealth in the world, and states will try to hoard as much of that wealth as they can within their borders to maintain an advantage over competing states. Wealth was extracted from the colonies in the name of building up the power of the state, rather than the independent corporations of the post-mercantilist era.

The competition among the major powers in the colonial era led to imperialist projects where the colonizing powers attempted to reduce the cultural influence of native populations to maintain complete political control over a colonized territory. Imperial competition led to tension among the great powers, which led to imperial wars such as World War I. As the major powers fought to control colonized territories, zones of influence and control were established which often became the borders of states which would later win their independence. One of the most famous examples of imperialism driving the creation of borders was the Sykes-Picot Agreement during World War I. The French, British and Russians made a secret agreement to carve up the Ottoman Empire into spheres of influence should the Empire be defeated. The agreement somewhat arbitrarily divided the Middle East into French and British spheres with little consideration for the religious and linguistic differences among the people who lived in the area. When the countries of the Middle East would later become independent states, they largely followed these borders. Many people point to the arbitrary nature of these borders as the source of

141

much of the contemporary conflict in the Middle East. Countries like Iraq, Syria, and Lebanon had ill-thought-out borders that led to nations without states, nations cutting across multiple states and the persecution of religious minorities.

Independence movements and democratization have shaped the political map since the end of World War II.

After the end of World War II, independence movements began to gain steam in Africa and the Middle East, leading to the creation of many new states. When these territories were under colonial control, they were depicted on maps as spheres of influence of the major powers without any real, hard borders. As the independence movements gained steam, the map was reshaped to depict states and their borders. Eventually, most of the world adopted the European model of state sovereignty, and political maps of the world became maps emphasizing the boundaries between states rather than colonial spheres of influence.

The creation of these new states often aligned with the borders of the zones of influence, and sometimes large territories under the control of one major power were broken into several states. For example, in South America, Spain had controlled most of the territory outside of Brazil. However, decolonization did not lead to one big Spanish-speaking country but many smaller ones. There were multiple fragmentations. Under the leadership of General Simon Bolivar, much of the northern part of South America was originally one country after winning independence from Spain. This new country, called Gran Colombia consisted of what is now Colombia, Venezuela, Ecuador, Panama, Guyana and the northern parts of Peru and Brazil. Economic tensions and a war with Peru eventually led to budding nationalist sentiment, and Gran Colombia broke up into the countries that exist today.

Gran Colombia before splitting into Colombia, Ecuador, Panama and Venezuela and losing territory to Brazil and Britain.

The fall of Communism ended the Cold War, led to the creation of newly independent states and changed the world balance of power.

While decolonization significantly changed the world map, resulting in the creation of many new countries, the second wave of new states emerged after the end of the Cold War. The Cold War itself saw the creation of many new states as a result of decolonization, with the Soviet Union and the United States competing to control these "third world" countries, which originally meant newly independent states not aligned with either side. Many of the "second world" countries, which were Soviet-aligned states, owed their origin to World War II when Russia assumed political influence over much of the territory of the defeated fascist powers. The Soviet Union was a federation which contained many nationalities, languages, and cultures held together by the communist ideology.

With the collapse of the Soviet Union and the fall of communism as a dominant ideology, the key aspect which kept these various cultures united no longer existed, and much of the former communist countries divided up along national, linguistic and religious lines. Parts of the Soviet Union such as Ukraine, Uzbekistan and Kazakhstan became independent countries owing to their cultural and linguistic differences.

The country of Yugoslavia split along religious lines, leading to a civil war throughout the early 1990s, as Orthodox Serbia, Catholic Croatia, and Muslim Bosnia fought for control of territory and attempted to expel followers of other religions from their territory. The dissolution of Yugoslavia was significant because, without the communist political ideology to unite the people, they reverted to their old religious identifications, putting neighbors at odds with each other. The dissolution of Yugoslavia is interesting because before the fall of communism, very few people in Yugoslavia felt much attachment to religion. Even though the three major parts had traditionally been followers of different religions, this was never a source of tension until communism disappeared. The internal wars in Yugoslavia did not result from the re-emergence of ancient hatreds, but a very modern phenomenon of people seeking a new belief system to replace communism. The new-found connection with religion as a dominant belief system created national identities where they had not existed before, leading to the creation of new states out of the civil war.

The fall of communism also had indirect effects in the third world. Previously, the major tension in these countries was between the political choice of staying non-aligned or siding with either America or the Soviets. After the fall of communism, this no longer became a choice as America emerged as the world's only superpower, and these internal political tensions were replaced with religious and ethnic tensions which led to violence rather than political debates and philosophical questions. Religious-based movements emerged as a driving force of conflict, and those movements are now seeking to change the political map. Groups like ISIS are attempting to redraw the borders of Iraq and Syria to carve out a fundamentalist Islamic state, and the Lord's Resistance Army in Uganda have created border conflicts as they engage in religious terrorism in the name of imposing Christianity.

Political Boundaries

> **Spatial political patterns reflect ideas of territoriality and power at a variety of scales.**

Spatial political patterns, including the shape of states and how maps are drawn, can reflect an attempt to project ideology and power. Political power and ideology can be projected through maps themselves. While political maps are often seen as a neutral and objective depiction of the different countries, the type of map projection used can lead to distortions. Since the Earth is a sphere, it cannot be directly mapped onto a two-dimensional square. To compensate for this, cartographers have developed systems to translate coordinates from the sphere to a 2D map. One of the most commonly used map projections is the Mercator projection, which is also one of the worst, as it causes huge distortions in the north. The Mercator is a reflection of Eurocentric ideology because it makes the northern hemisphere look much larger than the southern hemisphere. For example, in a Mercator projection map, Greenland looks to be about the same size as Africa. In reality, Greenland is tiny relative to Africa. Africa is 15 times bigger than Greenland, but you would never realize this by looking at a standard Mercator projection map.

Also, most maps place the U.K. in the center of the map, another expression of ideology as it places the U.K. and Europe at the center of the world, making it seem the most important. Since the Earth is a sphere, there is no center and maps could depict any point in the middle. At the same time, there is no up or down on a sphere, so the orientation of north on top and south on the bottom is another reflection of ideological notions about the northern countries being superior to the southern ones.

Political power is expressed geographically as control over people, land, and resources.

The basis of what defines a state is its ability to exert a monopoly on the use of force over a people in a given territory. Geopolitics comes into play when states are interacting with other states in relation to territory. Geopolitics studies how states interact with each other about the control of territory. There have been some theories to try to explain how geopolitics operates in any given era.

"Organic theory" argues that states are essentially living organisms which hunger for more land and natural resources and will naturally seek to expand to consume more and more of these resources. This theory can trace its origins back to Plato and Hobbes, but it was developed with geopolitics in mind by the German geographer Friedrich Ratzel in the late 1800s. Ratzel argued that borders should be given less emphasis in geopolitics as some states should expand to accommodate their biological-type growth, while others should be forced to contract or be swallowed up by hungrier states. Ratzel developed the concept of "Lebensraum," which translates as "life realm" or "living space," a concept which was appropriated by the Nazis to justify their border expansion and annexation of parts of neighboring countries.

World War II era German map indicating Lebensraum settler routes and destinations

In 1904, British geographer Halford Mackinder published an article outlining a theory of geopolitics which he called the *Geographical Pivot of History*, which was later shortened to *Heartland Theory*. Mackinder divided the Earth up into parts, positing Eurasia as the heartland of the Earth. He argued that whoever controlled this heartland (i.e., Russia) would have immense geopolitical power. Heartland Theory became very influential in the United States during the Cold War — because the Soviet Union controlled the heartland, it was believed to be primed for world domination. The United States became concerned with containing Soviet expansion because they believed that controlling the heartland would allow the Soviets to expand naturally. While there is little evidence to suggest that the Soviet Union was planning to expand into Western Europe, the American government believed this was inevitable and undertook a policy of containment to prevent Soviet expansion. Ironically, at the same time, the Soviets saw the Americans as expanding their influence of control dangerously close to Russian borders and engaged in actions meant to contain American expansion. Both countries ended up seeking to increase their spheres of influence because each thought the other was trying to take over the world.

Another prominent Cold War geopolitical theory that was popular in the United States was the *Domino Theory*. Americans believed that once a country became communist, this would lead to the neighboring countries becoming communist as well. Americans also thought that if the communist revolution was allowed to succeed in Vietnam, most of the countries of Southeast Asia were likely to fall in succession to communism. The Domino Theory was the main rationale for the U.S. invading Vietnam. After the U.S. lost the war and pulled out of Vietnam, allowing it to remain communist, the Domino Theory was proven incorrect, as the other countries of the region (the U.S. was in particular concerned about Thailand and India becoming communist) did not fall, like dominoes, to communism. The American invasion of Vietnam and the subsequent "carpet bombings" of Cambodia and Laos stirred up pro-communist sentiment in those countries as their people turned against the American aggressors.

The *Rimland Theory* was a modification of Heartland Theory developed by American International Relations theorist Nicholas John Spykman. Spykman argued that the Heartland Theory placed too much emphasis on the barren land of Siberia and ignored the influence of naval power. He argued the most important part of the Earth for geopolitical concerns was the rimland area of Eurasia that bordered Russia and was connected to the coast. The key to containing the Soviets according to the Rimland Theory was to control Western Europe, southern Europe, India, China, Japan, and the other countries along this large swath of Eurasia. In reality, there were so many different countries along the rimland that no one power could develop a sphere of influence which would allow global domination.

A more modern approach is *World Systems Theory*, which was developed by Immanuel Wallerstein in the 1970s. This theory is meant to be adaptive to history and change, as it divides the world up into core, semi-periphery and periphery countries, which can change over time. Core countries are ones with highly skilled labor forces which develop intellectual products. Periphery countries rely on extracting raw materials, and semi-periphery countries today primarily engage in manufacturing. The creation of an iPhone can be thought of in terms of World Systems Theory. The rare earth minerals are mined in poor peripheral countries in Africa, the phone itself is manufactured in semi-periphery China, and the phone was designed in the United States. According to World Systems Theory, geopolitical conflict and control throughout history can be explained largely through economics.

Territoriality is the connection of people, their culture and their economic systems to the land.

Territoriality is defined as creating ownership over a piece of land. It is largely an ideological mechanism that operates through culture and economics to foster the idea that a state or a people are intimately connected to a piece of land. Consider the state of Israel, which came into existence in 1948. As a relatively new state that involved pushing out the original inhabitants, Israel has had to work hard to foster a sense of territoriality that makes people believe that Israel should control this piece of land. Territoriality can have imperialist elements as well, as with Russia's recent annexation of Crimea. Russia fostered the idea that Crimea should be rightfully part of Russia through territoriality.

Russian soldiers without insignia deployed to wrest control of Crimea away from Ukraine

Boundaries are defined, delimited, demarcated and administered.

There are three main types of political boundaries which have often been used to mark off one state from another. Sometimes these boundaries are created on a map and then administered in reality, and other times they exist in the real world and are mapped after the fact. The first type of boundary is a *geometric boundary*, which is a straight line drawn on a map that ignores any physical or cultural boundaries. A famous example is the 49th parallel, which is the line of latitude that separates the Western United States from Western Canada. This is an example of a boundary that was drawn on a map and then enforced in reality.

The second type of political boundary is a *physical* or *natural boundary*. These types of boundaries separate states based on elements of the natural world, such as mountains, rivers or lakes. An example of a physical boundary would be Lake Ontario, which divides Canada and the U.S. between Ontario and New York State. The Pyrenees mountains are another good example, providing a natural boundary between Spain and France. Natural boundaries such as this have cut people off from each other in the past, leading to the development of different languages and cultures which would become separate nations and eventually be used as borders for states. Physical boundaries are boundaries that existed in the real world and then were later transposed to a map.

The third type of boundary is a *cultural boundary*. These boundaries roughly follow cultural differences, such as when one region speaks another language or follows a different religion. Originally, the concept of a nation-state was meant to follow cultural borders exactly, but it can be very difficult to map off clear divisions between different cultural groups. People like to mix with others and create new cultures, so using cultural borders as the basis for state borders has traditionally been very difficult. A more recent attempt to create a new state based on cultural borders was the partition of Pakistan from India, which was intended to be divided along the border of Muslims and Hindus. As stated earlier, this border area led to the formation of the syncretic religion of Sikhism, blurring any attempt to draw clear-cut cultural boundaries and eventually leading to violence.

Except free travel zones, such as the European Union, states generally enforce their borders and require travelers to go through customs to control who enters a country. In most cases, this is pretty clear-cut, as both sides are interested in controlling their territory. A special case is on a frontier, which is an area where borders are not clearly established or enforced. In some cases, a border frontier may exist simply because few people live in the area and thus enforcement is unnecessary. The border between Alaska and the Yukon that demarcates Canada and the U.S. is clearly established on maps, but it is a frontier because it is almost completely unenforced except at highway crossings. Someone could easily go through the woods and have no idea that he or she crossed an international border. The second type of frontier borders are ones which are not only sparsely populated and not enforced but also not clearly defined on maps. The border between Saudi Arabia and Yemen is often marked as a dotted line on maps because it is in the uninhabitable desert which is difficult to cross. As a result, neither country has felt the need to define where the border is clearly. Similar situations exist in the Amazon jungle between countries such as Venezuela, Brazil, and Guyana. The jungle is so dense that the borders are not clear and often change on maps as a result of new surveys of the area.

International boundaries establish the limits of sovereignty and can be the source of disputes.

Sovereignty is the ability for a state to exert full authority over its territory and rests on the principle that other states will not interfere with this authority. As a result, disputes often arise at borders for various reasons because these are areas of competing claims to total authority. There are various categories of border dispute which often combine, resulting in an exacerbated dispute.

A *definitional border dispute* involves disagreement over the language of a treaty establishing borders. Often, international borders were set before satellite imagery could give a 100% accurate picture of the entire Earth. The language of these border treaties can be open to interpretation, or one side may claim that, given today's more accurate maps, the border should be shifted slightly. An example of a definitional border dispute occurred in the late 1800s through the early 1900s between Argentina and Chile. The border between the countries had been defined as the highest peaks of the Andes, but various mineral-rich valleys lay between high peaks, which both sides claimed to be their own. Due to the imprecise language of the treaty, the two countries eventually had the dispute sorted out by a third-party arbitrator, but the border between the two countries has been a persistent issue down to the present day.

View from the Chilean side, the Cristo Redentor pass marks the border with Argentina.

A *locational border dispute* happens when both countries agree to the language of a treaty defining the border but disagree in its application to the map. A famous example of a locational border dispute was the Alaska Border Dispute of 1903. Both Canada and the United States agreed roughly where the border between the two countries should run on the Alaskan panhandle but placed it on different locations on the map. Canada accused the United States of trying to steal a large piece of Canadian land by drawing the border too far inland. Unfortunately for Canada, the United Kingdom still controlled Canadian foreign policy in 1903, and to improve relations with the Americans, they ceded a large portion of Canadian land to America. Canada was so angry at the United Kingdom for siding against them in the dispute that a sense of Canadian nationalism began to develop for the first time. Eventually, the Canadian Prime Minister would demand control over his country's foreign policy. While Canada lost a significant piece of land in the dispute, it helped Canada to become an independent country.

Operational border disputes are conflicts over how a border should function and are usually about the flow of migrants. The Mexico-U.S. border is a continual site of operational dispute because Mexico is much less interested in controlling the flow of migrant workers than the United States is. Calls to crack down on migrants by American politicians are often met with criticism from Mexican politicians. Other operational disputes are the manner in which Israel controls borders with the occupied Palestinian territories. Palestinians see Israel as unduly controlling their ability to move within their own territory freely and argue that the two territories of Gaza and the West Bank should not be cut off from each other.

Allocational border disputes are conflicts surrounding natural resources usually found underneath borders. The classic example is between Kuwait and Iraq in 1991, which eventually led to an American invasion on behalf of Kuwait. Kuwait accused Iraq of "slant drilling" by setting up oil rigs on the Kuwait border which drilled under the border and into Kuwait territory. Iraq argued that the border only applied to the surface of the Earth, and since their oil rigs were on the Iraqi side of the border, they were doing nothing wrong. Another example of such a dispute was between Canada, Spain, and Portugal in the early 1990s. Canada accused fishermen from Spain and Portugal of entering Canadian waters off the Grand Banks of Newfoundland and stealing their fish. Spain and Portugal responded by claiming that they were still in international waters. Canada's navy sent boats equipped with water cannons to blast the Spanish and Portuguese fishing boats back out into international waters. Since the stocks of cod were very low at the time, Canada was particularly angry at Spain and Portugal for illegally contributing to overfishing.

Boundaries can influence identity and promote or prevent international or internal interactions and exchanges.

Physical boundaries are often natural, cultural barriers in addition to being used as political boundaries. The Pyrenees Mountains which are today the border between France and Spain are also the historical border between the Spanish and French language. Due to the difficulty of crossing mountains and the clear separation between groups of people they provide, such natural features have often directly contributed to the formation of separate cultural groups. Another example of a major physical boundary is the Sahara Desert. When Islam was being spread to Africa, the desert proved to be a major obstacle to spreading the religion south, and today Islam is predominant north of the Sahara, with Christianity predominant south of it. Physical boundaries have also lessened cultural borders with time. States created in the modern era often have similar cultures, as in Latin America. The difference between the cultures of Colombia and Venezuela, for example, is not very marked, because the boundaries were established more recently, making any physical boundaries less of an obstacle to cross.

The Law of the Sea has enabled states to extend their boundaries offshore, which sometimes results in conflicts.

Coastal states are allowed to extend their borders out into the ocean as a result of the United Nations Convention on the Law of the Seas. The borders of a country extend 12 nautical miles from its coast out into the ocean. States can claim a further 200 nautical miles from their coast as their exclusive economic zone, in which that state has the exclusive right to fish and drill for oil. Since the Earth's coasts are not in a straight line, the extended ocean borders of countries are often hard to define. When multiple states claim that the same area of the ocean as part of their exclusive zone due to a curved coastline, the UN applies the median line principle and divides the ocean territory evenly between all who can claim it under the Law of the Seas.

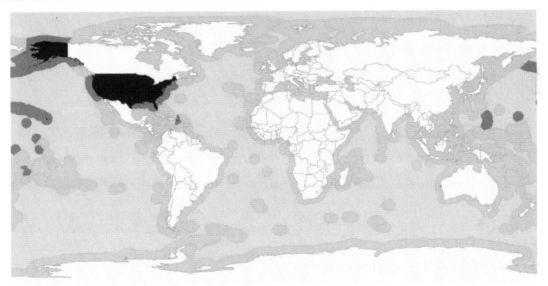

Map indicating the exclusive economic zones of the United States (dark shaded) and zones of other nations (lightly shaded)

Voting districts, redistricting and gerrymandering influence the results of elections at various scales.

Beyond the borders between states, there are internal political boundaries in many states. When states use the now outdated first-past-the-post electoral system (in which the country is divided up into districts with one member from each forming the legislature) the manner in which these districts are drawn is very important and often controversial. Countries may aim to make the districts have the same population, which leads to some districts being very large (for sparsely populated areas) and others being very small (for densely populated areas). Sometimes the goal is to make these districts conform to physical or cultural boundaries or the boundaries between urban, suburban or rural. This is very difficult and often leads to problems. In the United States, which is one of the few countries in which districts are not set by an independent body but by the state legislatures, gerrymandering is a problem. This is when a district is deliberately carved out to try to ensure that the governing party will be re-elected. This leads to unnatural districts with strange shapes, and it undermines democracy.

Due to these problems with districts, most countries use more modern voting systems that have some element of proportional representation, which provides representation based on population rather than geography. In Germany for example, part of the legislature is elected by winning districts, but part is also assigned based on the popular vote totals. This ensures that the legislature reflects how people voted and minimized the undemocratic distortions introduced by district-based systems. Most political scientists who study electoral systems argue that district-based systems, such as those used in the U.K., Canada, and the U.S., should be replaced with more modern systems that deliver proportional results. The U.K. and Canada have had major pushes for electoral reform but given that political elites in those countries support the existing district-based system, reforms have yet to happen.

Political boundaries do not always coincide with patterns of language, religion, ethnicity, nationality, and economy.

As mentioned earlier, political boundaries can be arbitrary and geometric, rather than following any boundaries between people. In many cases, borders were simply drawn on a map and enforced. The 49th parallel dividing Canada and the U.S. is a good example of an arbitrary border. The border between the Canadian province of Alberta and the American state of Montana has no relation to any actual boundary. People on both sides of the border speak English, are predominantly Protestant Christian, mostly white and have a similar economic situation. Many people in other parts of Canada often joke that people from Southern Alberta are more American than Canadian. At the same time, people in Vermont have a reputation of being fairly "Canadian" in their attitudes and politics. Incidentally, Vermont is separated from Canada by a geometric border as well.

Forms of governance include unitary states (centralized government) and federal states.

The type of government a country has is often a result of its geography. A unitary state is one in which the central government has authority on all matters, and any regional subdivisions do not have power on their own, only at the discretion of the central government. Much of Europe has unitary states because most of these countries are geographically small and without major cultural subdivisions. By contrast, federal states are ones in which sub-regions have their governments with their powers. Federal states tend to be larger countries with a lot of different sub-regions as well as cultural deviations all across its territory. Canada and the United States are examples of federal states, as their provinces and states have large amounts of power that are constitutionally guaranteed. Both countries are geographically large with different cultures in different areas.

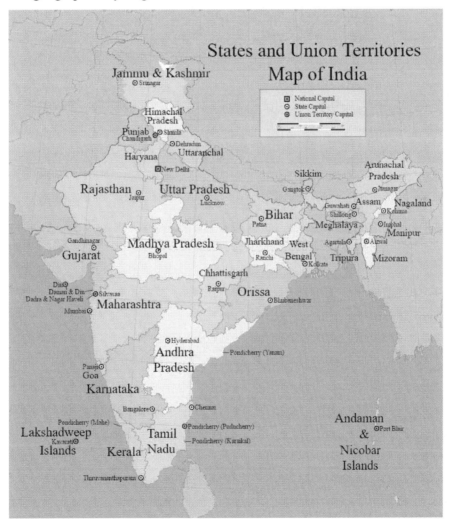

Map showing the many states that comprise India, the most populous federal state

Federal states and centralized states each have their advantages and disadvantages and, from a geographical point of view, one of the most important issues is maintaining control over the whole territory. Federal states are often susceptible to independence movements, as the sub-regions already have large amounts of power and may wish to break free and become independent completely. The United States had a civil war in which the Southern states attempted to break away and form their own country, while Canada has had the Quebec independence movement in which that province has attempted to become its own country on at least three occasions.

Centralized states give less power to sub-regions, but this can also create issues with separatist movements. Spain is a unitary state, but there are major cultural differences between the different parts of the country. These parts are given no real autonomy as they would have in a federal system, and as such, there have been independence movements in the Basque and Catalonia regions. Many argue that Spain switching to a federal system would give these regions more power and make them less likely to want to secede. At the same time, many believe that if Canada and the United States had had centralized governments with less power allowed to the provinces and states, their respective separatist movements would have never arisen in the first place.

Powers of the subdivisions of states vary according to the form of governance (e.g., the United States and Switzerland as federal states, France as a unitary state).

The powers of various sub-regional governments vary dramatically. In the United States, states are constitutionally given certain powers and have the power to pass their laws which may not correspond with federal law. For instance, marijuana is legal in Colorado while being illegal federally and in most other states. In Canada, provinces have extraordinary powers as the federal government is constitutionally mandated to allow provinces to control their education and healthcare systems, and all natural resources are owned by the province and not the federal government. By contrast, France's 18 administrative regional divisions have no legislative authority at all and cannot pass their legislation. This means that law and policy are consistent throughout all of France, while they can vary dramatically from province to province in Canada and from state to state in the United States.

State's morphology has economic, political and social implications.

States are often classified based on their territorial shape, which can impact various aspects of a country. *Fragmented states* are ones which are not contiguous over land and are broken into pieces. Indonesia, for example, is broken up over 16,000 islands. Another example is the United States, which includes Alaska (which is separated by Canada) and the islands of Hawaii. Fragmented states often foster independence movements if distant territories develop their own culture and nationality. *Elongated states* are long and thin in shape, like Chile and Vietnam. The shape of these states can cause political problems related to transportation infrastructure and are vulnerable to outside influences at the extreme edges.

A *compact state* is one which is close to a circle or a square, such as Switzerland or Hungary. Geopolitically these are often considered the ideal shape for a state since the capital can be placed in the center and all parts are roughly equidistant from the capital. *Prorupt states* have one piece that sticks off from the rest of the state, such as the southern peninsula of Thailand. Prorupt states can develop national unity issues because the area that juts out may often seek to join other countries or become independent.

Perforated states have a hole "punched" in them because they completely encircle another state. South Africa is an example, as the country of Lesotho is surrounded by South Africa. The relationship between the encircling state and the encircled state is often difficult, as many in the larger state will see the encircled state as rightfully part of the larger state.

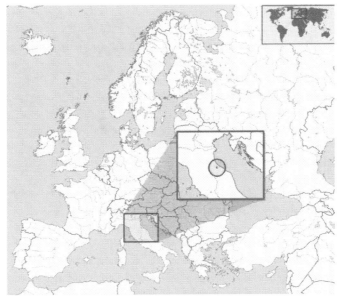

Italy, completely two sovereign nations, both San Marino (indicated in magnification) and the Vatican City is an example of a perforated state

---

Finally, *landlocked states* have no access to coast and are completely inland. Mongolia is an example of a very large landlocked state. Being landlocked can cause issues for trade, as most international shipping is water-based. This means that countries such as Mongolia must negotiate trade deals with neighboring countries to secure access to international trade.

Local and metropolitan forms of governance are subnational political units that have varying degrees of local control.

Cities are increasingly important in the geographical scale, as they have become the engines of economic activity in a globalized world. Increasingly, geographers are at the forefront of arguing that as we go further into the 21st century, the dominant economic entities will be cities, not states, meaning that cities should begin to be given more political power. The political power of cities is vastly different depending on the country. In Canada for example, cities have almost no independent political authority, and their governments exist solely on the whim of the province. In the late 1990s, the province of Ontario unilaterally redrew the borders of many cities, combining previously separate governments into one. The province also has the power to abolish city governments and change the rules for electing mayors and city councils at will.

In 1997, the residents of Mexico City won major reforms which granted the city some new powers, and by 2016 it was given the same powers as a federal state. This makes Mexico City one of the most politically powerful cities in the world, as it has its legislative authority. Unlike most countries, where the laws of different cities are relatively consistent for cities in the same region, Mexico City has broad legislative authority to pass its laws on almost any issue. Recently, the government of the city has legalized same-sex marriage, abortions, brought in no-fault divorce, euthanasia and developed a comprehensive social assistance program to help the poor. Many geographers see the scale of the city as the most important in a globalized world and argue Mexico City's power should be emulated around the world. Cities are increasingly what people identify with, and the culture changes more from city to city within a state or province than it does from state to state or province to province.

Globalization

> **The forces of globalization challenge contemporary political-territorial arrangements.**

Geographers were among the first to theorize the changing nature of political geography through the concept of scale. While many political scientists remain stuck in the traditional paradigm of international relations, which posits states as the most important actors, geographers have been quick to point out that the scale of the global was increasing in importance. Many geographers have also realized that the scale of the city is growing in importance as well. The concept of "the global city" is now an emerging area of study. Theorists of the global city argue that with economic globalization, cities are becoming more and more important as they are the drivers of economic growth. Global cities are no longer tied to the states they reside in; globalized economics means that each global city will have offices representing all major global corporations. Their cosmopolitanism and pluralism also mark global cities, and they increasingly attract people from around the world, leading to culturally and economically diverse cities that are less tied to the culture, economy, and politics of the state. Somewhat ironically, the increasing importance of the highest scale, the global, has led to the lowest scale, the city, also surging in importance.

With a robust community of international persons and companies,
Singapore is considered to very much be a global city of Asia

Some forces that may lead to supranationalism include economies of scale, trade agreements, military alliances, and transnational environmental challenges.

Supranationalism is the global level of political organization that is emerging currently. This level operates above and beyond the control of states and is so far primarily economic in nature. As corporations now easily move across the world and are not bound by regulations set by states, the scale of the economy today is truly global and above the power of states. The global as a supranational scale on the economic level is formalized by trade agreements, which more often than not function as corporate rights treaties and set forth the powers that globalized companies have to resist or overturn attempts by states to regulate them.

On other issues, the emergence of the global supranational scale has held less sway. Military alliances have become less important supranational actors in the era of globalization. During the Cold War, NATO and the Warsaw Pact were extremely important military alliances of multiple countries which promised to respond if one member attacked another. These two treaties were thought to have prevented the Cold War from becoming a hot war. Today, however, supranational military alliances are much less common and much less important. With the U.S. becoming now the world's only superpower, defensive pact alliances were no longer needed to keep two equal sides from blowing up the world with nuclear weapons. NATO was transformed into an instrument of American foreign policy, whereby countries would join with the American forces in the hope of receiving preferential economic treatment in exchange for participating, at least in a token way, in their wars. The second factor of the decline of supranational military alliances is the continuing idea that states must retain sovereignty. For this reason, the EU has not sought to create a military, leaving military issues up to the individual countries.

The environment is an issue that is inherently global in scale but attempts to transcend the state system and come to agreements to take action on issues like climate change have been repeatedly blocked. The lack of ability to enforce the Kyoto Protocol and make sure countries follow up on what they promise to do is an example of how the global scale continues to lack any political power, as states refuse to give up sovereignty and replace it with a supranational organization.

Supranationalism is expressed in the creation of multinational organizations.

Despite the continued failure to politically organize at the supranational global scale, multiple organizations have taken a smaller step by attempting to organize a few countries together for economic purposes. The European Union, ASEAN, and NAFTA are examples of economic treaties which operate at a level above states but are not quite global in scope. These organizations remain controversial because they have tended to shift authority on governing the economy away from democratically elected governments and into the hands of autonomous globalized corporations who are not democratically accountable.

Defenders of democracy see these organizations as an attack on the ability of people to decide their fate, as these treaties are often negotiated in secret and imposed on people against their will. The advocates of state sovereignty also have issues with these treaties as they give foreign corporations power over the state. NAFTA's Chapter 11 gives a foreign corporation the right to sue a government for passing legislation that may harm its ability to make a profit. Chapter 11 has most often been used against laws meant to protect human health or the environment, and it has led to corporations forcing countries to change their laws, violating the principle of state sovereignty.

Canada, Mexico, and the United States are the member states of NAFTA

The United Nations is often cited as a supranational organization, but this is largely incorrect. The United Nations is a mechanism to facilitate international relations, and it places the concept of state sovereignty as its highest ideal. The General Assembly of the UN is meant to be a forum for states to work together, not to create a supranational organization at a level above states. The only aspect of the UN which is supranational is the

Security Council. The Security Council has the power to approve or veto potential military actions by a member of the UN. Despite this power, the UN as a body has no means to enforce Security Council resolutions, as this is left up to individual states. This means that powerful states can ignore what the Security Council says, such as when the UN Security Council vetoed the American invasions of Iraq and Serbia, and the American government simply ignored it since no state had the military power to stop them.

Some forces that may lead to the devolution of states include physical geography, ethnic separatism, terrorism, economic and social problems, and irredentism.

Devolution is when a state grants more powers to a subnational entity. For example, in 1999, the government of the U.K. went through a process of devolution which granted significant new powers to Scotland. Scotland's past history drove this devolution of powers as an independent country. Many felt that Scotland was ill-served as part of a unitary British state and demanded either devolution or separation. Sometimes devolution can come from physical geographies, such as the many British and French overseas territories that were simply so far away it made sense to grant them some manner of autonomy over their affairs. Separatist and terrorist groups can also drive devolution as governments attempt to quash these movements by granting more regional autonomy, such as with the Kurds in Northern Iraq. *Irredentism* is any political movement seeking to reclaim a lost homeland. This lost homeland could be real, as in the case of Scotland, or rooted in mythology, as in the case of Israel.

Devolution is expressed in the fragmentation of states into autonomous regions, subnational political-territorial units or Balkanization.

Devolution can happen on many different levels and have different impacts. In 1999, Canada created the territory of Nunavut to be a region that was self-governed by the Inuit. Unlike provinces, which have their powers guaranteed by the constitution which the federal government cannot infringe upon, territories in Canada have devolved powers, which means that their autonomy only exists in so far as the federal government allows it. A similar form of devolution has happened in the United States with Native American reservations; these lands are autonomous by the grace of the federal government rather than through the law of the constitution. This means the federal government can change the status of both of these devolved entities any time it wishes, while it cannot change the status of a province or a state.

In some cases, subnational devolution has occurred to give more power not only to regions in unitary states such as in Spain and Belgium but also to federal states. Due to the strength of provinces in Canada, there is a constant push and pull struggle happening as provinces continually attempt to blackmail the federal government to extract more power and more funding. In many instances, provinces attempt to win more powers in exchange for giving the federal government something that it wants. This has made other provinces jealous, as they demand similar concessions in the name of fairness. Two major attempts to renegotiate federal-provincial relations in Canada in the late 1980s and early 1990s were largely a failure. The Meech Lake Accord unsuccessfully attempted to get Quebec to sign off on the new constitution of 1982 in exchange for more provincial powers, and the Charlottetown Accord of 1992 again unsuccessfully attempted to renegotiate political-federal relations.

Balkanization is a term used to refer to a state breaking up into a series of smaller states that are usually hostile towards each other. The term is derived from the history of the Balkan peninsula. This area of Europe was controlled by the Ottoman Empire but split into some smaller states from 1817 to 1912. These small states then recombined to form a new country, Yugoslavia, which broke up into smaller states again in 1989. Out of the former Yugoslavia, the new countries of Bosnia, Serbia, Croatia, Slovenia and the Former Yugoslav Republic of Macedonia were created. The term Balkanization usually has a negative meaning, as it is associated with instability and civil war. When the Quebec separatist movement was at its peak in Canada from the 1970s to late 1990s, many commentators opposed to Quebec independence warned that Canada would go through a process of balkanization if Quebec successfully separated. They argued that Quebec separating would lead to the disintegration of Canada into a number of smaller states.

In the Caucasus region of southern Russia, balkanization is a continual threat. Many of the cultural groups in that area are predominantly Muslim, and there have been pushes in Chechnya, South Ossetia, and Abkhazia to break away from Russia and become independent states. Chechens initiated two insurrections during the 1990s in an attempt to break away from Russia. The first insurrection led to a ceasefire, as Russia was undergoing economic turmoil. The second insurrection in 1999 was brutally crushed by the Russian military, who were ready to crack down on separatists by this time. Chechens increasingly identified with Islamic terrorist groups after September 11, 2001 and initiated a major terrorist attack in 2002 on a Moscow theatre in which over 900 people were taken hostage. Chechen terrorists occupied a school in 2004 in North Ossetia and threatened to execute the children if Chechnya was not granted independence. Russia feared losing more territory to balkanization, and, in the wake of the two wars and terrorist attacks, tightened its grip on Chechnya and the other regions in the Caucasus.

The Balkanization of Georgia can be seen in the breakaway

regions of Abkhazia and South Ossetia

Advances in communication technology have facilitated devolution, supranationalism and democratization.

Communication technology, and the internet, in particular, has played a role in reconfiguring geopolitics in the age of globalization. The internet has empowered both the supranational and the municipal scales. Increasingly, political movements are using the internet to organize, discuss and coordinate protests that demand more democracy "from the bottom up." The Arab Spring protests, which overthrew long-standing dictatorships in Tunisia and Egypt, were heavily integrated with the internet. Since the mainstream media in both countries were sympathetic to the government, activists used the internet to connect with other people who were likewise disgruntled with the regime. They then spread their own stories and organized protests, which they publicized through social media. In the case of Egypt, the dictatorship at one point during the protests cut off the internet entirely in an attempt to try to control access to information among the protesters, which only made people angrier and more determined to get out on the street and protest.

The internet can create an accessible public sphere in situations where the mainstream media is unreliable and overtly pro-government. By publicizing the street protests online, the activists were able to communicate directly with the people of Egypt and Tunisia without worrying about the mainstream media distorting or suppressing their message. The internet also helped facilitate global awareness and sympathy for the protesters from around the world. The experience of the Arab Spring protesters in successfully harnessing the internet to help their protests inspired activists in New York City to start the Occupy Wall Street movement, a protest against the U.S. government's bailouts and favorable treatment of those responsible for causing the 2008 economic crisis.

Occupy Wall Street protesters gathered on day 60

The Occupy movement began through online discussions, and after the initial street protests in New York, the movement's statement that they represented the 99% of Americans against the greedy 1% became a popular online meme. The Occupy protests spread across the world as ordinary people banded together to protest economic inequality and governments who seemed to be more interested in representing the interests of corporations than their people. In Nigeria, the Occupy movement was very successful in initiating protests aimed at President Goodluck Jonathan, who had begun a process of privatizing the country's oil reserves, causing the price of fuel to skyrocket for regular Nigerians. As a result of the Occupy Nigeria movement, public sentiment turned against President Jonathan, and he lost the ensuing elections. By organizing and spreading the Occupy movement through the internet, it was able to spread worldwide and foster democracy by allowing anyone to participate. The internet facilitated a form of global democracy that allowed people from far-flung regions of the world to participate in global political movements that demanded more democracy and less economic inequality. These protest movements are global and supranational in scale, as well as being local and democratic.

Centrifugal forces can originate in political dimensions, economic dimensions or cultural dimensions.

A *centrifugal force* within a country is any aspect that causes division among regions and threatens to push people within the same country further apart. At its extreme, centrifugal forces can tear a country apart and lead to balkanization. There are many different types of forces that can contribute to national disunity. The political dimensions of centrifugal force can include those countries with a strong cultural minority that sees itself as distinct from the cultural majority.

In Canada, the vast majority of people speak English, but in the province of Quebec, the vast majority speaks French. This causes national unity issues not only because the two parts of the country cannot talk to each other, but also because there are two separate sets of media; people in Quebec and the rest of Canada have two entirely different sets of popular cultural references. Television and film is a good example, as most people in English-speaking Canada primarily watch American TV and film. By contrast, Quebec has its own thriving French-language media industry that produces its TV shows and films. Quebecois film directors are world-renowned and often win major international prizes, while also being very popular within Quebec. However, these directors are often unknown in the rest of Canada. This causes national unity issues as the two linguistic groups feel they have little in common culturally. On top of this, education is controlled by provinces who have little interest in facilitating bilingualism, and children usually do not learn the second official language. In European countries, the school system facilitates national unity by ensuring that everyone has at least minor competence in a second important language.

A second political centrifugal force can result from the type of electoral system a country uses. Winner-take-all district-based systems tend to overemphasize regional divisions and can enable political parties with only regional support to win a disproportionate number of seats in a legislature. In the United States, the electoral college system has made certain states guaranteed victories for one party, diminishing the influence of voters in those states. It has also created the national unity wedge issue of dividing the country into red states and blue states. In Canada, the electoral system has played a major role in giving the Quebec separatist movement more influence and power than it actually has. In the 1993 federal election, the separatist Bloc Quebecois won the second most seats in parliament, making it the official opposition. This was even though the Bloc only ran candidates in the province of Quebec and placed fourth in the popular vote. Because the first-past-the-post system rewards regional concentration and punishes broad national support, a political party dedicated to independence for a province was able to play a major role in the federal parliament. As a result of this major win by the Bloc Quebecois thanks to the electoral system, Quebec nearly separated from Canada in a 1995 referendum, where Quebecers very narrowly voted to stay part of Canada by a margin of 50.5% to 49.4%.

Centrifugal political forces can also stem from armed conflict. This can happen in two different ways: when a separatist element takes up arms against the government or when the government gets involved in a war which a certain region of a country strongly disagrees with. Any time an armed insurrection occurs, it naturally divides the population. Sticking with the example of Quebec, in 1970 a terrorist group called the FLQ kidnapped and murdered a cabinet minister in the Quebec government. This turned much of public opinion in Canada strongly against the separatists in Quebec who had resorted to terrorism.

A Canadian infantry column deployed during the surrender of FLQ members

However, the federal government invoked martial law and suspended constitutional rights in the province of Quebec, even sending in the Canadian military. This heavy-handed overreaction by the federal government turned sentiment within Quebec strongly in favor of independence. Another example was during World War I, Canada decided to implement a draft which Quebec was opposed to because the people of Quebec saw Canada's involvement in the war as an example of Canada being a mere puppet of the British. The governing Liberal Party's Quebec wing split off in protest, and the Liberals formed a coalition with the Conservatives to stay in power.

Economic forces can also play a role in driving people apart. When governments focus on developing one region at the expense of others, this situation of uneven development can provoke unity issues. These unity issues can originate from both the poorer and the richer areas. In Bolivia, after the election of Evo Morales as president in 2006, the wealthier and mineral-rich Santa Cruz area began to inflame separatist sentiments as they feared Morales' focus on reducing economic inequality. Morales was elected with the support of the poorer indigenous population in the rest of the country, and his election set in motion centrifugal forces related to the uneven economic development of the country.

Stateless nations inside a country can often spur centrifugal forces as well. In Turkey, the Kurds in the southern part of the country have long agitated for more autonomy and sometimes even independence. The PKK movement has sometimes engaged in terrorism to agitate for their cause, and the Turkish government has often responded with mass killings of Kurds. Even when ethnic tensions do not lead to violence, it can be a centrifugal force. Belgium is roughly divided in half between Flemish Dutch speakers and French speakers, with many in Flanders wishing for independence, while many in the French part of Belgium wish their portion of the country to become part of France. These non-violent tensions came to a head in 2010 as political parties from both sides of the divide could not agree on how to form a government, leaving Belgium without any legislative government for 535 days. Belgium is complicated by the fact that each side of the country has its political parties, which in itself is a centrifugal force. The previous Belgian Prime Minister did not help matters, as at one point he was asked to sing the Belgian national anthem in French, and instead began to sing the national anthem of France.

Centripetal forces can originate in political dimensions, economic dimensions or cultural dimensions.

In contrast to centrifugal forces are *centripetal forces*, which bring people together and foster a sense of national unity among the various regions and cultures of a country. Large, diverse countries often invest in attempting to foster a sense of national identity that everyone can identify with to generate centripetal forces. Some countries are very good at defining national identity and using it to foster patriotism rather than identification with a region or subculture. The United States has been fairly successful in cultivating a national identity despite vast regional disparities and its history of internal conflict. Most people around the world can list a set of attributes or traits associated with American identity.

By contrast, Canada has been rather unsuccessful at cultivating a clear sense of what it means to be Canadian. Canadians are often confused with Americans when traveling, and Canadians themselves do not have a clear idea of what being a Canadian is, especially in light of the strong difference between provinces. In many ways, Canadian national identity has settled on a single negative trait rather than a list of positive traits; most Canadians define being Canadian as not being American. However, being so culturally, politically and geographically similar to Americans, simply saying one is not American has become enough to define oneself as Canadian regarding national identity.

Economic developments can often be a centripetal force, especially the establishment of transportation and media networks. The invention of radio (and later TV) was a major centripetal force throughout the world, as people in a country began to all listen to the same radio programs, which dramatically impacted the way people spoke. Maps demonstrating the change in dialects and accents in the U.K. since the creation of BBC radio demonstrate how the "BBC accent" came to predominate across most of the U.K. and how regional dialects and accents faded.

The building of transcontinental railroads in Canada and the United States were massive drivers of economic unity, as it became realistic to travel across the country in a reasonable time. The development of the interstate highway system in the United States and the TransCanada Highway in Canada further brought people together as trade integrated those respective countries.

Perhaps the biggest unifier is cultural. Sports especially can be a major unifying factor. The same Belgian Prime Minister who inflamed linguistic tensions by singing the national anthem of France declared that the only thing people in Belgium have in common is the Belgian national soccer team. Belgians set aside their language disputes and come together to cheer for the national team in their favorite sport. The same is true for hockey in Canada, where all regional differences fade away as Canadians from every part of the country, and every cultural background are all obsessed with hockey.

The Belgian national soccer team in 2013

Countries with a single dominant language have a natural advantage, as speaking the same language facilitates sharing a similar culture. This is why separatist movements in Latin American countries have tended to be relatively weak, due to the overwhelming hegemony of Portuguese in Brazil and Spanish everywhere else. Countries where most people follow the same religion also have a major advantage, as a similar religion is a major centripetal force. An even bigger unifying force is a commitment to secularism. Countries in which there is agreement that religion should stay out of politics and be a private affair tend to be better at fostering an attachment to the national identity.

In many cases, religious attachment acts as a rival attachment that can undermine a sense of belonging to a country. Many Americans were skeptical of President John F. Kennedy at first because he was Catholic. They were worried that he would be more loyal to the Pope and his Catholic religion than he would be to America. While this turned out to be false, it demonstrates how an attachment to other ideologies can be perceived as placing one's identification with the state in a secondary position.

More recently, in the United States, Republican Presidential candidate Ted Cruz proclaimed that he was a Christian first and an American second. He meant this as a positive affirmation of his religious belief, but many secular-minded Americans took this to mean that Cruz was not as strongly committed to America and its constitution as the other candidates. A similar issue has been occurring in Turkey, which was founded as a secular republic. Turks were united in their belief that Turkish national identity was primary and that religious identification as a Muslim was a private issue and not something that had anything to do with politics.

The current Turkish Prime Minister Recep Erdogan has been undoing the previously centripetal force of secularism by increasingly encouraging people in Turkey to identify as Muslims first and Turks second. Despite the fact that the Kurdish population is predominantly Muslim, this plan by Erdogan has backfired, as Kurds were also the most committed to the secular principles of the Turkish Republic. By attempting to undermine the secular basis of Turkey in the name of a common religious attachment, Prime Minister Erdogan ended up spurring a resurgence of Kurdish separatism; they have become more interested in autonomy so that they can return to a secular separation between politics and religion.

Notes

Chapter 5

Agriculture, Food Production and Rural Land Use

The origins of the domestication of plants and animals and the ensuing diffusion process of these advancements help explain why distinct patterns in diet, energy use and adaptation of biotechnology emerge in specific regions. Major agricultural regions are categorized as either commercial or subsistence and extensive or intensive according to their configuration and land use practices. Settlement patterns and landscape varieties typical of major agriculture types are key factors, as are land survey systems, environmental conditions, sustainability, global food supply issues and cultural and gender values that shape agriculture patterns. From analyses of these factors, theories and models of the patterns of rural land use and settlement emerge. Agribusiness, or large-scale commercial farms, exert a significant influence on food production and consumption.

Effects of Agriculture on the Environment

> The development of agriculture led to widespread alteration of the natural environment.

The development of human civilization is directly related to the alteration of the natural environment through agriculture. *Agriculture* is defined as the growing of plants or raising of animals for food purposes. This food can be primarily for personal use or sold at marketplaces to others. Before the creation of agriculture, humans were primarily hunters and gatherers who would gather wild plants and hunt roaming animals. This lifestyle necessitated a nomadic lifestyle that prevented humans from settling in one place. The creation of agriculture led to higher populations, more free time and the explosion of human culture and technology.

In Madhya Pradesh, India, Paleolithic cave painting
at the Bhimbetka rock shelters site depict early modern man hunting.

Early hearths of domestication of plants and animals include Southwest Asia, Southeast Asia, and the Americas.

Agriculture began as early hunter-gathers became familiar with the planting and seeding process by handling various types of plants that they gathered. Over thousands of years, humans figured out how to plant seeds and grow crops in one place, rather than traveling around finding these crops growing wild. Geographers place the development of agriculture at a number of different origin points called "hearths." Human agriculture is largely believed to have begun in Southwest Asia in the area of the Fertile Crescent, which includes the Nile River plains and stretches to the area around the Euphrates and Tigris rivers, which flow into the Persian Gulf. The Chogha Golan region of what is now Iran also shows evidence of domesticated wheat use as early as 10,000 BC.

Currently, geographers have identified at least 11 agricultural hearths in which agriculture developed. Many of these hearths developed independently from each other, while some interacted and spread know-how from one area to another. Many of these hearths have been traced to the original domestication of certain plants and animals. Some of the major hearths are the Fertile Crescent mentioned above, which began with the planting of figs and cereals and eventually incorporated the domestication of herd animals. Barley was an important early crop in the hearth of Western India, and millet developed in Northern China. Agriculture also developed in Ethiopia with the domestication of a small grain called teff. In Southern Mexico and Northern Peru, agriculture developed with corn in Mexico and squash, beans and cotton in Peru. Other sources of the independent development of agriculture were in the Sahel region of Africa just south of the Sahara Desert and in New Guinea in Southeast Asia.

Human agriculture began through vegetative planting, which involves cutting a part of a plant off and then planting it elsewhere. The discovery of the ability to harvest and plant crops from seeds in the Neolithic era is considered the first agricultural revolution. Seed agriculture led to a vast increase in yields, allowing early seed-based civilizations to grow in population and power. As these early seed-based civilizations (around 12,000 BC) were able to support higher populations and move away from hunting and gathering for good, they began to increasingly domesticate animals as well. These early civilizations were able to vastly increase the carrying capacity of their geographic region, which allowed the building of communities and the development of systems of governance, culture, religion and organized warfare. The development of seed agriculture occurred independently in some hearths, just like with vegetative planting.

Patterns of diffusion resulted in the globalization of various plants and animals.

The various agricultural practices of the hearths diffused out from their origins in various ways. The hearths of the Fertile Valley, Western India, and Northern China were influential in spreading agricultural knowledge not only to other hearths (leading to common patterns of crop and animal domestication) but also to other regions which were less agriculturally advanced. One example of agricultural diffusion was the Columbian Exchange, which resulted after the European colonization of the Americas in the 1500s. There was a massive transfer of crops, animals, and knowledge between the two continents who had previously only had sporadic contact. European traders introduced native species from the Western Hemisphere such as corn, potatoes, and tomatoes. These crops became staples in the European diet, as potatoes become synonymous with Ireland and tomatoes became a key ingredient of much of Italian cooking. Chocolate, which was originally developed by the Aztecs, also became very popular in Europe.

Modern boxed chocolates owe their existence to the processing discoveries of the Aztecs.

On the other end of the exchange, crops such as oranges were introduced into Florida by the Spanish, who had brought them from China. Coffee was introduced into Colombia and bananas into Ecuador. While today these crops are associated with these countries, before the Columbian Exchange, these were all unknown crops with no native origin. Native American groups, especially in the Western Plains, were quick to adopt horses that were imported from Europe to the point where horses are now ubiquitous in Sioux iconography. The Colombian Exchange also brought many diseases to the New World which would devastate the indigenous populations of many areas. Cholera, leprosy, measles, the flu, malaria, typhus, smallpox, and even the common cold, were unknown in the New World. The New World was largely at the receiving end of new diseases, as syphilis and Chagas disease are the only two that went back to the Old World to cause major health issues.

The natural environment influences agricultural regions.

The early agricultural hearths grew out of fertile river valleys in temperate climates. The major river systems around which human civilization and agriculture developed all shared the same properties of transporting mineral-rich sediment that acted as a natural fertilizer. The temperate nature of these climates allowed yearlong growing as well. The Fertile Crescent is also uniquely placed on the margins of Africa, Europe, and Asia, making it a hotspot of species transfer, which increased biodiversity in the region. For instance, the Fertile Valley was home to cows, sheep, goats, and pigs, which were then domesticated, while horses lived nearby and eventually became domesticated as well. Many of the major crops of the early agricultural era were also indigenous to the area, including wheat, barley, flax, chickpeas, and lentils. Having all these crops and animals naturally occurring in a fertile area without the extreme temperatures of cold regions or the tropics facilitated the development of year-round agriculture.

Populations alter the landscape to increase food production.

A major part of agriculture is changing the landscape to increase food production. Civilizations that developed in hilly and mountainous regions, such as the Inca of South America, often engaged in terrace farming. This involves flattening out sections of a hillside to create terraces on which crops are planted. By using this technique, steep hills that are inherently unsuitable for farming can be transformed into productive space. Other methods include draining wetlands and marshes so that crops are not constantly being flooded, chopping down forests to create open land for growing and grazing and running irrigation systems from nearby sources of fresh water to make dry land more fertile.

While each of these techniques alters the land to make it more fertile, they can often have negative consequences as well. Deforestation and the elimination of wetlands destroy the habitat for many species of plants and animals, and it also contributes to increasing greenhouse gas production. In Brazil, where the Amazon rainforest is being cut down to use as grazing land for cattle, this creates a double problem. The rainforest is a huge carbon sink, meaning that all the trees take carbon out of the atmosphere and help prevent climate change. Cutting down these trees eliminates this carbon sink and replaces it with cattle farming, which is one of the biggest sources of greenhouse gas emissions.

New technology and increased food production led to a better diet, longer life and more people available for work in factories.

The First Agricultural revolution was the adoption of seeds and took place in the Neolithic era. The Second Agricultural revolution revolved around the application of new technologies to farming and occurred alongside the Industrial Revolution. During the Middle Ages, farming was largely human-labor intensive; serfs only worked the land and had to give a large part of their harvest to the lords who owned it. With the collapse of feudalism and the advent of industrialization pushing people toward the city to work in the newly created factories, there was a demand for more efficient farming practices as the new urban industrial population needed to be fed.

C. 1310 depiction of English serfs harvesting crops under the supervision of a reeve

By the 1600s and 1700s in England and Western Europe, new farming innovations began to spread which increased efficiency. Fertilizer, irrigation and storage techniques vastly improved crop yields, allowing fewer people to farm and more people to work in factories in the city. By applying the principles of industrialization to farming, a side effect of capitalism was saving people from the drudgery of rural feudalism.

The Green Revolution began with the development of high-yield seeds, resulting in the increased use of chemical and mechanized farming.

The third major advance in agricultural technology is called the Green Revolution, which began in the early 1960s. The Green Revolution arose out of the advances in plant science and chemistry that allowed for the development of high yield seeds, which dramatically increased food production. Advances in chemistry led to the creation of synthetic fertilizers and pesticides. Farm work increasingly became mechanized in this period with tractors and other technologies dramatically increasing efficiency over previous labor-intensive farming practices. The Green revolution was particularly striking in the developing world, where the spread of these new practices and technologies doubled cereal production from 1961 to 1985.

Positive consequences of the Green Revolution include increased food production and a relative reduction in hunger at the global scale.

The Green Revolution brought in massive increases in food productivity. This massive increase in productivity allowed the population of the Earth to grow by 4 billion people since the start of the Green Revolution. Without these advances in food production, it is unlikely that the Earth would have been able to support so many people, and it is likely there would have been more starvation than there is today. India alone has seen its wheat production increased seven-fold since the start of the Green Revolution, preventing many people from going hungry. It is estimated that since the Green Revolution the average person in the developing world now gets 25% more calories in their diet, owing to increased food production.

Today, most of the issues with hunger and food insecurity are not related to a lack of production, as the world now produces much more food than is needed but are related to distribution issues. Hunger today is primarily an issue produced by uneven economic distribution rather than a lack of production capacity or a result of reaching the limits of the Earth's carrying capacity.

Negative consequences of the Green Revolution include environmental damage resulting from irrigation and chemical use and the cost of technology and seeds.

While the Green Revolution has vastly increased food production, leading to less starvation, it has had many negative consequences as well. Many argue that we are now into the second phase of the Green Revolution, which involves global agribusiness taking control of the world's food supply. This has caused issues for small farmers in the developing world because they now have to buy expensive seeds each year, as their traditional practice of seed saving from last year's harvests is being phased out due to corporate influence. This is especially an issue in India, where the first wave of the Green Revolution was government funded, which allowed many people to feed themselves as small sustenance farmers. Now, most of the farmland in India is owned by foreign corporations who charge small farmers to work their land. Critics of this second wave of the Green Revolution argue that it has increased poverty and decreased sovereignty despite continuing to increase food yields.

Indian farmer working the fields with an ox-driven plow

There have also been many negative environmental consequences of the Green Revolution. Increased chemical use has led to streams and rivers near farms becoming polluted with fertilizer and pesticide runoff. Due to the reliance on machinery running on fossil fuels, it has also led to an increase in greenhouse gasses and an increased dependency on nonrenewable resources. Others point to how the Green Revolution has popularized a small set of high-yield crops at the expense of others, reducing biodiversity and homogenizing the global diet. In many countries, the Green Revolution has replaced the problem of malnourishment with the problem of obesity, as highly processed foods are now cheaper than healthier, less processed fruits and vegetables. Early blanket uses of pesticides led to the near extinction of many types of birds in the 1960s as insect-eating birds pushed pesticides through the food chain.

The Green Revolution has also raised many questions about human health as a result of pesticide use. In developing countries where pesticide use is not tightly regulated, there have been many cases of pesticide poisonings, as well as links established between pesticide use on farms and cancer rates in nearby communities. Studies of villages in the Punjab region of India, which adopted Green Revolution farming techniques more recently, have demonstrated a statistically significant increase in cancer rates as well as having well over the recommended limit of nitrates.

Agricultural Regions

Major agricultural regions reflect physical geography and economic forces.

The most influential classification of the world's major agricultural regions is Whittlesey's Classification. This classification demonstrates how physical geography and economics can influence the types of agricultural production that dominate in a region. There are ten categories in the classifications, beginning with nomadic herding. *Nomadic herding* is common in desert and tundra areas. Generally, animals are herded based on seasons to find areas with food for the animals to eat. Due to the lack of fertile soil in the desert and tundra, animal herding becomes dominant. Nomadic herding was once a wealthy pursuit, as owning animals was more important than land, but today it is associated with poverty as stationary agriculture produces vastly superior yields.

Livestock ranching is common on large prairies such as the Western United States and Canada and the Patagonia region of South America. The type of livestock is generally related to climate patterns. Rainy regions have more cattle; dryer regions prefer sheep farming and goats and camels can easily survive in hot and arid climates.

Next is commercial dairy farming, which is associated with areas that can grow rich grass due to high rainfall. Dairy farming is more labor-intensive than meat farming and tends to fetch higher prices. It is associated with more developed countries such as France and New Zealand.

Commercial crop and livestock farming is a mixed agricultural region that dominates in temperate and dry continental climates. Commercial grain farming is predominant on the Great Plains of North America and involves intensive growth of grain for export. Commercial plantations are dominant in the tropics and tend to focus on cash crops such as bananas and coffee. Commercial gardening occurs in warmer climates and tends to focus on specialty crops.

Mediterranean agriculture is found in warm coastal regions and tends to focus on the production of citrus fruits such as oranges and lemons. Shifting cultivation is often practiced in highland areas and tends to be low productivity and associated with poorer regions. Finally, intensive subsistence cultivation tends to be associated with monsoon climates and regions with alluvial deposits. Rice tends to be the primary crop, and this type of cultivation is dominant in South East Asia.

Plant and animal production is dependent on climatic conditions, including spatial variations in temperature and rainfall.

As shown from Whittlesey's Classification, agriculture is highly dependent on both terrain features and climate. The best growing regions can support many types of agriculture and have an overlap of many of the ten different classifications. California, for instance, has a large overlap of multiple regions and produces a large variety of produce. Most of Canada relies on imports of food from California through the winter months when local produce is not in season. In the winter of 2015/2016, when California experienced a major drought and agricultural production waned, this had a major impact on fruit and vegetable prices in Canada and caused domestic inflation to surge.

Due to climate and growing season limitations,
many regions must import a portion of their produce

Some agricultural regions are associated with particular bioclimatic zones.

Mediterranean agriculture is associated with and named for the coastal area around the Mediterranean Sea in which this type of agriculture first became dominant. This region is famous for its production of olives, grapes, and figs, as well as grazing sheep and goats. Mediterranean agricultural practices include both intensive and extensive farming practices. What is said to be farmed extensively means that its growth is neither technologically nor labor intensive but relies primarily on the natural fertility of the soil.

By contrast, olives and grapes are farmed intensively, which means that a lot of labor and technology is used to enhance the yields of the crops dramatically. Grapes and olives are difficult crops that involve much work. Vineyards need to be pruned, and vines need to be carefully selected for replanting. Olives are also an intensive crop because it takes many years for olives to ripen, which means that branches from mature trees need to be carefully trimmed and replanted to try to speed up the ripening process. Wheat as an extensive crop is simply planted and then harvested without all the intensive work of cultivation.

Due to the popularity and profitability of the crops that are produced in the Mediterranean region, other regions which are similar in climate and terrain have been sought out to grow the same type of crops. Other Mediterranean agricultural regions have emerged in California, Chile, the southern portion of South Africa and the southern portion of Australia. These regions have a similar climate to the Mediterranean region of Europe, and they all have emerged as a major wine producing areas, which is an important and profitable crop that only grows well in this region. Agriculture in this region can be both sustenance and commercial, but the overwhelming trend is toward commercial agriculture.

Other regions which are associated primarily with one bioclimatic zone are shifting agriculture and pastoral nomadism. Shifting cultivation involves rotating crops to different fields to allow the soil to replenish itself. This is usually associated with subsistence farming, as it does not rely on fertilizer and has a much lower potential yield as a result. Shifting cultivation is associated with tropical zones and highland areas with a thin layer of topsoil whose nutrients are quickly depleted. Tropical rains can often contribute to washing away the layer of topsoil, causing even further problems. The pastoral nomad herding region is strongly associated with desert, tundra and other areas where the land is not arable enough to sustain permanent cultivation of crops. Pastoral nomadism is in extreme decline because simply moving across vast areas of land with one's herd is much more difficult in the modern political climate where land is owned mostly by individuals and borders are strictly enforced.

Agricultural production regions are defined by the extent to which they reflect subsistence or commercial practices, or intensive or extensive use of land.

The ten regions outlined earlier can further be divided based on whether they are predominantly subsistence or commercial and intensive or extensive. Take the dairy farming region as an example. There is a major difference between a region where most people own four or five cows or goats to produce milk and cheese to feed their family and a commercial factory farm with thousands of cows which produce milk and cheese to feed cities or countries. The type of land use will vary dramatically, and different problems will arise. Factory dairy farms are often responsible for major pollution issues as concentrated waste drains into nearby rivers, leading to possible nitrate pollution and *E. coli* outbreaks. Intensive and extensive practices also represent different land use patterns as well. An intensive cattle ranch, for instance, might involve a high-density feedlot which packs the cows into a relatively tight space and thus requires much human labor to manage disease and sickness, whereas an extensive cattle ranch might be very large, allowing the cows to feed naturally and essentially look after themselves. In both cases, the general trend is toward commercially intensive practices.

Small dairy farm

Intensive farming practices include market gardening, plantation agriculture, mixed crop/livestock systems, etc.

Intensive farming involves high amounts of capital invested per unit of land area. This means more technology, more labor, and less land. The main examples are market gardening, plantation agriculture, and mixed crop and livestock regions. The goal of intensive farming is to generate the maximum profit from the least amount of land through the application of technology and labor to make the land provide a higher yield. As a result, the vast majority of intensive farming tends to be commercial rather than subsistence and tends to resemble an industrialized factory rather than the traditional image of a family farm.

One notable exception are instances of intensive subsistence farming in which a farmer has a very small plot of land on which to grow enough food to feed his or her family. This sort of intensive farming is common in China and India, which are densely populated and force subsistence farmers to make do with very small plots of lands. These types of farmers will often attempt to get the most out of their small plot by double planting to try to harvest a crop more than once a year and by developing layered terrace systems and hanging plots to try to maximize growing space.

Extensive farming practices include shifting cultivation, nomadic herding, ranching, etc.

Extensive farming, which is common in shifting cultivation, nomadic herding and ranching regions, relies on producing yield from lots of land. The goal is to produce the most yield with the minimum amount of technology and labor, due to their cost. Extensive farming uses crop rotation instead of fertilizer and relies on natural grazing rather than factory farms. Most subsistence farming is extensive since these farmers lack the capital to invest in technology or hire workers and only a few people must work the land.

Large-scale commercial agricultural operations are replacing small family farms.

In many less developed countries agriculture is primarily subsistence-based rather than commercial. *Subsistence farming* is when the farmer only grows enough food to feed his or her family. Before the widespread adoption of industrialization and urbanization, these small family farms were the dominant occupation of many people in what are now the developed countries as well. People would primarily grow their food on their farms, a pattern that continued in larger countries like Canada and the United States after large-scale industrialization took place, owing to the vast tracts of fertile land.

In developed countries, there was a major shift in which farming became a primarily commercial activity due to land consolidation and advancing technologies. In commercial farming, plants and animals are primarily sold to be eaten by others. While many family farms and subsistence farmers sell any excess food that they cannot eat themselves, the difference is that with commercial farms their primary purpose is to sell the food. Today very few non-commercial family farms still exist in developed countries because large corporations have taken over the agriculture business and created industrialized factory farms.

The transformation of agriculture into large-scale agribusiness has resulted in complex commodity chains linking production and consumption of agricultural products.

An example of a large-scale commodity chain is grain farming. Large-scale grain production is dominated by the U.S. and Canada as these two countries export huge amounts of grain around the world. This grain is the basis of two separate sets of commodity production, it goes to feed livestock, and it goes to the production of grain-based products such as bread. During the Industrial Revolution, the advent of large-scale grain farming supplied the industrialized bakeries in the cities which could then feed a growing urban population.

Technological improvements have changed the economies of scale in the agricultural sector.

Large-scale grain farming was a result of some technological improvements that made producing more grain cheaper, creating a better economy of scale. In the 1830s, the McCormick Reaper was developed, which could effectively cut the standing grain in the field, vastly improving harvesting efficiency. The combine is a type of tractor which combines reaping, threshing and cleaning all in one machine that can be driven by one person. This vastly reduced the amount of labor required in grain farming. Dairy farming was vastly changed by the developing of refrigerated trucks. This allowed dairy farms to move further from cities and store products to deliver when it was convenient. Before this, milk had to be delivered as soon as it was ready directly to the customer. This was hugely inefficient, and refrigerated trucking moved to expand dairy production vastly.

Farmer using a McCormick Reaper in the Boise Valley, Idaho

Food is part of a global supply chain; products from less developed low-latitude regions are often consumed globally.

Globalization has affected food supply chains as well. As a result of trade agreements, such as the World Trade Organization WTO), poorer countries have been forced to remove protections for local farmers and controls on who can own land. As a result, many poorer countries have seen a dramatic shift toward growing cash crops such as coffee and bananas. Agribusiness corporations often buy out subsistence farmers and instead concentrate on growing a single crop for export. This is problematic because it often results in these poorer countries having food security issues as they now have to rely on food imports. The problem, however, is that trade agreements like the WTO do not apply evenly because the EU and the U.S. are allowed to maintain massive subsidies, which means smaller scale farms in the developing world cannot compete in those larger and richer markets.

Trade agreements have had devastating consequences for the food supply in many developing countries as imports are subject to higher prices. At the same time, when local farmers switch to cash crops, they are susceptible to fluctuating global prices. In 2012, Mexico faced a major problem when the price of corn shot up, as corn is a staple food in

Mexico. There was increased demand for ethanol (which is made from corn) which not only caused the price of corn to go up but also diverted corn crops toward fuel and away from food, leading to shortages in some parts of Mexico. When the Mexican government suggested putting in place price controls, the World Bank warned them that this could open Mexico up to punitive actions.

Patterns of global food distribution are affected by political systems, infrastructure, and patterns of world trade.

The uneven nature of trade regimes related to agriculture remains a continual issue for developing countries, who point out the existing world trade agreements are inherently unfair. Developed countries are allowed to provide huge subsidies to domestic agriculture, which means that exports from poorer countries are more expensive and uncompetitive. At the same time, poorer countries have been forced to eliminate their subsidies, meaning that exports from more developed countries are cheaper than food produced locally. The issue of agricultural subsidies is a source of economic tension, especially among the countries of North Africa and the EU. The North African countries want access to the European market but are shut out due to EU subsidies, while the North African countries are now awash in exports from Europe.

Settlement Patterns and Rural Land Use

Settlement patterns and rural land use are reflected in the cultural landscape.

Throughout history, the shape of a village and its spatial pattern was related to its function, purpose, and the environment. In much of early European history, for example, villages tended to be located on hills which left the flat fertile terrain around the hill for farming. Being on a hill also provided defense against invaders and allowed villages to watch over their farms from a higher vantage point. Eventually, these early villages often built stockades or walls, depending on whether wood or stone was more plentiful. Many Native American villages in the Northeast and Canada had elaborate wooden stockades, owing to the plentiful number of trees. By putting up walls around a village, it could be more easily protected from rivals. Most early villages were located near streams or rivers, as a source of fresh water was important for sustaining a concentrated population. Rivers, lakes, and coasts were also important sources of food and travel by boat.

Many early villages were characteristic of their environment as they had to rely on local building materials to construct their dwellings. In this sense, the cultural landscape was directly affected by the local terrain. Wood was, of course, a primary building material in an area that featured lots of trees. The Iroquois were famous for building large wooden longhouses out of the plentiful trees of the Great Lakes region in North America. Stone was a sturdier building material, but much more difficult to find and mine.

The depiction of a traditional Iroquois longhouse

More sophisticated ancient civilizations, such as the ancient Egyptians and Mayans, used the stone to build dwellings and even huge pyramids. In areas to the south which lacked trees, buildings were often constructed out of grass and brush. These forms of dwellings were common on the African savanna and among the Aboriginals of Northern Australia. Poles and sticks could be combined to wattle and weave together a meshing for structures in shrub-land areas. This type of building was common in West Africa. In the Middle East where the desert is common, sun-dried bricks made of mud were originally used to build structures, eventually being replaced by oven-baked bricks. One of the most impressive structures made of mud brick is the Great Mosque of Djenne in Mali, which was built in the 13th century by the very wealthy Mali Empire.

Rural settlement patterns are classified as clustered, dispersed or linear.

There are various settlement patterns that early villages adopted. A clustered settlement pattern is one in which there is a central feature that the houses cluster around. This was often a castle or some other defensive feature in early history. Later, the central feature evolved to be a public square where people could gather for political purposes or a religious building such as a church or a mosque. Clustered patterns are most visible in older settlements, and many cities in Africa, Europe and Asia still have features of the original clustered village pattern.

Today many small towns grow and cluster around a central business area, such as a small strip of road with stores. Political geographers are especially interested in village settlement patterns because it can reveal what the early settlers thought was the most important aspect of their lives. A cluster around shops, a church or a public square tells what the early settlers valued more because they placed it at the center of the settlement and clustered around it.

In contrast to a clustered village is a dispersed settlement pattern. Dispersed rural settlements tend to have various farms scattered through an area without any central feature or village linking them together. Dispersed rural settlements were fairly common in England and other parts of Western Europe, later being imported to North America. This settlement pattern is also common in Papua New Guinea, Southern Italy and the Alps area of Austria, Germany, and Switzerland. Typically dispersed rural settlements involve smaller farms with irregularly sized plots of land, often lined with trees. This settlement pattern is often a result of the more modern settlement, as people fled the crowded and polluted cities of the industrial area and sought to return to a life of farming. While very early settlements would cluster together for protection or some other public function, by the time of the industrial revolution, this was no longer an issue, and people sought to move farther away from others to claim their plot of land.

A linear settlement is one which expands along a straight line, usually a river or central roadway. Hong Kong is an example of a linear settlement that grew along the base of a line of steep mountains which constrained the direction of the city's growth. Another famous example is the plots of land along the St. Lawrence River in Quebec, Canada. This area was settled by farmers who divided the land into long narrow strips, with each having small access to the river. At this time, the St. Lawrence was a hugely important transportation route settlers relied on because of their unfamiliarity with the Canadian interior. As a result, instead of dividing the land into even squares or clustering around a central feature, they developed very long and narrow fields which are still visible today. Linear patterns such as the farming communities along the St. Lawrence River contrast to a ribbon development, which is a form of urban settlement which expands further and further outward from an original central street.

Other settlement patterns include polyfocal settlements and planned geometric settlements. Polyfocal settlements occur when two communities expand to the point where they begin to overlap and eventually become indistinguishable. A prominent example is the city of Minneapolis-St. Paul in Minnesota. Originally two separate settlements, they eventually expanded to the point where they became basically a single city. The capital city of Hungary is Budapest, which is another polyfocal settlement. Today Budapest is one city, but it originally began as two separate villages, one called Buda and the other called Pest.

Budapest was united into a single city in 1873

As urban planning rose to prominence, many new settlements followed a specific planning structure. Savannah, Georgia in the United States was based on a system of connected squares, all with a central park feature. Eventually, grid-based cities such as New York and San Francisco became very popular. There are also special cases of entirely planned cities which were created from nothing. Examples are the capitals of Brazil and Australia, which were designed to be new capital cities. The planned city of Bello Horizonte in Brazil divides the city into a series of neighborhoods divided by diagonal roads which cut the city into a series of diamonds.

Von Thünen's model helps to explain rural land use by emphasizing the importance of transportation costs associated with distance from the market.

Johann von Thünen was a German economist who came up with a model to predict the layout of agricultural practices in relation to a city marketplace. The model is based on the assumption that farmers located around a city all sell their products in the city at the same central marketplace. The model also assumes that the farmers are motivated by seeking higher prices and will only sell for the highest price. The model also assumes that all farmland is equally productive and there is only one mode of transportation to take the produce to the city market to sell. As a result of these assumptions, von Thünen argued that the most important factor was the distance from a farm to the market as measured in terms of transportation costs.

The model is then used to predict agricultural settlement patterns by positing a number of concentric rings around the central marketplace in the city. The land in a ring closest to the city will be intensive agriculture; it becomes more extensive the further it is from the city center. The furthest regions will be ranches and grazing pastures, and the closest to the city will be horticulture and dairy farms. The land closest to the city will be the most expensive, so intensive farming that can extract more yield out of less land will dominate closer to the city, while cheaper land further outside can be used for extensive farming. Transportation cost also matters, as when von Thünen was coming up with his model in the 19th century, dairy farms would have to transport milk directly to the customer due to a lack of refrigeration. It was cheaper in transportation costs for dairy farms to be closer to their customers than further afield. At the same time, an extensive grain farm can be further away since it can be transported in bulk for relatively cheap. Anything that is expensive to transport will be close to the city, and anything that is cheap to transport will be further away.

Von Thünen's model helps explain the contemporary distribution of agricultural regions.

Von Thünen's model has limited usefulness today. While it may have strongly predicted the location of dairy farms and grain farms in the 1800s, modern transportation costs are much different. The average city today that is surrounded by farmland can be compared to the Von Thünen model, and geographers today are more interested in how von Thünen's model rarely predicts the contemporary distribution of agricultural regions because transportation costs are now not the sole variable that determines farmland. Take for example contemporary farmers' markets in cities. Usually, a large city will have many different markets, often specializing in different farm products. The concentric ring approach cannot explain or predict land use since there is no single center point. As soon as there are multiple locations, the model breaks down.

Vendors and customers at a farmers' market in Boston, Massachusetts

A second problem is the assumption that farms can all produce the same yield. In reality, modern cities are large and cover many different terrain types. As cities have expanded through suburban sprawl, what used to be the extensive outer areas of large fields are now directly outside the city, with the more intensive farming now the furthest from the city. Some cities also have different types of terrain, where the land may not be fertile in one area, resulting in different agricultural layouts and causing the Von Thünen model to break down.

Perhaps the biggest problem with the Von Thünen model is the central assumption of distance as the most important factor. Today, many farms around a city export much of their crop around the world rather than sending it directly to the city. Distance to market today is not a factor on a city-rural basis but an international basis. Food now travels tens of thousands of miles to market, meaning in a globalized context, the Von Thünen model has almost no explanatory power at all. There is one exception, however, which is the resurgence of the local eating movement. People concerned about the greenhouse gas emissions caused by airplanes carrying food around the world have begun advocating for people to focus on eating food produced in their local area. In regions with a strong "locavore" movement, the Von Thünen model becomes relevant again as local distance once again becomes a factor. Many locavores specifically use concentric ring diagrams to map out the maximum distance they want their food to travel.

Regions of specialty farming do not always conform to von Thünen's concentric rings.

Specialty farming areas which focus either on a single cash crop, such as oranges in Florida or grapes in California, conform to the von Thünen model even less than most contemporary globalized cities. In these regions, there are large fields of single crop producers side by side whose primary market is not a local city but around the world. Florida oranges are not produced and eaten only by people in Miami or Tampa; they are sent around the country and exported around the world. The same is true for California grapes and wine, and it is true for most modern forms of agricultural production in the context of globalized supply chains. The Von Thünen model only explains the agricultural patterns of the 18th century and has very little relevance in a globalized world.

Environmental systems are affected by land use/land cover change.

Agricultural land use can dramatically change environmental systems in a region. Irrigation can allow farmers to water crops in areas where they otherwise would not grow due to a lack of water, but the water needed for irrigation must be transported from somewhere else. In many cases, this can cause the draining of water tables in other regions and potentially threaten drinking water supplies. The American southwest has made extensive use of irrigation, but it also has led to water shortages as watering crops and livestock has meant less water available for human consumption. In many developing countries where water is even scarcer, farmers often resort to using polluted water or even sewage for irrigation purposes. This can lead to the spread of diseases and pathogens, which leads to public health crises. In some cases, rivers are diverted and even partially drained for irrigation purposes, leading to issues for people downstream and plant and animal life.

Another problem is *desertification*, the spread of desert-like conditions to areas that were once more fertile. Desertification is caused by a loss of vegetation, which is responsible for maintaining soil richness and preventing rains from creating landslides and washouts. A major cause of desertification is animal grazing, as the livestock eat all the plants. This is especially problematic near existing deserts, as it causes the desert to spread, with major deserts like the Sahara growing rapidly and eating up all the arable land. Another major cause of desertification is climate change, as it leads to increased regional warming, causing more drought.

An abandoned building in Kolmanskop, Namibia is increasingly claimed by advancing sands

Related to desertification is *deforestation*, which involves chopping down all the trees in an area. This is especially a problem with the Amazon rainforest, as poor farmers practice slash and burn techniques to remove the jungle so they can work the land. The loss of rainforest is problematic because it is home to many different species of animals. Many medical researchers also point to a large number of unique plants which might hold the key to developing new medicines. Rainforests are also major carbon sinks that counteract climate change since trees take in carbon dioxide and breathe out oxygen. Deforestation was once a major problem in Europe because much of the forest was cut down for farming, but efforts to replant have proven successful at beginning to grow back some of the lost tree coverage.

Wetlands are extremely important for their ability to purify water, control floods and replenish groundwater supplies naturally. Unfortunately, wetlands continue to be drained to make areas more habitable by humans. Wetland destruction is often provoked by expanding suburbs and real estate developers who want to build new houses. In the past, draining wetlands was done to create farmland. It is estimated that half of the world's natural wetlands had been drained by the mid-1990s, prompting renewed calls for conservation, given their important natural functions and traditional home to many species of animals. Given the increased attention to the problem of climate change, preserving wetlands is especially important because they can act as both a carbon sink and are also useful for naturally controlling water levels.

Food Production and Consumption

Changes in food production and consumption present challenges and opportunities.

Advances in technology have dramatically changed food production. As previously mentioned, the first, second and third (green revolution) revolutions in agricultural production have each drastically increased yields. Today, farms resemble industrial factories and are controlled by large agribusiness companies. These agribusiness companies operate on a global scope and sell their products around the world. Contemporary agribusiness integrates all the stages of food production and merchandising under one corporation. This means the same corporation is often responsible for not just growing the food, but processing, packaging, distribution, advertising, research and development, and fertilizer manufacturing.

As a result of the shift away from family farms to large agribusiness corporations, employment in the farming industry has dropped dramatically. In 1950, 12% of Americans were employed in farming; now that number is less than 1%. The shift to globalized agribusiness has presented many opportunities because it has enhanced food production, but it also creates challenges such as food security issues and higher prices for consumers.

Agricultural innovations have resulted in ongoing debates over environmental, cultural and health impacts.

Agricultural innovations continue to happen and are not without controversy. Biotechnology is enabling the creation of genetically modified organisms (GMOs). Genetically modifying a plant or animal involves manipulating its DNA, often through splicing with other organisms, to introduce new genetic resistance to a crop. Corn is the most popular GMO, as today around 85% of corn grown in the U.S. has been genetically modified to be resistant to herbicides. This makes the corn resistant to herbicides used to kill weeds, allowing the corn to be sprayed with herbicides indiscriminately without fear that the weed-killer will kill the corn. Another major GMO crop is soy, which has been spliced with properties of olives to give it a high level of oleic acid, which can help reduce bad cholesterol levels.

GMO Kenyan corn (maize) field

A much more controversial example is giving cows recombinant bovine growth hormone, which causes the cows to produce more milk. These hormones have been banned by the EU, Canada, Japan, and most other developed countries but remain common in the United States. After scientific review, the EU found that milk from cows injected with bovine growth hormones was linked to increased instances of cancer in people who consume this milk, compared to people who drank milk from cows that were not injected with the hormones.

Canada banned the hormones for animal welfare reasons, as the hormone which stimulates increased milk production also negatively affects the health of the cows; their udders are not equipped to handle the increased milk production, leading to a much higher instance of infection. This results in the cows being given large doses of antibiotics, which then show up in milk which people drink, which in turn is contributing to a massive build-up of antibiotic resistance in humans. This makes humans more susceptible to bacterial infection because our bodies build antibiotic resistance, making this less effective as a medicine. Despite bans of the hormone in the rest of the world, the powerful agribusiness lobby in the United States has so far been able to keep the hormones legal.

While bovine growth hormones are problematic for a number of scientific reasons, plant-based GMOs are largely safe for human consumption but are still controversial. Some people believe that these GMOs have not been tested for long-term effects on human health, but the scientific consensus today is that these crops are safe. There is a second issue with GMO crops, however, which is the corporate control of food. In many cases, the crops are genetically modified, not to create any real benefit such as making them healthier or resistant to drought, but merely so that a corporation can apply for a patent and then charge royalty fees and control seed distribution.

In some cases, the herbicide-resistant crops are only resistant to one herbicide, which happens to be produced by the same company that controls the patent on the GMO crop. This locks farmers into buying not just seeds from a single company but also their herbicide products. This hurts competition and drives up the price of food. This problem is especially bad in poorer countries where farmers traditionally had saved the seeds from the year before and replanted them but are now required to pay foreign corporations because of patent law controls.

Even though many GMO crops increase yields and have the potential to reduce hunger, they are much more expensive, and profits go to transnational corporations. The higher expense leads to a situation where there is more than enough food produced, but it is not accessible due to its high cost. Most agribusiness corporations argue that GMO crops can end world hunger, but they fail to point out that hunger is a problem because of economic inequality and distribution, not due to the inability to produce enough food.

As a result of fears about GMOs, some unfounded and some based in science, the organic farming movement has taken off. Organic farming involves growing crops and raising animals without the use of chemical pesticides, using natural fertilizer and without using hormones and antibiotics in animals. The goal of organic farming is to maintain environmental sustainability and avoiding what is deemed as harmful agricultural practices.

Organic farming is controversial in itself, especially on the side of growing crops. Many critics see organic farming as simply a marketing ploy that convinces consumers to pay higher prices thinking they are buying into more environmentally friendly farming practices when in reality many of the larger "organic" farms do not follow the principles of organic farming. Other critics point to the ban on using GMO crops as scientifically unfounded, as these crops have not been found to have any negative human health consequences. While chemical fertilizers and pesticides used in large industrial farms often cause major pollution problems, the organic argument against GMO crops is considered flimsy.

Chickens allowed to move around in a free-range environment

On the livestock side, organic farms are much less controversial because they respond to real animal welfare issues. Organic livestock farms do not use growth hormones and generally aim to provide animals with a more natural environment, rather than to stuff them into tiny pens in which the animals are so confined they often cannot even turn around. Organic meat farming also became popular at the time of the Mad Cow Disease scare, in which it was found that eating meat from cows with this disease would lead to degenerative brain disease in humans. The cause of Mad Cow Disease was that large industrial factory farms were feeding cows ground up cow meat as part of their feed to save money. Organic meat farming focuses on feeding animals their natural diet, which makes the meat safer to eat.

Aquaculture is the farming of marine animals such as fish. It involves confining fish to pens and purposefully breeding them, in the same manner as livestock. Since the 1990s aquaculture has skyrocketed as wild fish stocks continue to decline due to overfishing. The most popular fish to be farmed worldwide are carp, salmon, tilapia, and catfish. Outside of fish, shrimp, prawns, oysters, and geoducks are the most common species to be farmed. Currently, China accounts for over half of the world's production of aquaculture, while in the U.S. and Canada aquaculture is the fastest growing form of agriculture.

While aquaculture can lessen the impact of overfishing on wild fish stocks, it is not without its issues. There have been accusations that China's fish farming industry is much smaller than reported. China has been accused of illegal fishing which is then reported as the product of aquaculture in an attempt to get around fishing regulations and conservation efforts. Currently, there is a major debate about whether aquaculture is better for the environment or not. While on a global scale aquaculture has been instrumental in helping stop the depletion of many species of fish, on a local level the individual farms can be quite damaging to the environment. Fish farms create concentrated amounts of organic waste which reduce water quality nearby and harms wild fish. Some species of farmed fish, such as salmon, are fed wild fish that are caught. This leads to a situation in which many pounds of wild fish need to be caught to produce one pound of farmed fish, making these forms of aquaculture inefficient and diminishing the local stocks of smaller fish. Furthermore, catching all these small fish on an industrial scale leaves nothing for the wild salmon stocks to eat. Salmon aquaculture has been accused of actually contributing to the decline of wild salmon, a problem which it sought to solve.

Another issue with aquaculture is the high rate of escapees, who can then go on to breed with wild fish, which dilutes the gene pool of the wild fish. This makes the wild fish more susceptible to diseases and generally makes their population weaker. Since the fish need to be farmed in waters of their natural environment, fish farms often end up destroying natural habitat. In 2016, a toxic algae bloom killed many wild fish and $800 million worth of farmed fish in Chile. Scientists at Concepcion University in Chile cited the increase in aquaculture as a contributing factor, as it changes the chemicals that are present in the water and the seabed. Shrimp farming in Indonesia and Thailand has contributed to the destruction of 20% of the region's mangrove forests, which are vital habitats for many different species.

Fish farm management in Shanghai

Environmental issues related to agriculture include sustainability, soil degradation, reduction in biodiversity, overgrazing, river and aquifer depletion, animal wastes and extensive fertilizer and pesticide use.

In addition to controversies over new agricultural technologies, there are some ongoing environmental issues associated with agriculture. Many of the critiques surround *sustainability*, which is the ability to continue producing food indefinitely without destroying the natural environment that makes this possible. One major issue is soil degradation in the form of erosion. Erosion and soil degradation occur when vegetation is removed to clear the land for agriculture. Plowing the land exposes topsoil which can then be blown away by wind or washed away by rain. This degrades the quality of the soil by removing nutrients and making it less fertile.

Erosion at its extreme can lead to the creation of deserts where very few plants can grow, and no farming can take place. Certain crops are especially bad for causing soil erosion, including soybeans, corn, coffee, cotton, rice, and wheat. Brazil alone loses around 50 million tons of topsoil every year, which leads to farms being less productive in the future and requiring more chemical fertilizers that cause pollution from runoff. A lack of solid topsoil layer can also increase flooding and in hilly regions increases the chance of dangerous landslides.

Overgrazing by animals can also lead to erosion and desertification. If animals do not have a large enough space to roam, they will eat all the vegetation and leave the topsoil exposed and vulnerable to being blown or washed away. Overgrazing can have devastating impacts on regions close to deserts because it can contribute to the expansion of deserts. Overgrazing is also unsustainable. Animals eating all the vegetation to the point where it cannot grow back means that the land will not be able to support livestock in the future.

Another major environmental impact of agriculture is on water systems. Agriculture is by far the world's largest consumer of fresh water, with farming consuming 70% of water globally, as compared to industry with 23% and human consumption with 8%. In many cases unsustainable methods are the problem, as farms use leaky or faulty irrigation systems or attempt to grow crops unsuitable to local conditions, requiring a disproportionate amount of water. Farming is the biggest source of groundwater table depletion and pollution. Fertilizer and pesticides used on farms can run off into local rivers or seep into the ground, causing water pollution.

Perhaps the biggest issue today for agriculture in relation to the environment is climate change. Livestock farming is one of the largest contributors of greenhouse gasses that cause climate change. Methane gasses, which are released during the digestion process of animals, contribute around 15-25% of total greenhouse gas emissions globally. This has led to many environmentalists advocating for reducing meat consumption as the activity that can have the biggest impact in reducing climate change. Studies of the carbon footprints of various diets back this claim up; the single biggest way to reduce one's climate impact is to eat less beef, as cows are especially bad for producing methane gas. Scientists have found that for the average American red meat consumption contributes more to greenhouse gas production than driving a car. Another study of the diets of people in the UK demonstrated that a vegetarian diet produces half as many greenhouse gas emissions compared to the average diet. One of the main reasons for this is related to the fact that livestock production is food inefficient, as grain is grown, then fed to animals, then people eat the animals. Directly consuming the grain is more efficient and removes a step of intensive farming which produces large amounts of greenhouse gasses.

Packaged red meats

Patterns of food production and consumption are influenced by food-choice issues.

One of the biggest changes in agricultural production of the last 20 years is the way that consumers have started to become more informed about what they eat. With issues such as obesity, the environment and ethics causing more people to think about what they eat, agricultural production is increasingly being driven by consumer choices. Organic farming took off as a result of concerns with the overuse of chemical pesticides, fertilizers and growth hormones given to cows. Organic farming is often linked to the local eating movement, which seeks out local organic farms to minimize the impact of transportation, both in terms of greenhouse gas emissions and food freshness.

A renewed focus on ethics is also driving consumers. The push for fair trade, especially in coffee, reflects this ethical concern. The fair trade movement seeks to buy coffee at fair prices from independent farmers in developing countries. This is in contrast to having major agribusiness corporations buy out all the farmers and take over the land for themselves. It is called fair trade because globalized agribusiness corporations rely on "free trade" agreements to exploit the land and farmers of other countries, making it so the local government cannot stop them. Fair trade seeks to protect the livelihoods of farmers in developing countries while still facilitating trade and allowing consumers in richer countries to import coffee beans.

Another major ethical concern driving changing agricultural practices is animal welfare. While most people have the image of a family farm when they think about where their steak came from, in reality almost all meat comes from industrialized factory farms where animals are squeezed into tiny spaces and often spend their lives sick and even unable to walk. Concern for the welfare of livestock has led to changes in production in places like the EU, which has been a world leader in pushing for animal welfare. The EU is phasing out the caging of egg-laying chickens, requiring that they have space to roam around, as well as many other regulations driven by popular concern with animal welfare. By contrast, many other countries lag on animal welfare issues. Developing countries, as well as the United States and Canada, have very few regulations which mean that factory farms are common and animal cruelty is standard practice. As a result of the backward condition of animal welfare in the U.S. and Canada, many consumers are choosing to become vegetarians and stop eating meat altogether. This has led to a new industry of meat-free products which seek to replicate the taste of meat without the cages and cruelty.

Eventually, the next big revolution in agricultural technology will be the ability to grow meat in a lab and eliminate the need to raise and kill livestock altogether. Lab-grown meat has the potential to dramatically reduce the impacts of climate change, free up huge amounts of land and water and vastly reduce animal cruelty. Once lab-grown meat becomes commercially viable and widespread, it will have a dramatic global impact possibly larger than the previous three agricultural revolutions.

Factors affecting the location of food-processing facilities include markets, economies of scale, transportation, government policies, etc.

The location of food processing facilities is varied, but they are usually placed based on where it is cheapest to do so. While in the past they were often found in every city, as food processing techniques made canning more common and globalization brought in international shipping, food processing sites are now usually located in places where the labor costs are the lowest. As part of an integrated global supply chain, a single agribusiness corporation will have different locations around the world. A grain company may grow its grain in the Western United States, ship it to Mexico where labor is cheaper to process it and then sell it in Western Europe.

The role of women in food production has changed.

The role of women has changed in relation to food production throughout history. In hunter/gatherer societies women were predominantly the gatherers while men hunted. This is an example of socially enforced gender roles that shaped early human societies and their religions and attitudes toward women. In the traditional farming culture that developed with the founding of human civilization and existed until the recent industrialization of agriculture, farming was strongly tied to gender roles. A *gender role* is a social perception that one sex must perform specific tasks, regardless of ability. In the United States, the traditional family farm tended to enforce a gender split where men worked in the fields and women worked in the farmhouse. Men would plow the fields and tend to the animals, while women would process the food and prepare meals.

Female farmer working the field

By the mid-20th century increasing industrialization and centralization of food processing led to many of the aspects of the feminine gender farming role being industrialized and moved to factory processing plants. Many scholars argue that this led to a change in the role of women that disempowered them, as they are no longer active participants in the farming process. This marked the shift from the female gender role of homemakers to housekeepers. Homemaking was considered an active task that was necessary to ensure that crops and livestock were processed into edible food, while housekeeping implies a passive role, brought on by the fact that by the 1950s many families were beginning to buy finished products in grocery stores instead of growing their food.

The regression of the status of women brought about by industrialization led to a second wave of feminism in the 1960s when women began to demand an equal role in the business world. While at first these feminist activists were considered radicals for trying to disrupt the status quo, today woman now play prominent roles in all sectors of the economy and the female gender role is no longer one which tells women that they cannot have jobs. In places that have yet to be affected by strong feminist movements, women are often still confined to gender roles that involve staying in the home. In many parts of the developing world, women are expected to be the farmers while the men go to the city to look for waged work. As a result of this gender division, it is often the men who control the cash in a family, giving the male gender role more power. International development efforts often focus on empowering women in developing countries since a strong feminist movement may be key to developing the economies of the industrialized countries.

The role of women has changed the types of food a family consumes, and the way food is prepared.

Food consumption has also changed along with changing gender roles. On the family farm, the woman would make food based on what the farm grew. This often led to fairly bland food with low nutritional value — often the same meal every day. As women entered the workforce en masse beginning in the 1960s, there were often two adults working, and many conservatives lamented the fact that women were not home to make healthy meals for their kids anymore. In some cases, TV dinners and fast food restaurants became more popular as they were faster ways to prepare food after a long day of work. Eventually, men began to share cooking duties, as recently the obesity epidemic has focused people in the developed world on the need to cook with fresh ingredients and rely less on processed foods.

Notes

Chapter 6

Industrialization and Economic Development

Discussion of industrialization and economic development intrinsically draws upon geographic elements of past and present patterns of industrialization, types of economic sectors and the acquisition of comparative advantage and complementarity. Helping to explain why the world is divided into economic cores, less-developed peripheries and semi-peripheral areas are models of economic development, such as Rostow's stages of economic growth or Wallerstein's world-systems theory.

Further means of gaining an in-depth understanding of the subject are through the analysis of contemporary patterns of industrialization and their impact on development, as well as applying measures of development (e.g., Gross Domestic Product (GDP), Human Development Index (HDI)) to grasp economic difference patterns. Weber's industrial location theory, accounts of economic globalization, the ways in which countries, regions, and communities confront economic inequality patterns, the global financial crisis, consumption pattern imbalances, women's labor force role, energy use, resource conservation and pollutions effects on both the environment and quality of life are go-to topics whose study can increase knowledge competence regarding geographies of interdependence in the world economy.

Industrialization

> **The Industrial Revolution, as it diffused from its hearth, facilitated improvements in standards of living.**

The Industrial Revolution began in England in the 1760s and later diffused across Western Europe. It was characterized by the use of steam-powered machinery and the introduction of factories, especially in the textile industry. Many historians argue that the increased economic efficiency created by the adoption of these new industrialized technologies led to a sustained increase in the standard of living for the general population for the first time in history. Jobs were plentiful and average income increased dramatically, especially as people moved from rural areas to cities. This represented a shift from subsistence farming to waged employment.

Early factory in the Kingdom of Saxony featuring machinery invented by Richard Hartmann

Industrialization began in response to new technologies and was facilitated by the availability of natural resources.

The early Industrial Revolution was a revolution in power production, which began by using water power to turn mills. Mills needed to be located alongside rivers with significant flow, and the natural geography dictated much of the locations of the early industrial era. Later when steam engines began to rise to prominence, they required large amounts of coal for fuel. As early factories shifted away from water power to steam power, factories began to clump around coal fields so that mined coal would not need to be transported far. The coal fields of northern and central England led to the growth of industrial cities such as Manchester and Liverpool, which grew from backwaters to the economic powerhouses of the Industrial Revolution. In the late 1770s, the newfound importance of Manchester caused its population to double over a period of just 15 years. Liverpool grew from a village of 6,000 people at the start of the 18th century to a thriving city with 80,000 people by the end of the 18th century.

These population booms led to the creation of working-class housing districts which were often extremely overcrowded and poorly crafted. Many families often crowded together in the same house, causing major public health issues. At the same time, the constant burning of coal caused massive air pollution issues as black clouds of soot commonly floated over the city, making the air difficult to breathe. City infrastructure was unable to keep up with population growth, and the working-class neighborhoods were often neglected, leading to polluted drinking water and dirty streets that were not cleaned of horse manure. Coal miners and factory workers in these areas began to form political movements to demand better conditions.

The diffusion of industrialization led to growing populations and increased food supplies, which freed workers to seek industrial jobs in cities.

As industrialization took root, its principles also spread to agriculture, leading to the Second Agricultural revolution. This allowed farms to vastly increase yields as they began to adopt industrial technologies. With food now plentiful and relatively inexpensive, many rural farmers, who were still living in situations not very far removed from the peasant serfs of the Middle Ages, began to move to cities in search of a better life. While subsistence farming kept families fed, it left people in abject poverty as they generally had very little left over which they could sell for money. Life in the city working for a wage meant they could not only have the cash to buy food, which was now plentiful and cheap but also have money left over so that people were not completely destitute. The new urban workers of the industrial revolution were by no means well off, but their lives were better than if they spent their lives merely trying to grow enough food to feed themselves.

Industrialism also meant the final triumph of capitalism over feudalism. Subsistence farmers were often still essentially locked to the land as serfs because they rarely owned the land they worked. Working at a factory meant the full commoditization of labor, as workers sold their labor to capitalist factory owners for a set hourly wage. With labor seen as a commodity, the workers were often not treated as human beings but as industrial inputs. This meant that there was very little regard for the well-being of workers in this era, who were often required to work 16-hour days. Small children were commonly employed in factories, with one of the first successful labor reforms in the UK being the Cotton Factories Regulation Act of 1819, which set a minimum age of 9 to work in a factory and a maximum workday of 12 hours for workers under 16 years old. After a constant barrage of strikes and political activism, women and children were granted a 10-hour work day in England by 1847, and all workers won a 12-hour work day in 1848 as a result of the French Revolution.

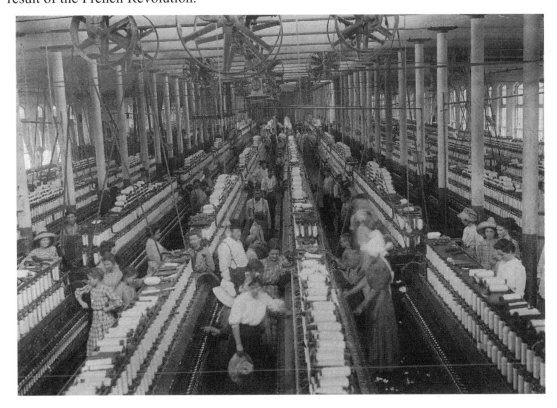

Children cotton mill workers

Safety conditions in the factories were also abysmal. Workers commonly lost fingers and limbs and were often badly burned as a result of the reliance on steam power. Coal mines were especially dangerous — death was a common occupational hazard. At this time, there was no compensation for being injured on the job, and thus even a small injury that prevented someone from working would often shortly lead to death as people became homeless and starved.

Increased industrialization led to demands for raw materials and the search for new markets and was a factor in the rise of colonialism and imperialism.

Industrialization required raw material inputs, in particular coal, to constantly fuel the factories. This led to an expansionary thrust to find newer and cheaper sources of raw materials, both in the Americas and in Africa. By the early 1800s, the industrial revolution had spread to North America, and European powers began to focus on attempts to colonize Africa in search of raw materials for domestic industries. This push to colonize new territories was driven not only by the industrialization process but also by political factors such as the nationalistic desire to control more territory, build empires and to compete geopolitical concerns. By 1914, the colonial projects of the European powers came to a head as their competing imperialist projects for control of land and raw materials led to World War I, which was a war directly caused by imperialist expansion.

The economy consists of primary, secondary, tertiary, quaternary and quinary sectors.

The economy can be divided into five industries or industrial sectors which work together to form a supply chain. These different industrial sectors are important for understanding economic development as more finished products can be sold for more money, while raw materials tend to cost less and be subject to price fluctuations. Economic development is usually associated with moving up the chain from primary all the way to the quinary industry.

Primary industry involves extracting raw materials from the Earth. Farming, fishing, mining, cutting trees and extracting fossil fuels are all examples of primary industries, as they are extractive in nature. More developed countries usually have fewer of these industries because in many cases they have already extracted their resources, which is the case with the UK, or they have moved up the production chain, and now their industry is focused on producing value-added goods, rather than just extracting raw materials. Industrialized countries tend to rely on imports of raw materials, and their population usually involves fewer people. One major exception is oil, which because it is used globally for fuel, it can be a strategic geopolitical advantage not to have to rely on imports from other countries. Oil, however, is still a commodity and its price can fluctuate wildly. When the price is high, countries may make much money taxing oil production but then see a major drop in revenue when the price of oil declines, which stalls the economy. The oil price fluctuations of the 2010s had dramatically affected Canada and Venezuela, first leading to economic booms, then to recessions when the price dropped.

The secondary sector involves processing and refining raw materials into a finished product that is more useful and therefore more valuable than the raw material alone. Manufacturing of all sorts is a secondary sector, and it can include anything from the production of furniture to food processing to refining oil into gasoline. Since refined products are more useful and more valuable, countries which can transition from primary to secondary industry tend to develop economically and become wealthier. Oil, for example, is much less useful in its crude form than refined gasoline. A country that has many oil refineries is going to be wealthier and more developed than a country that merely extracts oil and then sells it unrefined. Refineries and manufacturing also provide better jobs which tend to pay more and be less physically strenuous than primary sector jobs as well. For example, it is much better to work at a diamond refinery that transforms mined material into finished products which can be used in jewelry than it is to work in an actual mine. Countries with more secondary sector employment tend to have a better standard of living as a result of higher wages and less physically exhausting and dangerous working conditions.

The tertiary sector involves moving, selling and trading products made in the secondary and sometimes primary sectors. For instance, the financial sector is part of the tertiary economy as it involves buying and selling future contracts for oil and gasoline which determine the commodity price in the global economy. The tertiary sector is also called the service sector, as it involves jobs which are not involved with production but with transferring goods to the consumer. Wal-Mart for example, is a tertiary sector company, as it does not produce goods but sells them to the consumer.

Boeing airplane factory in Everett, Washington

Sectors of the economy which involve maintenance on finished products are also within the tertiary sector. A carpet cleaning company or a computer repair company are both tertiary. In today's globalized economy, most of the wealthier countries now have very little manufacturing, and the bulk of their economies takes place in the tertiary service sector. Whether this represents more economic development or less is open to dispute. In many cases, workers in the tertiary sector are paid significantly less than the secondary sector. For example, a cashier at Wal-Mart makes significantly less money than someone employed in manufacturing, leading to a decline in real wages for the working class in developed countries since the onset of economic neoliberal globalization.

The quaternary sector involves information and knowledge creation and transfer. Sometimes called the information economy or the knowledge economy, this sector is often positioned as the sector countries should strive to dominate to compete in the global economy. Computer programmers, scientists, university professors and anyone working in industries related to producing or transferring knowledge are part of this sector. This sector tends to be high paying and very profitable, but the promise of it providing mass employment for increasing the average wages of the working class has not panned out. Increasingly this sector is outsourced just as much as the secondary sector, which puts workers in developed countries in direct competition with workers in developing countries who are willing to work for drastically lower wages. As a result, only a select few benefit from employment in this sector, despite its continual importance in the information era.

Finally, the quinary sector, whose existence is sometimes disputed, involves high-level decision making. This would be the level of government, as legislatures and executives make decisions, as well as senior management within corporations. Given that this sector is merely a function of management which operates on top of the other sectors, many dispute the value of classifying it as a separate sector. For example, a government may develop a natural resources extraction policy which focuses on logging and oil extraction, which are primary industries. Despite the government developing policy related to primary industry, it would be considered quinary sector since it was the government making a high-level decision. Most economists, however, would simply argue that such decisions are part of the industrial sector they relate to, so the example of a government making decisions about resource extraction would really be part of the primary sector of the economy.

Alfred Weber's model of industrial location emphasized the owner's desire to minimize transportation and labor costs and maximize agglomeration economies.

In the mid-1900s the German economist Alfred Weber developed the Least Cost Theory of Industrial Location in order to predict and explain the location of factories as well as their potential for growth. Like the von Thünen agricultural model, Weber's model attempts to use location and transportation cost to describe where factories are likely to locate based on where it was cheapest to do so. The primary determinants in cost, according to Weber, were shipping costs of the finished goods. Shipping costs could be determined by looking at the distance from the factory to the end market as well as the weight of the goods being shipped. Lightweight goods could be shipped further for less money, while heavier goods would be more expensive to ship further and would tend to be located closer to the endpoints.

For the model to have any explanatory power, Weber's model was based on a number of assumptions which held the most. First is that transportation cost is entirely determined by a combination of distance and the weight of the goods. Industries are all aiming to maximize profits and thus minimize shipping costs. Industries have fixed locations where they sell their finished goods which are known in advance. Labor only exists in certain locations and will not move to follow a factory. Moreover, finally, that physical geography is not a factor.

Shipping by sea is typically the cheapest method of transporting goods and materials

In the era of globalization, some of these assumptions become very problematic. Today, the final location of goods is often anywhere in the world and certainly not known in advance; this makes determining an ideal factory location based on shipping costs impossible. Second is the idea that transportation distance and weight are the biggest determining factors for where a factory will be placed, which in today's globalized economy have almost no relation to where factories are placed. Today, factories are located based on where labor is cheapest, which is often as far as possible from the end market. A Wal-Mart in New York where the bulk of the merchandise is manufactured in China is going to have very high shipping costs for the factory to ship all the goods all the way around the world.

However, the fact that the labor costs are extremely minimal in China makes locating the factory there cheaper overall despite the higher transportation costs. For this reason, Weber's model has no relevance in the globalized world where labor cost is the most important factor driving factory location. There have been many examples of factories moving around to avoid increased labor costs. Textile manufacturers, at one point a huge industry in the U.S., began moving to Mexico in the 1980s and 1990s for the cheaper labor costs. As Mexican workers organized, these factories then moved to Indonesia and Vietnam and now are beginning to move to Myanmar. This is called "the race to the bottom," and it explains how manufacturing relocates again and again in a globalized context: factories move around to find low labor costs.

Weber's model, however, is useful when thinking about earlier eras of factory production. For instance, in the industrial revolution when coal was a primary input, many factories were located next to coal fields and mines because coal was very heavy and expensive to transport. Papermaking is an example of a manufacturing process which takes a heavy raw material and then creates a very light final product. Weber's model would rightfully predict that the paper factory would be located close to the forests that timber was being extracted from because timber is heavy but also could be located far from the cities where the paper was consumed because the paper is very light and cheap to transport. Paper is an example of a weight-losing industry. Weight-gaining industries, by contrast, will be located further from the raw material inputs and closer to where the product is consumed. For this reason, many beverage bottling factories were located in cities, as the inputs of water and ingredients were lighter than the filled bottles which were produced. There are also what are called *footloose industries*, which take in light materials and produce light finished products; these industries are much less restricted in where they will locate a factory.

Notes

Measures of Development

Measures of development are used to understand patterns of social and economic differences at a variety of scales.

Development is measured through the improvement of material conditions at a variety of scales, ranging from local to national to global. Countries are often generally broken into two groups: developed countries and developing (or underdeveloped) countries. To determine which country fits where, and to measure development over time, some measures are used to quantify development, including economic factors such as gross domestic product and social factors such as income distribution. Categorizing countries into developed and developing is often difficult to quantify since a country may be economically poor but have very high levels of education, healthcare, and income equality. An example is Cuba, which, on a purely economic level, is an underdeveloped, developing country. On a social level though, Cuba scores very high with healthcare measures; for example, on infant mortality rate, it scores better than wealthy countries like the United States. On the other side are countries such as Saudi Arabia, which is very wealthy, but scores very low on social measures.

Measures of social and economic development include Gross National Income (GNI) per capita, sectoral structure of an economy, income distribution, fertility rates, infant mortality rates, access to healthcare and literacy rates.

It is important to understand various measures of development and why each has strengths and weaknesses for comparing the development process between countries and over time within a single country. The most common measure of economic development is *Gross Domestic Product* (GDP), which is the total value of all goods and services produced within a country over a year. This is usually expressed on a per capita basis, which means the total value is divided by the number of people in a country. Developed countries usually have GDP levels of over $20,000 per capita, while poor countries often have GDP levels less than $1,000 per capita. *Gross National Product* (GNP) includes the value of goods produced by all citizens of a country, regardless of where they live. GDP is based on what is produced inside a geographical area, and GNP is based on what citizens of a country produce, regardless of where they live. Gross National Income (GNI) is the GDP plus GNP with the GNP of foreign residents subtracted.

As purely economic indicators, GDP, GNP, and GNI are problematic because they tell nothing about the social development of a country or how the wealth produced is distributed. Take the example of the country of Equatorial Guinea in Africa. It has the highest GPD per capita in Africa and is comparable to relatively developed countries such as Argentina, Hungary, Poland and Croatia in its GDP. By looking at GDP alone, one might assume that the development situation in Equatorial Guinea is similar to that in South America or Eastern Europe and far and away better than anywhere else in Africa. In reality, the wealth is the result of oil fields which have enriched the President Teodoro Obiang, who has an estimated net worth of $600 million. President Obiang took power in a coup d'état in 1979 and has ruled as an authoritarian dictator since. Despite the country's immense oil wealth and low population, less than half of the population have access to clean drinking water, and infant mortality rates are extremely high, with 20% of all children die before they reach age 5. Despite having a GPD comparable to Eastern Europe, Equatorial Guinea is much less developed than Poland, which has a modern healthcare system and no problems with access to clean water. For reasons like this, measuring development purely based on economic statistics is fallen out of favor as it can be extremely misleading.

Another way of looking at development is by analyzing the type of sectors which are dominant. Quaternary sectors involved in information technology, research and the knowledge economy tend to be the most technologically advanced with the highest levels of incomes, while countries that rely on the primary sector of resource extraction tend to be the least developed. Going up the sector chain used to mean increasing levels of industrialization and professional occupations in the economy, but with globalization, this has changed. According to free trade theory, countries should focus only on sectors in which they have a comparative advantage, rather than trying to move up the sector chain and become high tech knowledge economies. This has led to some countries becoming more economically vulnerable due to having natural resources. In the 1960s and 1970s, Canada was primarily a manufacturing economy as it was a highly industrialized country with state-of-the-art technology. With the advent of free trade, Canada was encouraged to focus on the primary sector due to its comparative advantage of having lots of natural resources. Canada refocused to emphasize the primary economy of oil extraction, timber, and mining, and this has led to a decline in the strength of the Canadian economy as it is now dependent on commodity prices. When commodity prices drop, Canada is at the mercy of international markets. Prior to the era of free trade when Canada was primarily a secondary sector manufacturing economy, it had a much higher level of economic strength and development.

Canadian log boom operations in Gold River, British Columbia

An important measure of development is income distribution, which is measured by the Gini coefficient. The *Gini coefficient* is a measure of statistical dispersion among income values of a frequency distribution. What this means is that Gini measures how spread out people's incomes are. For example, in a country where everyone made the same salary, the Gini coefficient would be zero; more unequal countries get further away from zero. Gini is useful because it can help correct for the fact that GDP is an average, which leads to countries such as Equatorial Guinea having deceptively high GDP levels. The Gini coefficient for Equatorial Guinea is estimated to be around 0.67, making it one of the most unequal countries in the entire world. By contrast, Norway, which is considered by the UN to be the most developed country in the world, has one of the lowest Gini coefficients of 0.25. A better picture about whether or not everyone is benefitting from GPD can be found by looking at how wealth is distributed.

In addition to these economic measures of development, social measures such as infant mortality rate, fertility rate, and literacy rate can be used to measure human development. If one looks at the life expectancy of a country, they can see where healthcare is better and also where there is less likelihood of violent death from war or murder at an early age. Part of human development means living a full life, which can be measured by looking at health statistics. If one returns to the example of Equatorial Guinea, it can be seen that it has a life expectancy of just 56 years old, the 14th worst in the world. By contrast, the comparable countries in terms of GDP of Eastern Europe have much higher rates, with Poland having a life expectancy of 77, Hungary 75 and Croatia 78. Therefore, even though GPD per capita is higher in Equatorial Guinea, you're more likely to live a long life in Eastern Europe. This tells that despite the wealth of Equatorial Guinea, the government is not investing this money in healthcare and is not using it to make the country a better place to live for the average person.

Measures of gender inequality include reproductive health, indices of empowerment and labor-market participation.

Another important aspect of human development to measure and consider is gender equality. Even by combining economic and social indicators, a full picture of development may not be understood if only half the population is benefitting. For this reason, gender equality is an important indicator of development as it tells how much of the population is benefiting from development. Gender equality in itself is also a measure of development, as having unequal relations between the sexes is a sign of traditional cultures which have failed to embrace the modern world. Many different measures such as reproductive health assessments, labor market participation, and political rights are often combined into a hybrid gender equality measure. The Gender-Related Development Index (GDI) seeks to measure gender gaps in life expectancy, education and income. It does this by taking a country's HDI (discussed in the next section) and applying penalties to its score where there are large gaps between men and women.

Women professionals taking part in a panel discussion

The Gender Empowerment Measure (GEM) has more of a political focus and attempts to measure the equality of access women have to positions of political and corporate power, as well as how much money women make compared to men. This is measured by looking at the percentage of seats held by women in the legislature of a country, the percentage of women in decision making positions in the private sector and comparing the income of men and women. For example, a country such as Saudi Arabia would have a GEM of almost zero, as women are not allowed in government and not allowed to have a position of any importance in the economy by law. This means that women do not have incomes and are entirely dependent on husbands or male relatives. By contrast, countries such as Norway and Sweden have parliaments in which women hold half the seats, women are prominent in managerial positions throughout the economy, and the income of women is comparable to that of men. This is a useful measure because, despite the fact that Saudi Arabia has a very high GDP and generally good scores on health and education, it has an abysmal record when it comes to women, which demonstrates that Saudi Arabia is not nearly as developed as other countries with the same GDP.

The Human Development Index (HDI) is a composite measure used to show spatial variation in levels of development.

Since GDP was the dominant measure of development despite its problems, in the 1990s the Human Development Index was developed by economists Mahbub ul Haq and Amartya Sen to provide a better measure of development that included social factors along with economic wealth. The HDI was quickly adopted by the United Nations and used to rank countries regarding their human development rather than simply their ability to accumulate wealth. The UN Development Program describes the HDI as the ability for people to be able to "be" and "do" what they desire, rather than simply their ability to purchase goods. The UN uses the HDI to rank countries and group them into four levels of development: very high development, high development, medium development, and low development. This data is then mapped, making it easy to compare neighboring countries and look for examples of countries with good development policies as well as identify countries lagging due to poor development policies.

Before 2010, the HDI was calculated by combining life expectancy, literacy rate, college/university enrollment, and GDP into one statistic. Due to the problems with GDP not being evenly distributed and thus being a bad measure of economic prosperity, in 2010 the UN changed the formula for calculating the HDI. The new formula considers life expectancy, an average number of years of schooling and an adjusted measure of GNI which includes a country's Gini coefficient. Norway is considered the most developed country in the world, and it has held this title for the last eight years in a row. The United States is currently ranked eighth. The least developed countries are Niger and the Central African Republic; although there have been no calculations for Somalia in the last five years, its score is estimated to be significantly worse than the other countries due to its unstable political situation, the rise of Islamic militants and the prevalence of pirates.

Models like Rostow's Stages of Economic Growth and Wallerstein's World System Theory help explain spatial variations in development.

How are the continued differences in development that are mapped by the UN's HDI explained? There are various theoretical models to explain this, with the Stages of Growth and World Systems Theory being two of the more widely known and discussed. The Stages of Growth Model was developed by Walt Rostow in the 1950s and argues that all countries move through the same five stages of development. The model is premised on the idea that every country will follow the same process of development before arriving at an end state of development. Stage One is "Traditional Society," which is a situation where most people are subsistence farmers, and there is a lack of excess economic production to invest in growth.

Stage Two is called the "Preconditions for Take Off" and involves a very small number of people within a country engaging in innovative industries which are beginning to earn excess capital that is reinvested. Stage Three is "Take Off," with the small companies in stage two beginning to experience rapid growth. The country's economy begins to grow exponentially as the economy industrializes and the population shifts from subsistence farming to factory work in the secondary sector. Stage Four is the "Drive to Maturity," where the conditions of industrialization and economic growth spread from the initiating city or region to the whole country. Stage Five is "High Mass Consumption," in which the economy becomes consumer-driven due to higher wages, thus shifting from secondary sector factory work to tertiary service sector work.

Rostow's Model became popular because of its simplicity, but many have pointed to its lack of applicability around the world. The model assumes that all countries will follow the same development path as the UK and the U.S. and that one stage will lead to the next. This is problematic because the development and industrialization of the UK, for example, happened because the country had plenty of an important natural resource (e.g., coal) just at the right time in history. What if the UK had no coal to drive its industrial process? This is the question that other countries ask, which this model does not consider. The Stages of Growth Model is also problematic in its linear interpretation of history. It assumes that once a country reaches one stage, it continues to develop towards the next stage and does not even consider the possibility of going backward.

Coal abundant regions in Britain that helped sustain industrialization

History is not a linear line, and there have been many examples of countries decreasing in development. Argentina is a good example, as by 1910 it was the world's tenth richest country. Having reached that high-level stage, according to Rostow, Argentina's situation should have only improved, but in reality, it has dropped backward among his stages, especially as a result of the economic mismanagement of the military dictatorship in the 1970s, which led to a period of hyperinflation throughout the 1980s. A further set of failed government policies in the 1990s led to total economic collapse by 2000. Another example is Kenya, which after independence from the UK was developing very rapidly through the 1960s and 1970s with an average annual growth rate of 7% of GDP during those decades. By the 1990s the Kenyan government switched to neoliberal economic policies and growth shrank dramatically while inequality increased. Kenya, which was once a potential candidate to become the most developed country in Africa, went back a stage in the Rostow model.

Rostow's model is also problematic because it assumes each country's economy is insular and not linked to the global economy. This is a particularly critical flaw in today's context of globalization, in which countries can face development issues through no fault of their own but due to global economic conditions. For example, countries whose economies are heavily dependent on the price of oil often face serious crises when the global price of oil suddenly drops. In these cases, even though nothing has changed inside the country, its economic situation will deteriorate rapidly. Rostow's model cannot account for this since it was created during a time when the global economy was not interlinked like it is today. Rostow also assumes the final stage of development will be characterized by high mass consumption, which is now problematic from an environmental point of view. Increasingly, a sign of modernization and development is a concern about the environment, which would lead to attempting to decrease wasteful consumption, which again is not accounted for in Rostow's model.

The other major model that seeks to explain uneven patterns of development is World Systems Theory, which was developed by Immanuel Wallerstein. It is based on the Dependency Theory, a theoretical explanation for persistent underdevelopment in South America based on the idea that countries get locked into core-periphery relationships. Core countries extract resources from periphery countries and then refine those resources in the core. This continuing relationship prevents the periphery countries from ever moving up a stage in Rostow's model as they get locked into a position of underdevelopment by the forces of the global economy. The periphery countries then become dependent on the core countries to both sell natural resources and for foreign aid, since the periphery countries are not able to develop their own secondary sector manufacturing economy because all of their resources continue to be extracted and transferred to the core.

Wallerstein took this observation from Dependency Theory and applied it to try to map out how the whole world is connected through a series of core-periphery dependent relations. Wallerstein also applies historical analysis to argue that the current relationships among countries are the result of colonial dependencies, which meant that countries were never competing on an equal basis, to begin with. Wallerstein also argues that as political and economic situations change, the global balance of power can shift with it; he identifies the UK and Western Europe as the original core of the 1700s-1800s, eventually giving way to the United States as the primary core country into the 1900s. In this sense, World

Systems Theory can explain exactly what Rostow's Stages of Growth cannot. It explains why countries can get stuck in a stage and never advance and also how countries can go backward in the model.

At the height of European colonial power in the 1890s, France, Great Britain,
the Netherlands, Germany, and Russia were part of the primary core

Wallerstein himself has addressed the main criticisms of World Systems Theory. Wallerstein points out that there are four common critiques of his model. The first is that it lacks hard data and that there is no objective way to determine which state is core and which is periphery (or semi-periphery). Wallerstein also points out that some have argued it does not provide enough emphasis on an economic class within a country and that it fails to take into account cultural differences in the role of persistent underdevelopment. A fourth criticism, which was leveled at him during the Cold War period (but proves the robustness of his model today), is that he assumed the entire world to be integrated into a single economy. His ability to predict the onset of economic globalization is today one of the strengths of the model, rather than a weakness as his critics in the 1970s argued.

The UN Millennium Development Goals help measure progress in development.

In 2000, the UN decided to lay down some concrete objectives to measure progress toward development for its member countries. At the Millennium Development Summit in 2000, all 189 UN member states agreed to work toward a list of eight development goals which were meant to be achieved by 2015. In 2005 the G8, which is a group of eight economically influential countries, agreed to work with the World Bank and IMF to cancel $40 billion of debt owed by the poorest countries.

As a result of the meeting, eight goals emerged which, ideally, were to be met by 2015. First was to eliminate extreme poverty and hunger. This would be measured by aiming to cut in half the number of people living on less than $1.25 per day, increase employment prospects and cut in half the number of people who go hungry each day. Goal 2 was to achieve universal primary education, ensuring every child attended and finished the first eight years of schooling. Goal 3 was to promote gender equality and to empower women, measured by the ratio of boys to girls in school, the number of women employed outside of agriculture and the number of women representatives in parliament. Goal 4 was to reduce child mortality rates, which is related to Goal 5: to improve maternal health, as measured by the number of women who died during childbirth and their access to contraception. Goal 6 was to combat infectious diseases such as HIV/AIDS and malaria by reducing their spread. Goal 7 was to promote environmental sustainability as measured by CO_2 gas emissions, the number of people with clean drinking water and the number of people living in slums. Goal 8 was to develop global cooperation to meet the previous seven goals.

Progress toward the goals has been uneven around the world, in part due to the ambitious nature of the goals and the lack of help poorer countries received from wealthier ones, especially after the 2008 global financial crisis. China, India, and Brazil were the most successful at meeting all or most of the goals, owing largely to their ability to act independently and not be reliant on foreign help. Those three countries had the advantage of having rapidly growing economies in 2000, giving them an advantage over other countries which had stagnant economies when the goals were set. Some countries made absolutely no progress whatsoever during this period. Benin in West Africa made no progress toward any of the development goals and remains in as bad shape as it was before the development goals were agreed to. Some countries, such as Nepal and Bangladesh, failed to meet most of the goals, yet still made considerable progress in reducing poverty and improving healthcare. Many consider these two countries a success even though they did not meet the specific goals. On a global scale, the number of people living on less than

$1.25 a day was cut in half, mostly because of the progress of China, whose economic development had little to do with trying to meet the goals.

One particular failure was the eighth goal of developing a framework of international cooperation to achieve the goals. Other than the debt forgiveness measures for a few smaller countries, there was very little progress on this front. Many of the wealthier countries failed to commit to helping the poorer countries meet their goals and actively undermined development by hijacking international conferences on development to promote economic "deals" that were advantageous to developed countries, such as forcing poorer countries to open their borders to agricultural exports from rich countries.

2007, a Kathmandu street suffering from inadequate garbage collection

The UN's Millennium Development Goals spurred much criticism from many different angles. Many critics pointed out that some of these goals were somewhat arbitrarily chosen and that giving every country the same goal was unfair. While China for example easily met its goals without really trying due to its rapidly developing economy, a poorer country such as Nepal which actively worked to reduce poverty and meet the goals was considered to have failed even though it did significantly reduce poverty. The poorer countries were especially critical of the wealthiest countries for failing to get involved to help them develop. They accused the richer countries of lacking the political will and simply signing on to help without actually doing anything. Others criticized the goals for lacking a focus on bettering the human rights situation, which is a prominent indicator of development.

As a result of the mixed success and many criticisms, after the 2015 deadline was met, the UN decided not to renew the same goals for the next 15 years but to switch gears and instead promote Sustainable Development Goals which give greater emphasis to environmentally sustainable development. The Sustainable Development Goals are a set of 17 goals which UN countries are meant to work toward by 2030. The UN sums up these goals with the following graphic. These goals place a much higher emphasis on environmentally-friendly development, as opposed to the Millennium goals which were primarily concerned with economic development.

In contrast to the periphery and semiperiphery, the core countries achieved dominance through industrial production of goods.

To expand on World Systems Theory, which was outlined above, the key aspect is that core countries developed by extracting raw materials from peripheral countries and then using those materials to manufacture finished goods. Since finished goods are more valuable, the core countries got richer while locking the peripheral countries into a cycle of dependence where they have little industry of their own and must focus on resource extraction. The core-periphery relationship of dependence is especially prominent today as the dominant form of global economic theory is neoliberalism. Neoliberalism argues that countries will develop to the extent that they focus on their comparative advantage. Essentially, for peripheral countries, this means being locked into resource extraction, which prevents development from happening. Since the predominance of neoliberal economics in the 1980s, many countries in Africa which were once poised to develop rapidly have gone backward.

The most notable exception is China, which has developed rapidly precisely because it has not opened up its borders, and, instead of resource extraction, it has focused on developing an industrialized manufacturing economy through government protection of those industries. If China stuck with its comparative advantage, it would be a primarily agricultural society and would be as poor as it was in the 1970s as a result. By not focusing on agricultural export and instead of having a government willing to invest in industrialization, China broke the cycle of dependency and has been rapidly developing. By contrast, most other developing countries have stagnant resource extraction economies and are heavily dependent on foreign aid to stay afloat. The primary way to develop is to break the cycle of dependence on both foreign aid and resource extraction. While from a political economy point of view this is somewhat obvious, it would involve a transformation of the global economy in such a way that it would no longer benefit the richest corporations in the world. As such, promoting real development is largely a problem with overcoming political obstacles, rather than a purely economic issue.

Although there are more women in the workforce, they do not have equity in wages or employment opportunity.

Many developing countries have seen a shift toward more women entering the workforce, but there are still cultural and religious barriers to equality. In many Sub-Saharan African countries, women are seen as the farmers while men are the wage earners, which can lead to discrimination against women who seek to enter the workforce and earn a wage. Many see this as a violation of gender roles, leading to women who do enter the workforce being paid less. In many countries dominated by strict interpretations of Islam and Christianity, there are often religious barriers that prevent women from being treated as equals in the workplace. The biggest obstacle to feminist principles and the promotion of equality are traditional religious views, and countries which are the most religious tend to have fewer rights for women.

Microloans have provided opportunities for women to create small local businesses, which have improved standards of living.

One new mechanism to promote economic development and empowerment among women are microloans. Microloans are very small loans, often only a few hundred dollars, which are given to people who traditionally do not have access to normal banking loans due to their situation of poverty. According to the advocates of microloans, small loans to women in developing countries can empower them to start small businesses or buy more advanced farming equipment, which ends up having a ripple effect throughout the economy, improving the lives of everyone involved. The idea is contentious, as many argued that focusing on microfinance was part of a neoliberal policy package which removed the responsibility of governments to develop infrastructure and have a serious plan to eradicate poverty by placing all the emphasis on individual entrepreneurs.

Thai female vendor selling food outside a temple complex

While originally microloans were touted as having a huge positive impact, further study has demonstrated that the early critics of microloans were generally correct. Numerous academic studies have demonstrated that microloans failed to spur economic growth, and the well-being of communities did not substantially improve as a result of having access to microfinance. The reason is that without the infrastructure (e.g., transportation, clean water, electricity, internet) any attempts to start small businesses in extremely poor rural communities simply remained extremely small or failed. In 2010, there was a large number of suicides in Andhra Pradesh in India, among people who had taken out microloans but could not pay them back. These people were not used to cycles of debt and repayment and viewed the inability to pay back a loan as a stain on their honor worth committing suicide over. As a result of this and the academic studies finding that microloans have no impact in reducing poverty, the brief enthusiasm for microloans has now almost completely diminished.

International Economics

Development is a process that varies across space and time.

Development has taken on many different forms both across the world and at different periods of history. This is an important thing to keep in mind as no two countries will develop exactly alike, and what worked in the past may not work now. Theoretical approaches to development that may have worked in the past may not be viable today as well. Based on World Systems Theory, a common approach to development was import substation industrialization (ISI), which argued that for countries to break the cycle of dependence they should focus on developing their domestic industries instead of importing the finished goods created with their natural resources that were produced elsewhere in the world. ISI was a common strategy that saw success in the 1950s through the 1980s in many countries such as Brazil and South Korea. Today, ISI is extraordinarily difficult to implement because of how integrated the global economy has become. ISI focused on developing national industries and making a country self-sufficient, which meant processing raw materials and using them in domestic factories while selling the finished goods domestically as well. Such a closed system is all but impossible today, and it also has serious consequences for countries which lack important raw materials such as oil.

Complementarity and comparative advantage establish the basis for trade.

As has been mentioned throughout, today the theory of comparative advantage forms the basis for models of development which focus on trade and open borders. Comparative advantage argues that certain countries will be better at producing certain products than others as a result of labor specialization, natural resources or other factors. According to comparative advantage, countries should then focus exclusively on producing those products where they have a comparative advantage since they will be able to make the most profit selling these products to other countries. At the same time, the country should import any product they do not have a comparative advantage in since to try to produce it domestically will be inefficient. If every country sticks to what it is good at, the economy as a whole will become more efficient through trade and everyone will be better off. This theory of comparative advantage was developed by political economist David Ricardo in 1817 to explain why international trade was beneficial.

For example, if Canada produces oil for $10 and computers for $30, while the United States produces oil for $30 and computers for $10, it would be mutually beneficial for these two countries if Canada produced all the oil and the United States produced all the computers. Canada would import cheaper computers, and the U.S. would import cheaper oil, while the overall economic efficiency would improve because neither country would waste time producing what could be produced more efficiently elsewhere. In theory, comparative advantage makes sense, but it has many problems when it comes to development because it leads to the cycles of dependency that can lock countries into a state of perpetual underdevelopment. For many developing countries, their comparative advantage is in the primary sector, so they end up exporting minerals and raw materials, which prevents them from moving along Rostow's stages of growth. Comparative advantage theory would argue that it is more efficient for those underdeveloped countries not to develop and not industrialize because it leads to more overall efficiency. However, this is, of course, problematic as the increased value from global efficiency does not evenly trickle down and benefit everyone. For example, the rare earth elements that are mined in Congo and Uganda for use in cell phones provide very little benefit regarding development or increased wealth to the people of those countries, while the huge corporations who make and sell the phones see a massive increase in profits.

Comparative advantage also has problems for developed countries as well. In today's global economy where factories can be located anywhere, countries with low wages and poor labor laws, such as China, have a huge comparative advantage in manufacturing. This means that jobs that used to pay well and were the basis of working-class prosperity in the United States have now shifted to China, being replaced by low wage service sector jobs at places that sell the products that were created with cheap Chinese labor. By playing to comparative advantage in the context of global free trade, American workers have become worse off, even if American corporations have become much richer. For these reasons, comparative advantage is often critiqued as an example of how economic theory can be out of touch with its actual real-world consequences.

Minnesota fast-food workers protested for higher wages and other benefits in 2015

International trade and trading blocs (e.g., EU and NAFTA) have become more important as a result of globalization.

In many countries, corporations have been able to lobby governments to sign onto trade agreements with important trade partners. A common misperception is that agreements such as NAFTA or the TPP are primarily about promoting trade and removing trade barriers. In reality, these agreements are almost always between countries which already are major trading partners. The agreements do not create trade but are about establishing the rules of trade. With NAFTA for example, Canada and the U.S. were already major trade partners, with the U.S. being the biggest import and export for Canada before NAFTA. What these agreements do is set up a framework of rules which go above the countries involved. This means that corporations can appeal to these rules to prevent countries from passing legislation that may undermine their ability to make a profit.

Trade agreements are often criticized for being undemocratic, both in their implementation and in the way they are negotiated. They are usually negotiated in secret and rushed through Congress without the public knowing much about them. They are criticized as being anti-democratic in their implementation because they give corporations the power to overrule legislation passed by a country. In the case of NAFTA, an American gasoline company was able to overturn Canadian law by appealing to NAFTA's Chapter 11. This undermines democracy as the elected governments are no longer able to make enforceable decisions for the good of the country, and it threatens state sovereignty because foreign entities can overrule the decisions of a state.

Geographies of interdependence in the world economy include global financial crises, the shift in manufacturing to newly industrialized countries, imbalances in consumption patterns and the roles of women in the labor force.

With the onset of globalization in the early 1990s, the world economy began to overpower the individual economies of various states. This has created a situation of global economic interdependence which has had various consequences. One of them is the contagion effect of financial crises. The 2008 global financial crisis began in the U.S. as the housing bubble collapsed, revealing that many investment banks were engaging in extremely risky practices. The collapse of major investment banks such as Bear Stearns and Lehman Brothers led to a global liquidity crisis and credit crunch, as banks in other countries had been buying these risky financial instruments from the American banks. As investment firms and banks around the world began to lose money because of the American banking failures, banks no longer had enough money to lend to each other to cover deposits, causing them to seek international sources, which spread the credit crunch around the world.

Meanwhile, the decline in the American economy meant that the U.S. was importing fewer goods, which caused problems for the U.S.'s major trading partners such as Canada, China and much of the developing world. This led to problems of consumer confidence around the world; when people feel the economy is doing poorly, they will save their money rather than spend it, which causes the economy to contract even further. Finally, the global nature of corporations means that they buy and sell products across the world. This meant that the stock markets of the world all experienced crashes at the same time, as there was no safe place for investors to put their money when all corporations today are global. These factors all contributed to transforming what was essentially a problem with over-inflated housing prices in the domestic American economy to a global crisis.

Similar economic contagion patterns emerged with the 1998 East Asian Financial Crisis. The countries of East Asia had begun to become a hot source of foreign capital as they opened up their borders to direct foreign investment in the mid-1990s. Thailand and Indonesia, in particular, were called the "Asian Tigers" and were seen as the next two countries that would become wealthy, fully-developed countries. Instead, a bubble formed as investors put money into building huge office towers and risky financial companies, while the government neglected basic infrastructures such as roads and sewers. When investors started to realize a bubble had formed and their investments were not worth as much as everyone had thought, everyone panicked and pulled his or her money out all at the same time. This caused a capital shortage in these countries, which led to the perception that all developing countries were risky, causing the crisis to ripple throughout the world. The spread of panics and crises in the financial sector is an example of how the globally-integrated economy operates. While risk tends to spread quickly, gains, unfortunately, tend to concentrate in the hands of wealthy elites and not get spread out to all countries and all people in those countries. As a result, the biggest victims of these financial crises are often not the big investors or the banks that collapse, but the working-class families who lose their life savings.

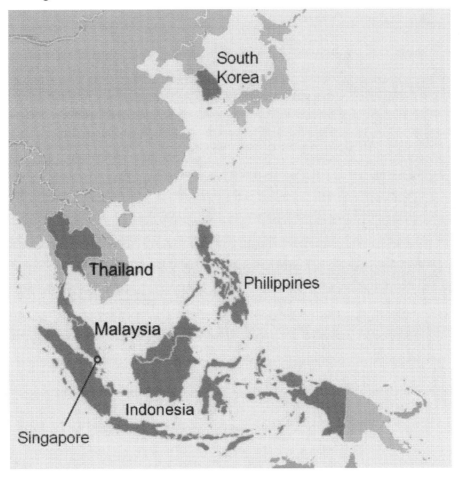

Nations worst affected by the 1998 East Asian Financial Crisis

Outsourcing and economic restructuring have led to a decline in jobs in manufacturing regions and the relocation of a significant segment of the workforce to other areas.

As mentioned above, globalization has hurt the working class in the developed countries as well. As a result of many years of labor activism and union organizing, manufacturing jobs in the United States had become well-paying and a good source of income that could allow a working-class family to lead a very comfortable life. With globalization, many of these jobs were outsourced to countries with few labor restrictions in which workers could be paid very low wages. The problem of outsourcing has been devastating for the industrial heartland of the United States, which is now called the Rust Belt, to indicate it is in a situation of decline. The city of Detroit was once the most prosperous city in America, being the heart of manufacturing and the automobile industry. Most of those jobs have moved overseas, and now Detroit is one of the poorest cities in the United States.

While outsourcing has been an undeniable negative for developed countries, many have argued that it has been a major gain for developing countries. This is a highly contentious argument that applies somewhat unevenly. Take the example of Mexico's maquiladoras, which were textile producing areas which relied on American companies outsourcing work to Mexico where the labor was cheaper. At first, this was a big gain for Mexican workers, as they had domestic jobs and could work for a wage which brought in more income than subsistence farming. However, after the Mexican workers began to organize and demand higher wages and better working conditions, the corporations who had outsourced these jobs realized that they could just as easily outsource the jobs to another country. The jobs that had moved from the United States to Mexico once again moved to China, Indonesia, the Philippines and now Vietnam and Myanmar. The current issue with migrant workers from Mexico illegally crossing the border to look for work in the U.S. is entirely a result of these shifting labor patterns. They were originally farmers, but they sold their farms to work in the maquiladoras. When the maquiladoras moved to East Asia, they could not go back to farming, and there are no other jobs in Mexico.

As mentioned earlier, this situation is called the "race to the bottom" and involves companies constantly shifting their production sites to the lowest bidder. This means that workers in the developing countries only get these jobs if they were willing to work for the absolute lowest rates of pay with the worst health and safety conditions. As soon as they organize and advocate for better conditions, the company will simply move to another country where there are still worse conditions. In an attempt to fight these exploitative conditions, many have advocated putting pressure on the companies who use these outsourcing practices by not buying their products.

The problem is that for most companies, outsourcing means simply buying finished manufactured products and then reselling them. Apple, for instance, does not make iPhones; the Chinese company Foxconn manufactures the phones according to Apple's designs and then sells the phones exclusively to Apple who then resells them as "Apple products." The exploited Chinese workers are not Apple employees, and Apple can deny that they have any involvement with this process; it's all the fault of their Chinese supplier. In the case of TVs, many Chinese manufacturers sell the same TV to many different companies who then slap their own label on it. A Samsung and Toshiba TV may be identical because they were made in the same Chinese factory, with the only difference being what brand name gets put on the front. This makes it very difficult to pressure the company that sells the consumer product because in many cases they have little to nothing to do with the actual production of the product they sell. They are merely marketing a brand rather than selling a product that they make and take responsibility for.

In countries outside the core, the diffusion of industry has resulted in the emergence of the international division of labor and manufacturing zones.

The situation of outsourcing and shifting of manufacturing to poorer countries has changed the international division of labor. The core countries are no longer the manufacturers who exploit the raw materials of the periphery. Today, the core countries are the consumers of goods who exploit the cheap labor of the periphery countries. Through the race to the bottom, secondary sector manufacturing is no longer the path to development and riches, as low-wage workers make these products while the brand-name companies reap the large profit margins from selling to wealthy consumers and not by the manufacturers in the periphery countries. The core-periphery model has changed along with globalization to focus on the callous exploitation of labor rather than exploiting the periphery's raw materials. Originally the division of labor would be within a single factory, using an assembly line. The people upstairs designed the product, the people downstairs worked on the assembly line putting the product together, and the salespeople would travel around selling the product. Now this division of labor is divided up across the world because companies have split apart with outsourcing and moved around the world.

Call center positions have increasingly become outsourced as globalization continues

In many cases, countries have sought to actively participate in the race to the bottom on a limited scale by designating certain parts of the country as special economic zones or as free trade zones. In these areas of a country, normal laws do not apply to tempt outsourcing companies to come in and set up factories. This means that companies within this region do not have to obey minimum wage laws, environmental regulations or workplace safety regulations, which makes labor extremely cheap and attractive for companies to set up manufacturing. The governments that set up these special zones argue it leads to jobs (even if they are significantly worse than jobs in the rest of the country) and that these zones can help lead to more development. In the case of the maquiladora zones in Mexico, the opposite was true; it ended up making the country worse off, with Mexico's real growth coming through the fostering of domestic-oriented industries such as telecommunications.

The contemporary economic landscape has been transformed by the emergence of service sectors, high technology industries, and growth poles.

In today's economic climate, the path to development is increasingly seen as being able to take part in the knowledge economy via high tech industries and the internet. This has led to certain areas such as Silicon Valley in California or Electronics City in Bangalore, India being concentrated areas where new technology companies form. In a globalized economy, states are less important than cities as drivers of growth, and high tech industry development tends to be very uneven. While Silicon Valley in the U.S. is the home of a thriving tech industry with high-paying jobs, other cities such as Detroit continue to lose population due to high unemployment. The same pattern is true in India, where

Bangalore is the home of cutting-edge technologies while other parts of India lack access to electricity and clean water.

While the initial promise of globalization was to shift the broad working class in the developed countries from manufacturing jobs to high tech employment, instead most workers ended up in the low-paying service economy. The biggest private sector employers in the United States used to be car companies like Ford and GM and manufacturing companies like General Electric. The advocates of outsourcing and globalization claimed that those workers would end up in computer industry jobs. In reality, however, the biggest employers in the United States today are not Google and Apple, but Wal-Mart and McDonald's, both of which offer low wages.

Government initiatives at all scales may help promote economic development.

Throughout the 1990s, with the dominance of neoliberalism as a development strategy, countries came to believe that government involvement in the development process was an overall negative which only restricted growth. Neoliberal development theory argues that if companies are free to compete in the global market they will thrive, and any attempts by the government to regulate industry or finance or to try to subsidize domestic industries, will only lead to failure. These "hands off the economy" policies were enforced by the World Bank and IMF, who required countries that needed loans to undergo structural adjustment programs to reorient their economies to adhere to neoliberal principles. According to this theory, any government involvement in the economy means that the government is artificially picking "winners" and "losers," which often leads to the more efficient companies failing while inefficient companies thrive because of corruption and political connections to the government. Neoliberal development theorists argue that allowing the market to determine which companies thrive and which fail leads to a healthier economy and more development. Due to the combination of neoliberalism becoming the dominant school of thought among professional economists and the power of the international institutions to enforce these policies, almost every country except China adopted neoliberal development policies by the late 1990s.

Activism against neoliberal economic policy has been growing in many countries

By 2008 however, it had become obvious that this policy package was an unmitigated failure. A lack of government regulation and oversight of the financial industry was a major contributor to the 2008 financial crisis, and the record of neoliberal development policy was extremely poor. Particularly in Africa, where there was the greatest acceptance of these policies, many countries went backward and became less developed after they switched to a practice of minimal government involvement in the development process. Meanwhile, China was the one exception, as the Chinese government was heavily involved in managing the economy and promoting growth, and it turned out that the one exception to neoliberalism was also the country which was most successful at achieving economic growth and development. As of now, the theory and practice of development are in flux. The dominant theory of neoliberalism has been disproven by events, and few advocate it after 2008. The example of China shows that government involvement in the economy is beneficial. A competing model has yet to develop to replace neoliberalism, and many developing countries continue to apply neoliberal principles while some are beginning to emulate China. Unfortunately, China's development policies are also connected to authoritarian government, and thus many are uneasy to hold China up as a model of developmental success because its economic victories have come at the expense of democracy and human rights.

Sustainable Development

> **Sustainable development is a strategy to address resource depletion and environmental degradation.**

As was pointed out earlier concerning the UN Millennium Development Goals, there has been a major shift in thinking about development due to the increasing problem of climate change. Pure economic development has often had devastating consequences. The industrialization of Great Britain and America during the 1800s relied on coal and led to massive pollution problems and greenhouse gas emissions. China's development is currently largely fueled by coal power plants, which is greatly diminishing the quality of the air. Development theorists have begun to question whether a country can be considered developing if its economic fortunes are improving but people are no longer able to breathe the air. As a result, development theory now focuses on promoting sustainable development, which considers the environment as well as economic and social factors.

Sustainable development addresses issues of natural resource depletion, mass consumption, the costs and effects of pollution and the impact of climate change, as well as issues of human health, well-being, and social and economic equity.

The goal of *sustainable development* is to maintain a rate of growth and resource consumption that is indefinitely sustainable. A simple example of sustainable development might be a community that eats primarily fish that are caught from the ocean. To develop sustainably would mean that the community would grow only when there were excess fish. If they were to catch all the fish to grow rapidly now, they would leave no fish to eat in the future. That would be unsustainable. Since the Earth only has a finite amount of natural resources, which are continually consumed, sustainable development seeks to preserve the capacity of human societies to continue to grow economically into the future. While often the environment is pitted against the economy, in fact, the real debate is whether long-term economic growth or short-term growth should be favored. Standard economic thinking argues for extracting resources as quickly as possible to increase short-term growth at the expense of long-term growth. Sustainable economics argues that finite resources should be extracted slower so that they are not all depleted, leading to continued growth over the long term.

While in theory sustainable development makes more sense since it preserves the ability to grow the economy indefinitely, the current configuration of global capitalism very much favors short-term growth at the expense of continued development. Corporations have to be responsive to shareholders whose primary interest is making money now, not 100 years from now. This puts pressure on companies to grow as quickly as they can now, even if it means they are likely to go out of business in 10 or 20 years when there are no more resources left to exploit. Corporations focused on short-term gains then see long-term gains as an obstacle to immediate growth, which pits them against sustainable development, even if it would be better for any individual corporation over the long term. Another barrier to implementing sustainable development is the fact that most governments operate on 4 or 5-year election cycles. Political leaders tend to focus on growth now so that they can be re-elected in the next few years. Sacrificing some immediate growth for the long-term benefit of the country has so far in most countries been a losing strategy since most people are primarily concerned with their immediate well-being. Switching to the superior sustainable growth model requires a changed mindset in voters to get them to think about the long-term well-being of the country they live in.

Highly-contended elections can influence politicians to focus too heavily on the short-term

Ecotourism is a strategy used by some countries to help protect the environment and generate jobs.

Some countries have been able to square sustainable development with immediate economic gain by promoting ecotourism. Rather than chopping down rainforests for immediate profit, they seek to attract tourists who'll spend money; not chopping down a rainforest can be just as short-term profitable as chopping it down. The country of Costa Rica in Central America is filled with rainforest and exotic plants and animals and has been able to promote sustainable development through ecotourism. The money being made from ecotourism allows people to improve their standard of living so that they are less tempted to cut down the rainforest for immediate profit. Costa Rica also has one of the cleanest electricity generating systems in the world. In 2015, 99% of its electricity was generated through sustainable sources such as hydroelectric dams, geothermal power stations, wind power, and solar generating stations. By switching to sustainable energy sources, it means that Costa Rica does not have to import expensive natural resources such as coal, oil or uranium which are not found locally. As a result of the 99% clean energy generation, electric bills in Costa Rica dropped by 12% in 2015 due to the savings on not having to import foreign fuel sources.

This also has the benefit of making Costa Rica energy independent, meaning it does not have to worry about complicated geopolitical tangles due to a need to import fossil fuels. The United States, for example, is often driven to get into wars or to support brutal dictatorships because of its reliance on imported fossil fuels. Many believe that U.S. involvement in Iraq was directly related to oil, as former Iraqi dictator Saddam Hussein had cut off oil exports to the U.S. and had abandoned the U.S. dollar for pricing Iraqi oil. The U.S.'s lack of domestic sustainable energy means that it has to play nice with authoritarian governments with terrible human rights regimes. Harsh dictators rule Saudi Arabia and Equatorial Guinea and both countries rank among the worst in the world when it comes to human rights. However, since both countries are swimming in oil, the U.S. has maintained close alliances with these two countries despite the complicated geopolitical situation it creates. Saudi Arabia has been implicated in funding anti-American Islamic terrorists around the world, and some Saudi government officials were named in Congress' 9/11 Commission Report. Even though Saudi Arabia continually undermines American foreign policy interests, the U.S. continues to maintain the alliance. As the example of Costa Rica demonstrates, energy independence through sustainable development can lead to a more humane foreign policy. Costa Rica does not even have a standing military since its energy independence has allowed it to promote a peaceful foreign policy.

Notes

Chapter 7

Cities and Urban Land Use

Urban geography is divided into two subfields. The first subfield is concerned with the study of city location placement. It is centered on numerous analyses, ranging from current and historical distribution of cities, the political, economic and cultural functions of cities, explanations for differential city growth and transportation types and communication linkages among cities. Settlement geography theories help frame discussions and understanding. The analysis of quantitative information, from topics such as population growth, migration, zones of influence and employment, gives critical insight into urban hierarchy changes.

The second subfield concerns itself with city form, internal structures, and landscapes, emphasizing the living, day-to-day conditions for residents. Topics covered under this subfield are topics ranging from patterns of urban land use, ethnic segregation, types of transportation and architectural traditions to cycles of uneven development and environmental justice. Both quantitative and qualitative data offer evidence-based insights. Models of internal city structure and development can be applied among different nations to assess their effectiveness in both a regional and worldwide scope.

Economic systems, housing finance, culture, architectural history, government policies, and transportation innovations are factors that feature prominently in the analysis of urban landscape spatial patterns. The study of cities worldwide illustrates how differing economic systems and cultural values can lead to variations in the spatial structures of urban landscapes.

Examination of current trends in urban development figures prominently in establishing framework understanding. Of likewise importance is an evaluation of sustainable urban planning initiatives and community actions that reduce energy use and protect the environments of cities of the future.

Urban Settlements

> **The form, function and size of urban settlements are constantly changing.**

What defines a city is not clear-cut because it is hard to set a specific population number to define an area as a city. Geographers instead tend to focus on the concept of urbanization, which is less about defining cities based on population and more about urban lifestyles and city landscapes. If someone can take public transit to his or her job in a skyscraper, this is characteristic of an urban lifestyle in a city landscape. Urban geography studies these patterns of culture, work and the urban use of space. Urban geography is often interested in historical perspectives as well, including how cities grow and shrink.

Site and situation influence the origin, function, and growth of cities.

When looking at the origin of cities, geographers focus on urban hearths, which are areas where urbanization first occurred. By looking at how patterns of urbanization grow and diffuse from these origin points, geographers seek to explain how and why cities have grown and how urbanization may or may not spread to the rest of a country. The earliest urban hearths grew out of the agricultural hearths; small farming villages grew into urban centers of trade and commerce around 5,500 years ago in Mesopotamia, India, Pakistan, Egypt, China, Mexico, and Peru. One interesting example of an urban hearth growing out of an agricultural hearth was the city of Cahokia Mounds in what is now Ohio. Early Native American cultures began to farm the area and build settlements around 600. By the middle of the 13th century, the population of Cahokia is estimated to have been around 40,000 people, making it the largest city in North American history until the population of Philadelphia surpassed 40,000 in 1780.

For the model to have any explanatory power, Weber's model was based on a number of assumptions which held the most. First is that transportation cost is entirely determined by a combination of distance and the weight of the goods. Industries are all aiming to maximize profits and thus minimize shipping costs. Industries have fixed locations where they sell their finished goods which are known in advance. Labor only exists in certain locations and will not move to follow a factory. And finally, that physical geography is not a factor.

The ruins of Eridu in Iraq are believed by many to mark the location of the world's oldest city

Cahokia, like many early cities, grew as a result of a location that made it ideal for trade. In addition to being located in the fertile land near the Mississippi River, it was in a central location that different Native American groups would pass through as they sought to trade with their neighbors. Located at the conflux of the Mississippi, Missouri and Illinois Rivers, it became a central spot for early trade in minerals such as copper. As a result of its location among the central waterways and its site as a place of trade, Cahokia developed a thriving economy based on manufacturing and selling tools for farming and pottery. Along with trade, a prime factor for the development of early cities was the centralization of religious ritual. Cahokia also fits this pattern because the inhabitants built extremely large mounds for religious burial purposes.

In ancient Greece and later Rome, a new pattern of urbanization developed related to the invention of politics and democracy. In ancient Athens, the fact that people had a democratic say in the government attracted them to live in the city, so they could more readily take part in deliberations and votes. While citizens often maintained land outside of the city to be farmed, it was usually worked by slaves, allowing the citizens to focus on urban political matters. During this time, even in cities which were tyrannies or oligarchies, power was centered in cities, and this was a strong attractor for population growth.

Transportation and communication have facilitated urbanization (e.g., Borchert's epochs of urban growth) and suburbanization.

In 1967 the American geographer John Borchert developed a model to conceptualize the growth of American cities. Borchert argued that changes in transportation technology were the key to understanding different eras of urbanization, and his model is divided into epochs based on the predominant form of transportation at the time. Borchert's model consists of five epochs. The first is the Sail-Wagon Epoch (1790–1830), in which cities near major ports and waterways grew the fastest due to sail-powered ships being the fastest form of transport, with smaller cities growing within wagon distance of major ports. The second is the Iron Horse Epoch (1830–1870) where steam power became predominant, leading to steam-powered railways and steamships being the fastest forms of transportation. Cities grew along rail networks, and port cities continued to grow in this epoch. Third is the Steel Rail Epoch (1870-1920), in which railroad technology advanced, leading to the creation of a national rail network facilitating the growth of previously isolated Western cities. Fourth is the Auto-Air Amenity Epoch (1920-1970) led by the gasoline engine and the expansion of cars and air travel. Commuter suburbs began to grow around cities, and airports facilitated regional commerce. Finally, the High Technology Epoch (1970-now) is when urban growth is driven by the expansion of the service sector and information technology rather than transportation. Cities with lots of information technology, such as San Francisco, San Jose, and Seattle, drive growth, while former manufacturing cities such as Detroit and Pittsburgh have experienced a decline.

Improvements in agriculture and transportation, population growth, migration, economic development and government policies influence urbanization.

After the initial wave of urbanization that grew out of the agricultural hearths which became urban hearths in the classical era, cities in Europe experienced a major decline in population, power, and influence during the Middle Ages. Power was now concentrated in the hands of distant monarchs and their local lords who controlled the serf population of small-scale farmers. Cities were primarily oriented towards being hubs of agricultural exchange and the sites of major churches and other aspects of Christian political authority. The structure of medieval European cities was based on clustering around occupations. The predominance of trade guilds would lead blacksmiths to concentrate in one part of town, for example.

With industrialization and the onset of the Enlightenment, cities began to increase in importance both economically and intellectually. Factory work and the shift from feudalism to capitalism led to a vast increase in urban populations, while the ideals of the Enlightenment helped undermine the authority of the Christian Church and shift political power from monarchs and priests to urban factory owners and secular power structures such as the nation-state. The second agricultural revolution enabled a huge spike in yields which facilitated the shift from an agriculture-based to an urban-based society. The early cities of the industrial revolution were primarily located near coal fields and often not found in traditional locations near ports and important waterways. Eventually, as trade increased, port cities became more important, especially as coal shipping became less expensive. By the early 1900s, the most important cities in the world were either industrial cities based on manufacturing, such as Chicago, Barcelona, and Manchester, or trade-based and located on major shipping routes, such as New York, St. Petersburg, Russia and Bombay, India.

Lower Manhattan with its many docks in 1931

In many of these industrial cities, the population growth was so rapid that governments could not keep up. Infrastructure lagged behind growth, and many of these cities had serious problems with pollution and squalid living conditions for workers. In many cases, the industrial cities which brought about the advance of capitalism were also the sites of working-class organization and nascent socialist movements. Chicago in the United States was the birthplace of working-class anarchist organizations which eventually led to shortening the workday from 12 hours to 8 hours. British working-class movements began in Manchester; Barcelona was the center of the Spanish Republican government which fought against the fascists during the Spanish Civil War of 1936-39.

World cities function at the top of the world's urban hierarchy and drive globalization.

In today's globalized world, the central hubs of economic activity and intellectual influence are large, diverse cities called "Global Cities" or sometimes "World Cities." These cities produce ideas, culture, and economic products that are influential and consumed around the entire world. These cities stand out for their economic power as centers of global finance and trade. In a globalized economy where national borders have become less important, global cities are increasingly what economic geographers focus on. Different industries have different global cities which attract talented people from around the world. Los Angeles attracts actors and film directors, Milan attracts the top fashion designers and London, and New York attracts the top financial firms and workers. This is a dramatic change from the previous era of national economies, where each city within a country might function as that country's top destination for film, fashion or finance, but today certain global cities are centers for these industries rather than one in each country.

Since these cities attract corporations and people from around the world, they have a tendency to be diverse melting pots of different cultures, which in itself makes these cities a microcosm of the world. This can lead to innovation in itself; for instance, the converging cultures of New York City have led to culinary fusion restaurants which combine cuisines (e.g., Mexican and Japanese). As a microcosm of globalization, these cities are primarily oriented toward the world rather than toward the country they are in. This can lead many people who identify strongly with a country to feel alienated by how diverse these global cities are. At the same time, they facilitate people from around the world moving there and fitting in easily. One can imagine the ease with which it is to move to a foreign city if it already has many aspects of your own culture contained within it, as compared to moving to a smaller, non-global city where one's culture is seen as completely alien.

Megacities are rapidly increasing in countries of the periphery and semi-periphery.

Megacities are any city with over 10 million people. There are many growing megacities in the developing world, as large cities offer one of the few attractive places for well-paying employment. Due to their sheer size, megacities exert an enormous amount of influence on a country's economy. As of data from 2015, there are currently 25 megacities in the world, many of which are also global cities. The largest megacity is Tokyo, with a metropolitan population of 38 million people. This means there are more people in Tokyo than in all of Canada. Other prominent megacities include Shanghai in China, Jakarta in Indonesia, Mexico City, Seoul in South Korea, Karachi in Pakistan and Delhi in India.

Megacities and world cities experience economic, social, political and environmental challenges.

While many of the megacities in developed countries such as Japan and South Korea have fewer problems because their governments are wealthier and can keep up with infrastructure demands, the rapid growth of megacities in developing countries can cause a number of problems. One of the primary problems is the growth of slums. *Slums* are poorly built and illegal settlements, often on the edge of the city, which are built by people who have come to the city in search of employment after leaving behind a life of subsistence farming. They have no money, to begin with and cannot afford to rent, so they build their own dwellings out of found materials. Slum dwellers often do not have access to proper sanitation or water systems, and owing to their dwellings' illegal status often avoid making use of government services such as healthcare and education for fear that the authorities will come and tear down their dwelling. This creates a recurrent cycle of poverty that megacities need to address.

As a consequence of slums and general poverty, crime and homelessness are often major problems in megacities. Cities often cannot pay enough police to patrol poor areas, allowing gangs to essentially establish control over certain areas of the city. This can lead to major problems with gun violence and murder, as well as drugs and robbery. Traffic also becomes an issue in megacities in poorer countries, as public transport becomes extremely overcrowded because cities lack the money to invest in upgrades. Streets are clogged with cars, scooters, and pedestrians, and it can be very difficult to get around efficiently. Poorer megacities often face major air pollution issues as well. Beijing and Shanghai in China often have air so thick with smog that it can be difficult to breathe. Air pollution stems from a combination of traffic and factories and coal-powered energy generation plants.

The Dharavi area of Mumbai is Asia's second largest slum

In wealthier cities, there are often an entirely different set of problems. Suburban sprawl can be a big problem, as many people want to live near the city but have their own detached house and yard. This leads to traffic gridlock and strains public transit. Gentrification is also a problem as wealthier people, especially in the United States, move back into the urban core from the suburbs. This can mean buying up of houses and businesses that served the working class, making cities less affordable to live in.

An example is Brooklyn, New York which used to be a fairly inexpensive place to live that was still close to Manhattan. It maintained a working-class culture with many businesses aimed toward the working-class population. Recently gentrification has pushed prices up and made it unaffordable for those people who traditionally formed the bulk of Brooklyn's population.

Notes

Understanding Cities Using Models

Models help to understand the distribution and size of cities.

One key aspect of urban geography is the spatial distribution of cities in comparison to each other. Geographers are often interested in understanding not just why cities are placed where they are but how they are relatively distributed to each other. Put together, a series of cities at various scales form an urban system which creates a spider-web type pattern of cities and connections between cities. Geographers are interested in how these cities interact and why some grow larger than others. To try to explain these patterns, models of city distribution and size have been developed.

Models that are useful for explaining the distribution and size of cities include the rank-size rule, the law of the primate city and Christaller's central place theory.

In the 1930s, German geographer Walter Christaller developed central place theory based on von Thünen's model of agricultural land use. Like von Thünen's model, central place theory starts with a number of assumptions that are somewhat unrealistic when one looks at how cities are actually placed. Central place theory assumes that the land of an area is all flat, and therefore physical geography is not a determining factor for where cities are placed. It assumes the rural population is evenly distributed across rural areas and there is no natural growth of cities out of rural villages. It assumes transportation is uniform and not hindered by physical geography, and it assumes a linear growth model where cities only get larger and larger.

According to central place theory, the original purpose of cities was to provide services to people in the surrounding rural areas, which are called "hinterlands." Each service has a threshold of people that it can serve, and services with higher thresholds will attract people from further out in the hinterlands. In practice, this means that specialized services such as a hospital will have a higher threshold than, say, a restaurant. People will travel further to reach a hospital than they will to a restaurant. It is also much easier to have numerous restaurants than it is to have numerous hospitals. City services are then affected by the number of people they can attract from the hinterlands and the threshold of how many people they can serve. Central place theory states that people in the hinterlands will be attracted to the nearest and best services while also avoiding overcrowding. This creates a hexagonal pattern of cities and towns, with a major city in the center holding some of the more specialized services. While people in the hinterlands may occasionally travel to the larger city for an amenity such as an airport, they will aim to go to the closest smaller city to find a coffee shop, for instance.

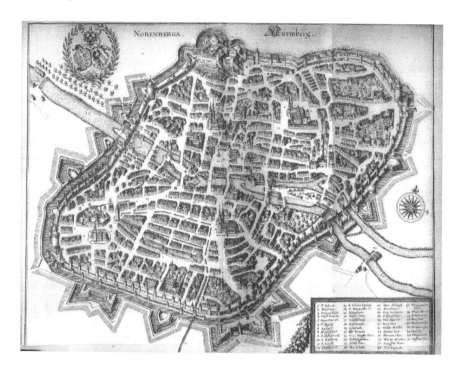

1648 Nuremberg city layout, areas outside the city walls being considered the hinterlands

Due to the pattern of major and minor cities, an urban hierarchy is created in which a few major cities are surrounded by smaller ones which offer small range and lower threshold services, with the major city having a high threshold and high range services. This hierarchy is shaped like a pyramid because there are fewer major cities but many more minor cities. In the United States, New York City, Chicago, and Los Angeles sit on top of the urban hierarchy, offering specialized services unavailable anywhere else. For example, New York City is home to Wall Street, the financial center of the entire United States, while L.A. has Hollywood, the primary location of the film industry. Second order cities serve as regional hubs, such as Miami or St. Louis, followed by many smaller cities that contain many urban services but lack specialized services that are only found higher up in the urban hierarchy.

Another model of urban distribution and size is the rank-size rule, which is a method of predicting a city's place within the urban hierarchy. The rank-size rule states that the nth largest city's population in a particular region will be $1/n^{th}$ the size of the largest city.

This means that the third largest city in a region should have a population that is one-third that of the largest city. The rank-size rule depends on what is considered a single region, but most areas of the United States more or less conform by this rule. In some countries, however, the rank-size rule does not apply because there is one city that is disproportionately larger than all others. These are called primate cities, as they break the rank-size rule because the second largest city is usually much smaller than half the size of the primate city. Examples of primate cities are London, Paris and Buenos Aires. In Argentina, Buenos Aires is ten times larger than the second largest city in the country. This means that Buenos Aires is a very strong primate city.

The gravity model is useful in explaining interactions among networks of cities.

The gravity model of migration is used to predict the degree of interaction among two places, in particular between networks of cities. It is based on the law of gravity, but it adapts it to model location and city importance. The basic idea is that as a city's importance increases, it will exert a stronger pull on nearby populations, just as a large mass creates a gravity pull on the smaller masses in gravity nearby. The gravity model is often used to predict traffic flows among cities in an urban hierarchy as well as migration patterns from smaller cities to cities higher up in the urban hierarchy.

As both the capital and fourth largest city in China, Beijing exerts strong influence well beyond its administrative boundary

Notes

Urban Analysis Using Models

> **Models of internal city structure and urban development provide a framework for urban analysis.**

In addition to looking at the spatial layout of different cities across a region, urban geographers are also very interested in the internal layout of cities. Models to explain and predict how cities might grow are useful for urban planners as they can help with the planning of city infrastructures such as roads, cycling paths, public transport, and sewer systems. These patterns are also interesting for urban geographers who study the politics and economics of cities, as they are interested in looking for patterns regarding integrating various cultural communities, alleviating poverty and trying to prevent the growth of economically bad neighborhoods where crime is high. By looking at models of city layout, these geographers can alert city services and politicians to areas which may become problematic in the future and could be targeted today to prevent them from becoming undesirable areas to live.

Classic models that are useful for explaining the internal structures of cities and urban development are the Burgess concentric-zone model, the Hoyt sector model, and the Harris-Ullman multiple-nuclei model.

The classic models focusing on the development of American cities all begin with the idea that a city grows out from its central business district (CBD). The first of these models was Burgess' concentric zone model, which depicts a city as having concentric rings around the central business district. Each of these rings has a different primary use. The first ring around the CBD is light manufacturing and wholesale, with the next ring being lower-class residential, then middle-class residential, then finally wealthy, upper-class residential. Burgess based this model on the real-life growth of Chicago. As a city grows, it can add rings like a tree, and it can also change the nature of a ring. The manufacturing ring might get transformed into an extension of the CBD, and manufacturing might end up being pushed to an outer ring, for example. The model works on the idea that when new people move to a city, they initially move to an area closest to the center, then later move further from the center. These changing living patterns account for why zones are often in transition. Sometimes land developers will speculate on which area will be next to be redeveloped and buy up land in advance. If the anticipated transition fails to take place, then these transition zones may linger on as permanent "skid rows" full of abandoned buildings and generally exist as undesirable areas of the city.

In the 1930s Homer Hoyt noticed that most cities did not follow the concentric model exactly and that zones tended to extend along major transportation routes. Hoyt realized that industrial areas tended to clump along railroad corridors, which often extended outward from the CBD. He also modified the concentric rings model because wealthier neighborhoods were not exclusively on the edge of town but located along major public transport sectors and highways leading into the CBD. Residential neighborhoods are clustered by class, but rather than simply the distance from the CBD; they are measured in the distance from transportation corridors that lead to the CBD. The city of Calgary, Alberta grew almost exactly according to Hoyt's model, even though Hoyt was also trying to model Chicago's growth.

By the 1940s, urban geographers argued that cities did not grow in even circles (or even in circles with exceptions for transportation corridors) but had much more uneven growth to the point where the CBD was not the sole center of a city. The multiple nuclei model argued that growth happens not just around the CBD but around other major features in a city such as a university, airport or seaport. Given that these hubs of growth were often located far from the CBD, this model predicted a decline in the importance of the CBD. This model also recognized that developments tended to occur in chunks rather than in slow waves of circular growth. A residential neighborhood or shopping mall would be zoned and built in one go, leading to square patches of zones within a city. This model was also an attempt to explain the urban layout of Chicago.

The galactic city model is useful for explaining internal structures and urban development within metropolitan areas.

The galactic city model was developed in the 1960s, based on the growth of Detroit, to explain the effect of private car ownership on city growth. With the ease of commuting, the city becomes more spread out, creating suburban sprawl and replacing public transit corridors with wider roads. In this model, the CBD is still at the center but becomes much less important, as major industries and businesses move further from the center to major highway intersections. Spread out from the CBD are various shopping malls, which are located in mostly residential areas and concentrate shopping areas into car-centric areas away from the CBD. Many businesses spring up in edge cities in the outer suburbs, and the CBD goes increasingly into decay because people can now go to these edge cities for shopping and entertainment instead of into the CBD. Increasingly office parks and manufacturing move to edge cities as well, and the CBD becomes virtually abandoned and the site of crime and decay.

Detroit in 1942, still a thriving community before job loss, crime and urban decay set in

World-regional models are useful (with limitations) for explaining land use and urban development.

The classic models listed thus far focus almost entirely on American cities (with a particular emphasis on Chicago) and are not necessarily applicable to urban areas in the rest of the world. Latin America is another target of urban development models because, like North America, the development of its modern cities is much more recent than in Europe or Asia. Latin American cities are interesting because, in the areas colonized by Spain, the Spanish government set out to purposefully apply urban planning policies, in contrast to the cities of Europe which grew organically. Unlike with North America, Latin American cities feature less prominent suburbs and more poverty and require a different model of growth.

The primary model of the Latin American city layout is the Ford-Griffith model. At the center, it places a large open plaza (which is also used as a market for people to sell handicrafts and vegetables) that is connected to a standard high-rise central business district. Extending from the CBD is a spine of commercial business which leads to a large mall on the edge of the city. Industrial parks are also located on the edge of the city, often with an industrial spine along a railroad leading into the CBD. Residential housing patterns tend to be the opposite of American cities, as closest to the CBD are the wealthiest areas, getting increasingly poorer the further from the CBD you go. Along the edge of the city is often a ring of squatter settlements which many cities do not service at all with infrastructure. Extending from the market are often disamenity zones, which are areas which have been passed over by basic infrastructure by the city and have become slums dominated by gangs.

Many African cities are notable for having essentially three different central business districts, which are sometimes nearby and sometimes spread out across the city. The first is the traditional market area, which dates to the pre-colonial era and is the space where farmers and producers came to sell their goods. These tend to remain in place because the open-air markets are filled with temporary stalls that are arranged in an often chaotic fashion. The second CBD is the colonial-era district which is dominated by European colonial architecture and tends to consist of single-story shopping. The third is a modern CBD featuring the typical high rise office towers.

Many African cities have these three CBDs as somewhat central features, with residential buildings outside of and encircling these three CBDs. Outside of the residential areas is often a district of industry, usually related to mining, recycling, and manufacturing, with an outer edge of squatter settlements outside of the industrial ring.

Landscapes and Social Space

Built landscapes and social space reflect the attitudes and values of a population.

The built landscape of a city reflects the attitude and cultural values of the population, often in a striking fashion. The growth of cities such as Detroit into galactic style cities, with edge cities in the suburbs becoming more important than the CBD, results from the U.S. obsession with car culture. Many North American cities at one time had electric streetcar systems which formed the basis of most public transit and were ripped out in the 1960s to reflect a car-centric cultural attitude. It is only recently that cities have begun to adapt to promote public transit and cycling infrastructure. Cities such as Amsterdam and Copenhagen have elaborate cycling infrastructure, which reflects the cultural attitude toward cycling in those cities. Some North American and Australian cities have almost no accommodations for cyclists, demonstrating a general attitude enshrining the primacy of the car.

The Brazilian Rocinha slum in Rio de Janeiro (foreground) bordering upscale high-rise buildings just across the highway

---

In many Latin American cities, infrastructure goes almost exclusively toward wealthier neighborhoods, leading to very stark contrasts between the poor and the rich parts of the city. The richest parts of many Latin American cities are often nicer than the richest part of any American city, yet the poor parts are completely neglected, leading to slums; in American cities there tends to be more of an effort to distribute infrastructure in a more even fashion. While this may not reflect the views of the general population in Latin American cities, it does reflect how political factors influenced historical patterns of development. This is called "uneven development" and can be seen as a reflection of political attitudes toward equality.

Residential buildings and patterns of land use reflect a city's culture, technological capabilities, and cycles of development.

One of the biggest issues facing city planners today, which is also a common source of study for urban geographers, is the issue of suburban sprawl. Suburban sprawl first began in the 1960s with the advent of widespread personal car ownership. Commuting to a job in the city center became easier when one could drive a car into the city rather than have to rely on public transit. As a result, cities began to spread out and cover more land, often encroaching on agricultural land on the edge of cities and turning it into suburban residential housing. In many American cities, the growth of suburbs led to the middle class vacating the city center. Eventually, edge cities sprung up, which meant that shopping and entertainment, and ultimately offices and work, were no longer in the CBD. This led to urban decay and continued reliance on car-centric urban planning.

Today, suburban sprawl is recognized as a serious problem for multiple reasons. First is that personal car ownership and commuting has led to major traffic problems. In car-centric cities with large amounts of suburban sprawl such as Toronto and Los Angeles, people often face commutes of one or two hours each way, most of which is spent sitting in slow-moving traffic. Due to the previous era's reliance on car culture, these outer suburbs are not serviced by public transit and often lack cycling infrastructure, making commuting by car the only option. Sitting in traffic hurts economic productivity as business and industry face increased shipping and delivery times due to commuter traffic. The second problem is greenhouse gas emissions from slow-moving cars, which contributes to climate change. As a result, a new wave of urban planning has focused on trying to contain suburban sprawl and promote alternatives to car commuting by establishing cycling and public transportation infrastructure.

Because commuting by car often takes so long, there is a new push for people to move back into urban cores in many American cities. This demonstrates how a cycle of residential development can respond to technological and cultural changes. Initially, wealthier individuals lived in the city, and then moved to the suburbs with the widespread acceptance of cars, leading to a cultural attitude about the inner city being full of crime and an undesirable place to live. Now wealthier people are beginning to move back into the inner cities since they no longer wish to waste two to four hours a day sitting in traffic; this has led to the revitalization of many urban cores. Many American cities are strong advocates of this return to the core, as suburbs have become their cities.

Economic development and interconnections within a metropolitan area are dependent upon the location and quality of infrastructure.

The key to all economic development is infrastructure. The more infrastructure a city has, the more attractive it will be for business. Industry requires airports, seaports, and railways for shipping. Commercial offices require public transit and a strong internet backbone connection, and shopping areas require a good road system for deliveries and proper water and sewage systems. Combined, all these city services are what makes one city more or less attractive to start a business. While politicians often argue that lowering taxes is what attracts business, this has the opposite effect. With lower taxes, there is less spending on infrastructure, which makes a city a less desirable place to do business.

The 2007 collapse of the I-35W Mississippi River bridge in Minneapolis represents catastrophic infrastructure failure and construction negligence

271

As an example, imagine Google wants to set up a new office and has two cities in mind. One city has much lower taxes, which means Google would make a higher profit, but it also means that this city has slower internet and lacks reliable cycling and public transit infrastructure which the highly-skilled Google employees want to be able to use to get to work. Meanwhile, the other city has higher taxes but has invested in upgrading infrastructure so that it has fast internet, a modern cycling, and public transportation system and many parks and recreation areas. In economics, there is a concept known as the "Laffer Curve," which argues that as an area increases taxes, it becomes less attractive to business as higher taxes eat into profits. According to the Laffer curve, Google would choose the city with lower taxes. However, in reality, Google needs fast internet, and its employees do not want to work in a city without amenities such as public transport and parks. This would mean that Google would have to create these services for their workers themselves, which would cancel out any tax savings. As a result, Google would always choose the city with better infrastructure even if the taxes were higher, demonstrating how the Laffer Curve is largely irrelevant to real-life economic situations. The Laffer Curve would argue that, theoretically, all businesses should relocate to Somalia, which, lacking a functional government, has no corporate taxation whatsoever. Of course, Somalia also has virtually no infrastructure that any modern company would need as a prerequisite. For this reason, economic development of cities depends on developing modern infrastructure, even if that means higher taxes.

Sustainable design initiatives include walkable mixed-use commercial and residential areas and smart-growth policies.

To adapt cities to the reality of climate change, some new policies to promote sustainable design have begun to gain influence. The first of these is creating mixed-use neighborhoods to promote walkability and lessen the need for long commutes. According to this design philosophy, a building will have commercial storefronts at street level, then a floor or two of offices, with the rest of the building being apartments. By mixing residential, commercial and office spaces together, a person could theoretically work in the same building they live in and only have to go downstairs to get groceries or do some other shopping. This is in stark contrast to the old philosophy of urban planning that involved dividing the city into very separate residential, commercial and industrial/office zones which are located far apart from each other. Mixed-use areas also reduce the strain on infrastructure by evening out demand; public transit and roads will be less crowded with commuters at certain times of the day, and the energy distribution system will not be overloaded in certain areas at certain times of the day. These policies make infrastructure development both more predictable and cheaper overall.

Another aspect of the sustainable design is the growth of new sustainable urban planning movements. One which has rapidly gained in popularity is the building of greenbelts, such as in Toronto, London, and Portland, Oregon. An area of land around the city is demarcated as green space, either as parks or simply as a forest which cannot be encroached on with growth. A greenbelt then places a limit on suburban sprawl, along with providing recreational space just outside the city. Forested greenbelts can also help fight climate change and air pollution. It can be difficult for cities to implement greenbelts because it places direct constraints on new suburban developments. Developers who build these new housing developments make much money and are often able to use their wealth to sway politicians. Intensification (i.e., shifting new residential development from the periphery to existing built places) is better for cities than sprawl since it adds new housing without expanding space, which is better for infrastructure and sustainability. However, intensification projects require developers to buy land that is already expensive and remodel existing buildings. Developers make more money buying a cheap lot of farmland than they do acquiring the rights to land already within the city.

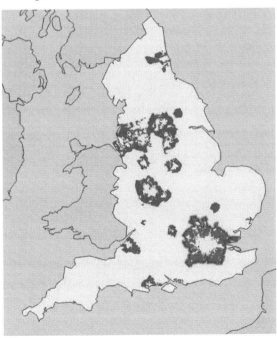

England's designated green belt areas

273

New Urbanism is an urban planning movement that began in the United States in the 1980s with the goal of creating environmentally-friendly, walkable neighborhoods. New Urbanism seeks to create diverse communities with housing for various income levels and jobs for people with various education and skill levels. Many newer parts of American cities were designed according to the principles of New Urbanism, which creates a master plan of design and prominently features pedestrian walking paths to connect residential and commercial districts, which are centered around a community feature such as a park or community center. One of the goals of New Urbanism is to ensure that every house in the neighborhood should be a maximum of a five-minute walk to the central feature. Examples of New Urbanism in the United States include newer sections of Miami and the towns of Seaside and Celebration in Florida, wholly planned using the principles of New Urbanism. Seaside, with Florida's unique layout and architecture, has made it a tourist attraction in itself, and it was even used as the set of the film *The Truman Show*, which depicted an entire town as a reality TV show based around the life of one person who does not know he is on a TV show.

Not everyone likes New Urbanism, however, as it has come under criticism from multiple points of view. Many critiques it as being a nostalgia movement, longing for a simpler time, and even that it evokes a kind of creepy, fake-1950s feeling which makes the towns feel unreal. This is part of the reason why Seaside was chosen as the location for *The Truman Show*. These critics argue that New Urbanism has a tendency to turn into enclaves for the very wealthy and argue that in reality it usually fails to meet its goal of mixed-income housing. Others argue that it is still essentially a car-centric design, as pedestrian paths are relegated to the backs of houses and businesses. Some argue that it can only be applied to small towns or semi-urban neighborhoods because it focuses on small homes rather than on intensive development through condo towers and high rise office buildings.

While New Urbanism became popular in the United States, in European cities such as Amsterdam and Copenhagen, the Smart Growth movement took shape. Smart Growth seeks to limit suburban sprawl by developing proper transportation networks which are designed entirely around public transportation and cycling, rather than cars. While New Urbanism still assumed the car as the primary mode of transport despite promoting walkability, Smart Growth assumes a car is for longer and infrequent trips, and the primary means of getting around will be either bicycle or public transit. This leads to a different design philosophy in city layout, even if Smart Growth shares a desire for walkability, mixed-use zoning and environmental sustainability with the New Urbanism movement.

Smart Growth has led to cities such as Amsterdam and Copenhagen becoming influential hubs of forward thinking in city planning. Some American cities have begun to attempt to adapt some of the principles of Smart Growth, notably complete streets (which make a street suitable for all forms of transportation equally, not just primarily cars) and transit-oriented development. Some examples of implementations of Smart Growth in the United States are in Arlington, Virginia, Minneapolis-St. Paul and Denver. Melbourne, Australia has also adopted Smart Growth as its primary design philosophy for all new housing developments.

Functional and geographic fragmentation of governments presents challenges in addressing urban issues.

A major problem in many American cities is that they are fragmented into an urban core city with a series of suburban cities around it. In cities which have had experienced a significant decline in urban populations as people moved to the suburbs in the 1960s, the urban core city often lacks a tax base to sustain it. This means that infrastructure starts to suffer, which causes businesses to leave the urban core city as well as the residents. This fragmentation is partly a result of the lack of planning for suburban growth which enabled the suburbs to incorporate as cities rather than having the existing city expand its territory to encompass the new developments. Part of the reason for this was related to the racial makeup of these early suburban vs. urban cities.

The 1960s civil rights movement helped open political doors for people of color

The move from the city to the suburbs by the middle class in the 1960s was when the middle class was predominantly white. This was called "white flight," and it left a perception of urban cores as being places for black Americans and Latinos. Due to the racist attitudes of white middle-class Americans, the growth of suburban cities was an explicit way to create a de facto form of political-racial segregation. With black Americans gaining power throughout the 1960s and increasingly becoming prominent political leaders, especially at the municipal level, the creation of predominantly-white suburban cities was a mechanism to avoid diversity on city councils and in the political system.

Detroit, for example, essentially went bankrupt because all the people with good-paying jobs who should form its tax base lived in the suburbs which are not part of the city of Detroit. This meant that the city's primary tax base of people who relied on using its roads and services were paying taxes to a different city. After many factories closed, the city of Detroit lost almost all of its revenue streams. Other examples are St. Louis, which had a million people in 1950, but today only has 300,000 because suburbs have incorporated into their cities. In many ways this is a uniquely American problem, as many Canadian cities were amalgamated in the 1990s, meaning that the suburban cities were dissolved and made part of the primary urban city. While this policy has led to some oddities, such as primarily agricultural areas being politically controlled by a major city, it has avoided the issue of urban cores losing their tax base.

Census and survey data provide quantitative information about a city's population.

Part of city planning and urban geography relies on looking at data, which can come from quantitative or qualitative sources. *Quantitative data* is statistical in nature and involves counting and recording hard facts. When countries conduct a census, they go house to house and count how many people live there and gather other facts about them. Cities then use this information about the population for planning purposes. If a city knows which parts are growing the fastest, they can predict where there will be increased strain on infrastructure and budget upgrades accordingly. This data is extremely important for city planning. Another manner of quantitative data is through using GIS software to visually map data that is collected through the census or by issuing surveys. For example, if a city wants to make sure that there is a park near every neighborhood, the easiest way to do this is to load up a map in GIS software which only shows a layer of parks. This will make parks the outstanding feature of the map and allows city planners to easily see where there are gaps and where they should target building a new park. They can also add survey data about parks to their map and correlate where people think there should be a park with these visible gaps in park coverage.

Qualitative data from field studies and narratives provide information about individual attitudes toward urban change.

While quantitative data is essential for high-level planning, when cities want to get an idea of what people think, they use *qualitative data* which cannot be measured in numbers. For example, if a new project is proposed, a city councilor might hold an open forum meeting where residents can come and voice their approval or disapproval of the project or any other concerns they might have. If common themes emerge, then the city can take these under consideration and adapt to accommodate the concerns.

An example of leveraging qualitative data about urban change occurred in Ottawa, Canada when the city decided to begin to build a light rail transit (LTR) system to replace its primary bus-based public transit system. Since it would take many years to replace the dedicated bus-only roads with a rail track, it would require the existing bus routes to all be changed since they could no longer run on their normal routes due to the light rail construction. First, the city looked at the quantitative data and determined where they could move these primary bus routes so that they could still service the same people yet not create traffic problems from running on the same road as cars. Based on their quantitative data of bus ridership and traffic congestion, they developed a new plan of where the buses would temporarily run until the light rail system was built.

They then held consultations with people living near the streets where the busses would now be running. While the quantitative data demonstrated that using the chosen streets would impact the fewest overall number of people, those who lived on the street of the new bus route were angry that the busses would be too loud or that the streets would become unsafe. After this was expressed at many public meetings, the city then used this qualitative data about safety and noise concerns to modify their plan by building a large noise-blocking wall along the new street in an attempt to both reduce noise and keep the streets safer by preventing access. By looking at both the quantitative and qualitative data, the city was able to plan for the best spot for the temporary bus route and also address the concerns of the residents who would be impacted by the changes.

Notes

Challenges of Urban Areas

Urban areas face economic, social, political, cultural and environmental challenges.

In addition to cities increasingly becoming the primary engines of the global economy, they face some unique challenges which municipal governments are often not equipped to handle. Because previous eras put all the power in the hands of the state as the primary economic, political and social force, cities have traditionally been politically constrained when it comes to facing these challenges. In federal states such as Canada and the United States, the municipal layer is not constitutionally guaranteed and exists merely at the whim of the province or the state. At the time that both of these countries developed, they were a federation of large regions which became provinces or states, but today these regional entities are vastly less important than cities. There has been some theoretical movement among some political thinkers to rethink federalism to include cities as constitutionally guaranteed entities granted as much or more power than states and provinces.

Political theorist and author Benjamin Barber

American political theorist Benjamin Barber has argued that municipal politics is the most democratic layer of government because city councilors and mayors are closer to the people they represent, which causes them to be more democratically accountable. Barber is an advocate of vastly increasing the political power of cities to meet the challenges of a global economy where cities are the primary instruments of economic growth and social and cultural development. To rearrange power structures in such a manner is a difficult task, as federal governments and state and provincial governments are never keen to cede authority to a lower level of government. This leads to policymaking at the national level that often ignores the role of cities, even while often unnecessarily pandering to the interests of individual state governments. Many urban geographers are at the forefront of pushing for more municipal political authority as a way to modernize political structures for the era of globalization.

Economic and social problems associated with the growth and decline of urban communities include housing and insurance discrimination, housing affordability, access to food stores and public services, disamenity zones, zones of abandonment and gentrification.

Many of the challenges that cities face relate to economic and social growth and decline. In American cities, ghettoization refers to an area of concentrated poverty inhabited by a single group of people. Originally, ghettos began in American cities as a result of immigrants of shared ethnicity living near one another, with prominent Irish and Italian ghettos. By the 1950s, as a result of increased Chinese immigration and the increased urban migration of black Americans, Chinese and black ghettos became prominent. One of the factors leading to ghettos as sources of poverty was housing discrimination policies that were implemented by banks and real estate developers. Real estate agents used to practice "racial steering" in which they would only show someone potential houses to buy in neighborhoods that matched their race. This applied to whites, blacks, and immigrants, and it was driven by attitudes in favor of racial segregation in the 1950s and 1960s. These practices prevented diverse neighborhoods from forming and were an unofficial form of racial segregation.

Another problem that existed up until the late 1970s was the practice of redlining by banks. Banks would refuse to issue mortgages for houses in certain parts of the city. In America this was predominantly in black neighborhoods; in Canada, it was done primarily in poor neighborhoods. The combination of racial steering and redlining meant that black Americans who had well-paying jobs and saved enough money to buy a house were still locked out of ownership. The only houses real estate agents would show were in predominantly black neighborhoods where banks would simply refuse to issue a mortgage, even if it were clear the person applying could easily pay. These policies locked these ghettoized neighborhoods into a cycle of race-based poverty, as it ensured that blacks could not own their own homes and ensured that rent money kept flowing to the white owners. In

Canada, redlining was used on any neighborhood that was perceived as working-class or lower-income, which created a class barrier. The working class was prevented from owning their own homes by banks who acted to enforce class division, even when the applicant could easily afford the mortgage.

With the growth of suburbs, many white people moved out of the urban core in what was called "white flight" to the suburbs. Those whites who remained in the urban core tended to be seen by racists as traitors who were inappropriately mixing with other races. To try to force these remaining white families out of the urban core and into the suburbs (where new housing developments meant more money for real estate developers), real estate developers would engage in the practice of *blockbusting*. This involved purposely bringing in minority families to the remaining white neighborhoods in an attempt to try to scare them into the suburbs. Real estate agents also profited from this practice because if they could scare away an entire block of people by playing on racist fears, it would mean that many people would attempt to sell their houses. Real estate agents only make money when people buy or sell a house, so blockbusting was also a way to manufacture business by artificially inducing people to sell their houses.

Harlem in 1943, a black cultural center

As a part of the general civil rights reforms passed in 1968 as a result of the advance of the civil rights movement led by Dr. Martin Luther King, the Fair Housing Act of 1968 was passed, which aimed to prevent racial steering. The act also sought to combat redlining by making discriminating against a person based on race for lending purposes illegal; however, the banks continued the practice of redlining since they argued that they were not discriminating against individuals based on race since their redlined areas were unavailable for mortgages for whites and blacks equally. To fight the continued practice of redlining, many black Americans joined together to start banks which had the sole purpose of fighting the racist practices of other banks. One such example was the creation of ShoreBank in Chicago in the early 1970s, which had an explicit agenda of combating redlining by offering mortgages to people who wished to purchase a house in areas the other banks had redlined. This helped to empower black Americans and also to reverse urban decay, as being unable to sell a house in these areas led to many crumbling and abandoned buildings. Finally, in 1977 the federal government took action to ban redlining once for all with the Community Reinvestment Act, which required banks to apply the same lending criteria in all parts of a city. It then became illegal to discriminate against buyers based on race and based on where they wanted to buy a house.

In Canada, the problem of redlining remained through the 1980s despite efforts by the federal government to combat it. Poor areas were largely the target of redlining in Canada which led to discrimination against the working class and prevented class mobility. After World War II, when returning soldiers who had fought for Canada in the war were unable to purchase houses, the Canadian government created the Canadian Mortgage and Housing Corporation (CMHC), which is a government-owned corporation which provides mortgage insurance. Instead of compelling the banks not to discriminate, as in the U.S., in Canada, the CMHC provided mandatory insurance on "risky mortgages" in order to encourage banks to expand their lending practices without taking on further risk. While the CMHC insurance did not stop redlining right away, it eventually conditioned the banks to realize that lending to poorer people was extremely profitable because if they defaulted, the bank would not lose any money because of the CMHC insurance.

The CMHC enabled the expansion of housing ownership in Canada, but by the late 2000s was being blamed for having a role in creating a major housing bubble. The CMHC went from encouraging banks to lend to poorer people to become a safety net that enabled banks to give mortgages to just about anyone, even if they had no money at all. If the person defaulted, CMHC would pay the bank, and the bank would not lose any money. Due to how easy it was now to get a mortgage, housing prices have skyrocketed in Canada. The average price in major cities such as Vancouver and Toronto is now over $1 million, making buying a house completely unaffordable for the working class and middle class alike. In this sense, CMHC worked a little too well and has now reintroduced the problem of the working class being unable to buy a house.

This leads into the second issue cities face, which is housing affordability. When housing prices go up disproportionate to income levels, it makes cities unattractive places for the working class to live. This can cause a strain on the economy as people move further outside the city looking for cheaper housing, increasing commute times and leading to more traffic gridlock and suburban sprawl. When housing prices begin to rise very fast, it can lead to gentrification, in which older neighborhoods with cheaper housing get bought up and redeveloped to be made into more expensive housing. Gentrification is a hotly debated issue since it has very positive effects and very negative effects at the same time. On the plus side, it can reinvigorate rundown neighborhoods as they become redeveloped and attract wealthier people and more business, making these areas overall nicer places to live. Gentrification can also help combat suburban sprawl because instead of moving out into the suburbs, wealthier people can move into a redeveloped urban neighborhood with modern amenities in the city center. It can also lead to mixed neighborhoods and combat ghettoization. For example, in Brooklyn, New York's Williamsburg area, young professionals have led a push for gentrification which has turned a formerly Jewish ghetto into a mixed and racially diverse neighborhood with a variety of different shops and businesses.

London community activists resist ongoing gentrification

On the negative side, gentrification is an example of uneven development as it simply makes areas more attractive to the wealthy while pushing the poor out. In doing so, it contributes to housing unaffordability, as most cities now have very few areas which are affordable. The new businesses that gentrification attracts often are unaffordable to a neighborhood's original inhabitants, as they target the wealthier newcomers exclusively, making the neighborhood more expensive for shopping as well as housing. To combat the negative effects of gentrification while preserving the positive effects, some cities have begun to implement policies where redeveloped areas are required to maintain a certain number of units of affordable housing.

For example, if a row of older townhouses is torn down to build a new condo tower aimed at wealthy investors, then one or two floors will be required to provide rental units at below-market rates. City planners hope that this can not only counteract the effect of gentrification driving out the poor which often leads to homelessness but also that by mixing people of various classes it may provide opportunities for poorer residents to socialize and make connections with the richer residents who can perhaps offer them a better job.

With the problem of obesity becoming more of an issue, one challenge for cities is ensuring that residents in all parts of the city have access to grocery stores. Urban geographers have become interested in studying what they call "food deserts," which are areas of cities which do not have easy access to grocery stores. There have been studies published linking such food deserts to obesity, as the lack of easy availability of purchasing fruits and vegetables can lead people to eat at fast food restaurants, contributing to health issues related to obesity. Food deserts are especially problematic in low-income areas where many people may not have easy access to cars. Traveling long distances for groceries on foot, bicycle or public transit is inconvenient, especially if there are fast food outlets in close proximity. Geographers studying food deserts have found that grocery stores tend to target new locations in wealthier suburbs, leaving poorer neighborhoods to become food deserts. This emerging field of urban geography seeks to advise city planners and zoning regulators.

One of the ways to combat food deserts that have been proposed is expanding small-scale farmers' markets into food desert areas. In some cities, there are even mobile farmers' markets that go to nearby farms, collect produce in a large covered truck, then schedule a day in various food deserts so that residents can easily have access to fresh food. Cities have also been encouraged to change bylaws to encourage urban gardening and community garden plots and to allow people to keep one or two chickens in their backyard to have access to fresh eggs.

As seen with the model of Latin American cities, disamenity zones are a problem which relates to food deserts. *Disamenity zones* are areas that lack most city services, often including electricity and clean water in many cities in developing countries. These zones are often just outside the core of the city and turn into slums. This can lead to abandoned zones as well, which are increasingly becoming a problem in North American cities. After the 2008 financial crisis, many parts of Detroit were simply abandoned en masse as residents had their houses foreclosed by the bank and moved away. To save money, the city has taken to turning off the street lights in these areas and generally neglecting city services, which turns an abandoned zone into a disamenity zone.

Land use and environmental problems associated with the growth and decline of urban communities include suburban sprawl, sanitation, air and water quality, remediation and redevelopment of brownfields, farmland protection, and energy use.

While cities have become the drivers of economic growth and political and social power in the age of globalization, they are also the primary sites of environmental problems in an era that is increasingly concerned with climate change. Suburban sprawl is at the forefront of these environmental problems. While other problems with sprawl have previously been discussed, it turns out that cities with low density have much larger per capita carbon footprints than cities with higher density. So in addition to the other problems with suburban sprawl, such as loss of farmland, increased traffic problems, the strain on city infrastructure and political fragmentation, it also turns out sprawl is quite bad for the environment.

Part of the reason why sprawl leads to a higher carbon footprint is that it leads to commuting longer distances by car and larger houses with fewer people in them but which use more electricity. While cities have focused on combating suburban sprawl by promoting urban intensification and redevelopment, some urban geographers believe that suburbs can be transformed to become more environmentally friendly. Given that suburbs tend to have no high rises blocking the sunlight, houses could easily be equipped with solar panels to turn suburbs into solar farms generating their electricity.

Los Angeles suburban sprawl

Another major problem that cities face, especially in the developing world, is air pollution. While air pollution used to be a bigger issue in the developed world, as industry and manufacturing have shifted to developing countries, air pollution has shifted with it. Beijing has become one of the worst cities in the world for air pollution and smog, far surpassing cities such as Los Angeles which used to be notorious for air pollution. Air pollution is not only bad for people's health and the environment but also has major economic consequences as well. In Beijing, the air quality can become so bad that the city has to shut down schools and prevent any outdoor work such as construction from occurring. Air pollution has also been the subject of many protests in Beijing, which have made it a sensitive topic for the national government, which likes to maintain an image of social cohesion and harmony. The primary causes of Beijing's air pollution problems are vehicle traffic, coal-burning power plants and emissions from industrial factories. Beijing is also prone to dust storms which blow in from neighboring dry areas and contribute to making the air an even lower quality.

The government of Beijing has taken some steps to try to improve air quality. They have introduced a vehicle registration quota, allowing only 20,000 new vehicles on the road each year. Registrations for these vehicles are awarded by lottery to preserve fairness and prevent corruption. Beijing is notorious for its traffic jams, with one jam on a highway outside of the city lasting for five whole days, with travelers only able to advance one kilometer (0.62 miles) per day. On holidays a major expressway leading out of the city toward Hong Kong that is 50 lanes wide can turn into the world's largest parking lot. Idling cars get people nowhere and increase pollution, so the Beijing government has begun to implement congestion charges, which are taxes people pay for driving into a traffic jam and are meant to discourage people from contributing to these major jams. The city government has pledged to spend $2.5 billion in 2016 to upgrade municipal vehicles to newer lower-emission models and replace coal power plants with cleaner alternatives. Despite this large investment, Greenpeace estimates it would cost over $250 billion to clean up Beijing's air pollution issue for good.

While air and water pollution are major issues in developing countries, in developed countries, a major issue relates to grown pollution left behind by factories which have since shut down. These sites are called *brownfields* because they are areas within a city in which the ground has become polluted or contains dumped toxic waste. Given that industrial sites were once on the edges of the CBD in many developed cities, these brownfields are now a problem as they are often located in prime areas of a city, sticking out as ugly, undeveloped spots. Many developers would love to build new buildings on these sites but cannot do so because the ground is so polluted, which leaves them to simply be fenced-in lots. Cleaning up this land for re-use can be very difficult as pollutants have seeped into the soil and toxic waste can make building atop these areas problematic.

Abandoned since 1958, the Packard Automotive Plant still stands undeveloped in Detroit

Despite the problems with brownfields, many cities have been able to develop successful re-use plans. One of the largest and most successful brownfield redevelopments is Atlantic Station in Atlanta on the site of the former Atlantic Steel Mill. The most polluted area was turned into a park, and around it is retail and housing developments, all designed to be energy-efficient and environmentally sustainable. Seattle has also been successful in transforming former brownfield sites into parks. Owing to its past as a major industrial city, Pittsburgh had many abandoned brownfield sites which it is now redeveloping after spending a lot of time and money cleaning up the polluted land. Brownfield redevelopment is beneficial because it not only cleans up polluted land but also allows new developments to be built on land inside the city rather than on the edge of the city. In this way, brownfield redevelopment is a major way to fight suburban sprawl. While cleaning up brownfield sites can be very expensive since eliminating ground pollution is so difficult, the federal EPA has introduced a system of tax credits to help cities and developers offset some of the cost of cleanup.

To promote energy efficiency, many cities have adopted policies such as tax credits and preferential treatment for developers who build according to LEED certification. *LEED* stands for Leadership in Energy and Environmental Design, which was developed by the American Green Building Council. LEED consists of some energy-efficient and environmentally-friendly design criteria that all new buildings can be judged on. Four levels of certification can be achieved, with "platinum" as the highest level of energy efficiency and environmental sustainability. To encourage LEED buildings, many cities have developed incentive programs. Cities want LEED buildings because they use less energy and generally are better places to work and live. Cincinnati, Ohio offers all buildings that are LEED-certified a 100% exemption from paying property taxes. In Maryland, all new public buildings are required to be built to at least LEED "silver" status. Canada's CMHC offers discounted insurance rates for people buying LEED-certified homes and property. Despite cities being a major source of energy consumption and pollution, through initiatives such as green building and LEED, cities are also on the forefront of developing new technologies and standards that can lead to future environmental sustainability.

Appendix

Glossary of Terms

A

Absolute barrier – a feature or condition which completely prevents *Diffusion*.

Absolute location – the exact position of a *Place* on the earth's surface.

Accessible – a *Place* which is easy to reach.

Accessibility – how easy a *Place* is to get to.

Accretion – the addition of land to a state or other area by natural processes such as the gradual shift in the bed of a river or the creation of land from alluvial *Deposition* or volcanic activity.

Active volcano – a volcano that has erupted recently and is likely to erupt again.

Activity segregation – most often used to refer to the different and unequal use of space by men and women; occurs because men and women are assigned different roles to play in *Gendered* divisions of labor; the concept is flexible and may also refer to similar situations related to different aspects of identity.

Acculturation – the exchange of cultural features that results when groups come into continuous first-hand contact; occurs when the "weaker" of two cultures adopt traits from the more dominant culture.

Acquisition of rights – one state's granting of the use of territory by another state without title or sovereignty changing hands; such transfers of rights take the form of leases and servitudes (e.g., Hong Kong during its period as a British crown colony).

Adaptation – adjusting to a transition based on the cultural *Environment* of the target language.

Adaptive strategies – the unique way in which each *Culture* uses its particular physical *Environment*.

Administration (of boundaries) – the final phase of *Boundary making* in which countries are sharing a common border establish regular procedures for maintaining boundary markers, settling local disputes, regulating the use of water and waterways in the border area and conducting other administrative tasks.

Affirmative gerrymandering – a type of *Gerrymandering* designed to enhance the ability of minority groups to elect representatives who will best serve their interests.

African Union (AU) – formerly the Organization of African Unity (OAU); the premier supranational organization for all of Africa; patterned after the *European Union* and given greater powers than those of the OAU; allows for intervention in the affairs of member states to resolve conflicts and prevent genocide and gross human rights violations; also working toward greater economic integration with plans to introduce a common currency for all of Africa.

Age-sex pyramid (population pyramid) – a series of horizontal bars that illustrate the structure of a population; the bars represent different age categories, which are placed on either side of a central vertical axis; males are to the left of the axis, females to the right.

Ageing population – a high proportion of elderly people who have survived due to advances in nutrition and medical care; creates problems since these people often do not work and have to be provided with pensions, medical care, social support, sheltered housing etc. from the taxes paid by a proportionally smaller number of younger workers.

Aging population structure – a population pyramid with a narrower shape, broad at the top, found in MEDCs; reflects their low *Birth rates* and the greater proportion of elderly people.

Agglomeration economies – savings which arise from the concentration of industries in urban areas and their location close to linked activities (e.g., a car factory attracts component suppliers to locate close by, saving on transport costs); other savings are made in labor and training costs and the use of the services found in urban areas (e.g., housing, banking, roads, electricity, etc.).

Agricultural density – the number of farmers per unit area of arable (farmable) land; compare with *Arithmetic density* and *Physiological density*.

Agriculture – the systematic cultivation of plants and animals; highly variable over space and time; generally speaking, agriculture can be divided into two classes: subsistence agriculture and *Commercial agriculture*; in the contemporary world, *Commercial* systems predominate and are expanding at the expense of older subsistence systems.

Allocational boundary dispute – a *Boundary* dispute that involves conflicting claims to the natural resources of a border region.

Amenities – services that people find very useful but are not essential, like swimming pools, libraries, parks, etc.; may be within the home or outside the home.

Andean Community – originally the Andean Group; a supranational organization composed of Venezuela, Colombia, Ecuador, Peru, and Bolivia; has created a *Customs union* and is working toward a *Common market* among its members.

Animism – the belief that inanimate objects, such as trees, rocks, and rivers, possess souls.

Annexation – an extension of a state's law to territory and inhabitants in an attempt to legitimize acquisition of the territory; at the local scale, it is a technique often used by cities and towns in the United States and other countries in which a municipality extends its borders to encompass neighboring unincorporated areas.

Antecedent boundary – determined prior to intensive settlement of an area; before *Development* of a distinct cultural landscape.

Apartheid – literally, "apart-ness;" the Afrikaans term for South Africa's pre-1994 policies of racial separation; a geographical system that produced highly segregated socio-economic patterns and racial control; operated at three scales: petty, urban and grand (see Recitation 8); sought to totally control the movements and locations of all people of color.

Arab League – the League of Arab States, commonly known as the Arab League; the primary supranational body for countries whose populations contain an Arab majority or a significant Arab minority; the Palestinian Authority is also a member.

Arable farming – a farm or area that only grows crops.

Arbitration – a formal, expensive and time-consuming method of third-party participation in dispute resolution; the parties to the dispute agree in advance whether the findings will be binding or merely advisory, select one or more arbitrators and agree to a set of principles and rules of law that apply to the case; the arbitrator(s) take testimony, study it and render a decision.

Archipelagic state – a state that is composed of one or more *Archipelagos*, perhaps including other islands, with baselines, not exceeding 100 nautical miles and a specified ratio of land-to-water territory within the baselines (e.g., Fiji, the Philippines); the special requirements effectively disqualify other countries such as Japan from this category.

Archipelagic waters – the internal waters of an *Archipelagic state*.

Archipelago – a group of islands, parts of islands, interconnecting waters and other natural features that are typically viewed as forming a single geographic feature.

Architectural form – the look of housing, affected by the available materials, the *Environment* the house is in and the *Popular culture* of the time.

Arithmetic ("regular" or "crude") density – the number of people per unit area of all land; compare with *Agricultural density* and *Physiological density*.

Articles of Confederation – a 1781 agreement whereby representatives of the people of the original 13 American colonies initially sought to establish the United States of America as a confederation.

ASEAN – the Association of Southeast Asian Nations; the primary supranational body in Southeast Asia working toward closer economic integration.

Assembly industries – see *Screwdriver industries*.

Assimilation – in cultural convergence, occurs when the original traits of the weaker *Culture* are completely erased and replaced by the traits of the more dominant culture; the process through which people lose originally differentiating traits (e.g., dress, speech, particularities, mannerisms) when they come into contact with another society or culture; represented a pillar of former French colonial policy whereby the French colonial authorities sought to impose French language and *Culture* upon the indigenous peoples of their colonies.

Assisted areas – see *Development areas*.

Assumptions – a statement or condition agreed to be true for a particular model; such statements or conditions may not hold in the real world but are made to simplify a system and isolate important variables.

Astropolitics – the geopolitics of the cosmos.

Asymmetric conflict – a conflict that features an imbalance of power between combatant groups; in such cases, the weaker side may opt for guerrilla warfare and/or terrorism rather than risk defeat by engaging superior forces in conventional warfare.

Autarky – a national policy of economic self-sufficiency and non-reliance on imports or foreign aid.

Attractive countryside – areas of pleasant scenery such as mountains, rivers, lakes, and coasts.

Authenticity – the truthfulness of origins, attributions, commitments, sincerity, devotion, and intentions; the quality of being authentic.

B

Balance of trade – the value of *Exports* minus the value of imports; there may be a trade deficit or trade surplus.

Balkanization – the process by which a state breaks down through conflict among its various ethnicities into smaller, often hostile political units; the term was coined by German sociologists in the 1920s in reference to conflicts such as the Balkan Wars that preceded World War I.

Bantustan – created by the *apartheid*-era government of South Africa; quasi-independent territorial divisions designed to concentrate various tribal peoples in economically undesirable territories; served as administrative tools for subjugation and were not recognized by the international community; reincorporated into South Africa in 1994.

Barrio / favela – a shantytown in or near a *City*; slum area.

Barriers – in diffusion studies, the term given to something that slows, stops or transforms a *Diffusion* event; see *Absolute barriers* and *Permeable barriers*.

Bid-rent curve – a graph which plots the relationship between how much rent people are willing to pay for land given its *Distance* from a specified point (usually the center of a *City*); essential for understanding the *Von Thünen model* and the *Concentric zone model* of the city.

Bilateral negotiations – occur between two states without the involvement of other parties.

Bilingual – people or societies that commonly use two languages in their daily affairs.

Biological determinism – the theory that the various cultures, social systems and economic and political conditions of groups from around the world correspond with and are created by the innate genetic makeup of individuals or races or ethnicities.

Bipolar world – the world as it appeared during the Cold War in which power was balanced between the capitalist West, led by the United States, and the communist East, led by the former Soviet Union.

Birth Rate – the number of live births per 1,000 people per year.

Boundary – a linear feature marking the edges of territory between separate states, regions, civil divisions or other *Places*; a border.

Boundary making – the process of definition, delimitation, demarcation, and *Administration of boundaries*.

Boycott – a form of economic sanction that prohibits some or all imports from a country, group of countries or region; counterpart to an *Embargo*; can also be applied at the local level as in the case of consumers boycotting the products of an unpopular company.

Break of bulk location – a location such as a coastal port which takes its advantage from a position where there is a forced transfer of raw materials or goods from one form of transport to another; coastal locations are favored for iron and steel plants in the UK since the coal and iron ore raw materials are now imported.

Break of bulk point – the *Place* where goods have to be unloaded (e.g., a port).

Bridging Point – a settlement site where a river is narrow or shallow enough to be bridged; the bridge becomes a route and trading center and is the natural location for a market.

Brownfield land – urban land that has previously been developed, such as the site of a demolished building or factory.

Brownfield site – an *Inner-city Derelict* site which can be cleared and reused for new industry.

Buddhism – religion; belief that enlightenment will come through knowledge, especially self- knowledge, elimination of greed, craving and desire, complete honesty and never hurting another person or animal.

Buffer state – a small neutral state between two rival powers; a state that separates ideological and/or political adversaries (e.g., Afghanistan served as a buffer state separating British-controlled India and Tsarist Russia (later the Soviet Union) for much of the nineteenth and twentieth centuries).

Buffer zone – a set of countries that collectively serve as interrelated buffer states (e.g., Ukraine, Belarus, and Finland provide a buffer zone between Russia and NATO, although the entry of the three Baltic States into NATO creates a substantial *Gap*).

Bulge of young male migrants – on a population pyramid; young males move to urban areas due to push-pull factors.

Bulk (or weight) gaining industries – such industries add weight or bulk during the production process; finished commodities are heavier or bulkier than their constituent parts; typically located closer to markets than to their sources for *Components* because transportation costs are lower before manufacturing; contrast with *Bulk (or weight) reducing industries*.

Bulk (or weight) reducing industries – such industries remove weight or bulk during the production process; finished commodities are lighter and less bulky than their constituent parts; typically located closer to their sources for *Components* and raw materials than to their markets because transportation costs are less after manufacturing; contrast with *Bulk (or weight) gaining industries*.

Burgess model – an urban land use model showing five concentric zones, based upon the age of houses and the wealth of their inhabitants; see *Concentric ring model*.

Business parks – new offices built in pleasant surroundings on the edge of cities; mainly found on edge-of-*City* greenfield sites, although some are part of *Inner-city* redevelopment schemes; usually over 70% of the land is converted into ornamental gardens and lakes; ideal locations for high-tech industries such as electronics and research institutions.

By-pass – a road built around a busy urban area to avoid traffic jams.

By-products – what is left over after something is made (e.g., chemicals following the refining of oil); some by-products can be treated to make other products.

C

Cabotage – coastwise maritime trade that may or may not be reserved for national flag carriers.

Capital – wealth in the form of money or property owned by a person or business and human resources of economic value; value that is created from and reinvested in the production of commodities; capital may take different forms as production and exchange occurs and manifests itself as the ability to purchase (or invest in) machinery, raw materials, and labor.

Capitalism – a specific form of economic organization in which workers (those who produce things) are separated from the ownership of the means of production; in which labor is treated as merely another *Commodity* in the production process; value created by labor accrues not to the laborers, but to the owners of the means of production; see *Exchange value*, *Use-value* and *Marx*.

Capital intensive – an activity which requires much money.

Cardinal points – the four main points of the compass (N, S, E, W).

CBD – Central Business District or *City* center; the *Commercial* and business *center* of a town or city where land values are at the highest; the most *Accessible* part of the town or city; high land values lead to intensive use of the land and buildings are built as high as possible to maximize office space and rental income.

Census – a counting of people by the government every ten years to gather data for the planning of schools, hospitals, etc.; unreliable for a number of reasons.

Central place – any settlement that provides goods and services for smaller neighboring settlements.

Centralization – a process of concentrating increasing power in a central authority.

Central place theory – a normative theory devised by economic geographer Walter Christaller (1893-1963), among others; accounts for the size and *Distribution* of retailing *Functions* within urban places and their hinterlands by emphasizing the concepts of range and threshold.

Centrifugal forces – forces that act to divide a country's people into rival groups based on religious, ethnolinguistic, ideological or other differences.

Centripetal forces – forces that act to unite a country's people into a single nation based on religious, ethnolinguistic, ideological or other similarities.

Cheap labor – see *Overseas competition*.

Child dependency ratio – the number of children in relation to the number of working (economically active) population; usually expressed as a ratio.

Chokepoint – a narrow international waterway through which ships must pass to travel between larger bodies of water; may be natural, such as the Strait of Malacca and the Bab el-Mandeb, or artificial, such as the Panama Canal and the Suez Canal; the Cape of Good Hope is also viewed as a chokepoint between Africa and the stormy seas of the Southern Ocean.

Cholera – water- and feces-borne disease of the intestine; studies of the *Diffusion* of cholera have been important in the *Development* of both geographical and medical knowledge.

Christianity – **a** religion based on the life and teachings of Jesus.

Citizens – citizenship implies a particular relationship to government, one in which citizens have a voice in the affairs of their government; a highly contested ideal, in that while people of different classes, *Genders*, races or ethnicities may have won formal rights as citizens over time, they may nonetheless actually be excluded from effective citizenship through poverty, policies of discrimination or social processes of disempowerment (such as bigotry and sexism).

City – cities are urban *Places*; usually large (more than 20,000 people) and economically self- sufficient (unlike a large *Dormitory* or *Suburban town*).

City-state – a sovereign state compromising a *City* and its immediate hinterland.

Clan – a sub-tribal group, formed by families with close ancestral linkages.

Clean-up – a method of getting rid of pollution.

Cleavage model – devised by Liset and Rokkan; explains persistent regional patterns in voting behavior regarding tensions pitting the national *Core area* against *Peripheral* districts.

Clustered settlement pattern – a settlement where buildings are clustered around a particular point.

Cohort – population subgroups for a given region, country, civil division or another unit that are based on age and sex (e.g., females aged 20-24, males aged 25-29).

Colombo plan – Asian supranational organization; *Functions* as a review agency to coordinate bilateral and multilateral aid programs between donors and recipients.

Colonialism – the rule by a sovereign state over an alien people and land which involves formalized political and legal control; an asymmetrical economic relationship that favors the colonizer and a social system in which the colonizers dominate the colonized; compare with *Imperialism*.

Colonial period – the structure of world trade today had its origin in the colonial period when MEDCs used LEDCs as sources of raw materials for their *Factories*.

COMESA – the Common Market for Eastern and Southern Africa; a supranational organization devoted to building closer economic integration among 20 States in eastern and southern Africa.

Commercial – describes the business activities of trading and buying or selling goods.

Commercial agriculture – crop growing and livestock breeding is undertaken primarily to realize exchange value (rather than use value) in local, national or international competitive markets; contrast with *Subsistence agriculture*.

Commercial center – where business activities such as shops and services are concentrated.

Commodification – the process through which something is given monetary value.

Commodity – a thing or process that is produced to be bought and sold; its value is realized as exchange value, more so than use value.

Common market – a *Customs union* plus the free movement within the group of *Capital* and labor as well as goods.

Commonwealth of Independent States (CIS) – a supranational organization composed of former Soviet republics; the result of an attempt by the dying Soviet Union to preserve something of the former USSR; primary emphases are security and economic integration.

Communications – how people, goods and ideas move from one *Place* to another; usually refers to roads and railways.

Commuting – the process by which people are living in one *Place* travel to another place to work.

Compact – formal agreement or covenant (e.g., the Pacific Ocean Resources Compact facilitates cooperation among U.S. states of the Pacific Northwest as well as British Columbia in efforts to preserve valuable marine resources).

Compact state – a state in which the *Distance* from the center to any *Boundary* does not vary significantly (e.g., Cambodia, Poland, Zimbabwe).

Comparative advantage – economic concept suggesting that the people of a country or region benefit if they engage in economic activities that they can perform more efficiently than their neighbors and acquire through trade other goods and services that would be costlier for them to produce on their own.

Comparison goods/services – high-order (usually expensive) goods such as antiques, jewelry and some clothing and electrical equipment; so called because people like to compare prices, quality, and other features before buying them; usually sold in shops in *City* centers or large out-of-town shopping centers; people visit comparison shops only occasionally, so they need a large market area.

Components – parts of a product that are transported to a factory (plant) for final assembly (e.g., brakes, lights, wheels, glass, seals, etc. are all car components).

Comprehensive redevelopment – an area, usually in the *Inner city*, where the whole urban landscape was demolished before being rebuilt on a planned basis by the council or city government.

Concentrated population distribution – where people are grouped densely in an urbanized area; see *Port, Bridging-point, Route center, Wet point site, Market town, Mining town,* and *Resort.*

Concentric ring model – see *Burgess Model.*

Concentric zone model – a model of urban land use based on inferences from *Bid-rent curves*; suggests that different social groups and land uses sort themselves into a set of concentric rings around the peak land value intersection; see *Rent gap* and *Gentrification.*

Conciliation – a method of third-party intervention in which states' designated intermediaries consider the positions of the disputants and offer a compromise solution to the problem.

Condominium – a territory that is jointly administered by two or more states (e.g., Sudan, which was jointly administered by Britain and Egypt until it achieved independence in 1956).

Confederation – a political alliance or league; unlike a *Federal state*, the constituent members of the confederation possess greater political power than the central authority; Canada is still a confederation, although it *Functions* as a federation in many aspects.

Conference of Berlin – a meeting of 14 mostly-European countries on how to divide up Africa amongst themselves that disregarded African input or *Ethnic groups*.

Conflict resolution – the process whereby international governmental and non-governmental actors pursue peaceful solutions to conflicts (pacific settlement of disputes) among states and nations.

Confluence – where one river joins another.

Confluence town – a town that grows where two rivers meet.

Confucianism – a philosophy of ethics, education and public service based on the writings of Confucius.

Congestion – overcrowding on roads causing traffic jams.

Connectivity – the degree of connection or separation between people, *Places,* and things.

Conquest – the seizure of territory by military force.

Consequent boundary – a *Subsequent boundary* that is created to accommodate a region's cultural diversity.

Conservation – the protection of the *Environment*.

Conservationist – people who care for and look after the *Environment*.

Consumer – people who buy products or services; as trade in goods and services increases, the power of the consumer increases; industries must create what people want (or think they need).

Consumption – the use of a thing or process; the geography of consumption is an effort to understand how resources and commodities are used, how they are distributed and how that use and *Distribution* is geographically uneven; studies of consumption often rely on such concepts as *Cultural hegemony* to understand why consumption is uneven and to understand who has power in consumption systems; studies of consumption also often focus on the symbolic qualities that commodities possess.

Contagious diffusion – a form of *Expansion diffusion* in which an innovation (or another phenomenon) spreads across contiguous space after direct contact between the innovator(s) and the potential adopters of innovation (or another phenomenon); contrast with *Hierarchical diffusion*.

Containerization – goods being packed into large metal boxes for transport by road and/or sea.

Continent – a large area of land; there are seven continents: North and South America, Asia, Europe, Africa, Australia, and Antarctica.

Continental shelf – the portion of continental landmasses lying in relatively shallow water (normally less than 660 feet) between the coastline and the continental slope; the continental slope marks the point where the seafloor plunges to the much greater depths of the mid-oceanic (abyssal) plains.

Contiguous zone – a zone extending 24 nautical miles from the baseline used to establish the territorial sea; in the zone beyond the territorial sea (12-24nm), states may exercise jurisdiction in customs, fiscal, health, and immigration matters, but do not have the same rights as in the territorial sea.

Contour – a line drawn on a map connecting *Places* of the same height above sea-level.

Contraception – using birth control to prevent pregnancy.

Conurbation – a large urban settlement which is the result of towns and cities spreading out and merging.

Convention – a multilateral treaty among three or more states or other entities.

Conventional warfare – armed conflict between states and/or nations in which combatants appear in organized military units that are often outfitted with standard uniforms, weapons and equipment; typically involves major combat operations that overtly seize control of territory, inhabitants, and resources.

Convenience goods/services – low/order goods; inexpensive things that vary little in price, quality or other features that are bought regularly (e.g., newspapers, cigarettes, bread); convenience shops are found on most street corners where they have a small market area of people who visit the shop on most days.

Core / periphery / semi-periphery – the idea that the core houses the main economic power of the region and the outlying region and the periphery houses lesser economic power with the semi-periphery in-between the two.

Core area – the nucleus of a state or other political unit; its central, essential, enduring heart; may be ancient or relatively new but generally supports a large share of a state's population, may be focused on a particular *City* and contain important agricultural, industrial, political, social, transportation and other systems.

Core region – an area at the heart of *Economic activity*; a well-off industrial region of a country (e.g., South East England); see *Industrial development certificates*, *Cumulative causation*, *Multiplier effect,* and *Agglomeration Economies*.

Corner shop – a shop typical of the *Inner-city* zone (but also common in all zones except the CBD) found on every street corner that sells a range of every-day needs; see *Convenience goods* and *Low-order goods/services*.

Council of Europe – a supranational organization, composed of virtually all of the countries of Europe; primarily a consultative body.

Counter-urbanization – the movement of people from the MEDC cities to the countryside seeking a better quality of life; many still commute into the *City* to work, but increasing numbers are moving to completely change their lifestyle and work in the rural area, often by *Teleworking*; see *De-urbanization* and *Urban-rural shift*.

County – a common civil division in various parts of the world; a second-order civil division in the United States.

Creole – a language that began as a pidgin language but was later adopted as the mother tongue by a people in place of the mother tongue.

Critical – given to careful, precise judgments; precise analysis.

Critical geopolitics – the view that geopolitics should take a broader perspective than that provided by orthodox geopolitics; taking into account alternative viewpoints reflecting the complexity of geopolitical interactions throughout the world.

Cross-section – a diagram showing by means of a side view the slopes and heights of the land surface.

Crude Birth Rate (CBR) – the annual number of live births per 1,000 population in a given area.

Crude Death Rate (CDR) – the annual number of deaths per 1,000 population in a given area.

Cultural boundaries – *Boundaries* that are based on *Culture* traits.

Cultural adaptation – adjusting to a translation based on the cultural *Environment* of the target language.

Cultural appropriation – the process by which cultures adopt customs and knowledge from other cultures and use them for their benefit.

Cultural convergence – continuing contact and interaction between one *Culture* and another that results in both becoming more similar.

Cultural divergence – the separation of cultures through less and less contact and interaction between them; restriction of a *Culture* from outside influences.

Cultural diffusion – the spread of *Culture*.

Cultural landscape – the *Environment* as humans alter it via the construction of built forms; see *Landscape*; contrast with the *Natural landscape*.

Cultural hegemony – a phenomenon in which one group seems to willingly submit to the political, social and cultural practices of another, more dominant group, fostering the acceptance of inequality as "natural;" almost always contested in one way or another, even if only subtly; used to describe processes as diverse as the perpetuation of racism or patriarchy in the U.S. and the aggressive export of European or American *Popular culture* to other countries.

Cultural identity – the way people categorize their culture, sometimes by the way they dress and what they eat.

Cultural imperialism – seeks to influence peoples' behavior rather than establish direct military control (e.g., French efforts at *Assimilation* of colonial peoples and communist propaganda during the twentieth century).

Cultural integration – the process of combining cultures into one.

Cultural regions – a portion of the earth's surface occupied by a population sharing recognizable and distinctive cultural characteristics.

Cultural shatter belt – an area of instability between regions with opposing political and cultural values.

Cultural pluralism – the manner in which two or more population groups, each practicing its own culture, may live adjacent to one another without mixing inside a single state.

Cultural-political boundary – a *Boundary* that is delineated based on the pattern of settlements of different cultural groups.

Cultural realm – the entire region that displays the characteristics of a culture.

Culture – an abstract concept that refers to 1) the "total way of life" of a group of people; or 2) to a system of signification (i.e., signs, symbols) that gives meaning to people; or 3) to the works of art, music, literature, etc. of a people; or 4) to that which is not nature.

Culture complex – a unique combination of *Culture* traits for a particular culture group.

Culture hearth – **an** area where innovations in *Culture* initially began and from where such cultural elements spread.

Culture realm – a cluster of regions in which related *Culture* systems prevail.

Culture region – a region within which common *Culture* characteristics prevail.

Culture trait – a single piece of a culture's traditions and practices.

Culture system – **a** collection of *Culture complexes* that shapes a group's common identity.

Cumulative causation – the process by which one region of a country increasingly becomes the center of *Economic activity*; see *Agglomeration economies* and *Multiplier effect*.

Customs union – a *Free trade area* plus a common external tariff; members trade freely among themselves and also form a single unit for trading with nonmembers; customs duties are commonly pooled and used either for common purposes or apportioned among the members.

Cyberspace – the intangible space created through electronic communication, especially on the Internet or other computer networks.

Cycle of decline (deprivation) – as traditional industries close, job losses lead to less money in the area, with a domino effect on other businesses such as suppliers, shops, etc.; more businesses are forced to close, and the problem becomes worse and worse; the ablest workers move away to other areas; the area becomes more run-down with high crime, vandalism, etc. and an *Ageing population*.

Cycle of deprivation – a sequence of events experienced by disadvantaged people in which one problem (e.g., lack of work) leads to other problems and so makes things worse.

D

Death rate – the number of people dying per 1,000 of the population.

Decentralization – 1) the process whereby states or other political entities devolve more power to lower-order civil divisions; 2) the movement of shops, offices, and industry away from urban centers in MEDCs and NICs into retail and *Business parks* in the suburbs.

Declining region – one where traditional heavy industries are closing down leading to high unemployment and out-migration (e.g., South Wales); see *Deindustrialization* and *Cycle of decline*.

Decolonization – whereby previously colonized territories obtain independence from imperial rule.

Defensive site – a *Place* where a settlement can be easily defended against attack, such as on a hilltop or surrounded by water.

Definition phase in boundary creation – the first stage in *Boundary making* in which the exact location of a *Boundary* is legally described and negotiated.

Definitional boundary dispute – arises when parties disagree over the interpretation of the language used to define the *Boundary*.

Deindustrialization – the sustained and cumulative diminishment of the importance of industry (especially manufacturing) in the economy of a particular *Place* caused by declining profits and changes in local and global economic conditions; associated with the systematic decline of a place or region as a center of mass-production and assembly-line manufacture; sometimes refers to the actual process of closing down a particular factory and throwing people out of work; contrast with *Industrialization*; see *Post-Fordism*.

Deforestation – the clearing and destruction of forests, especially tropical rainforests, to make way for expanding settlement *Frontiers* and the exploitation of new economic opportunities.

Delimitation phase in boundary creation – the translation of the written terms of a *Boundary* treaty into an official cartographic representation.

Delta – a flat area of deposited river silt found at the mouth of a river.

Demand – the willingness and ability of consumers to pay for a particular good or service; as long as the supply of goods and services meets the demand, prices remain the same (stable).

Demarcation phase in boundary creation – phase in which the *Boundary* is visibly marked on the landscape by a fence, line, sign, wall or other means.

Demographic collapse – a rapid, devastating decline in population, as happened to Native Americans when Europeans brought disease, differing economies and new forms of warfare to the "New World" after 1492.

Demographic transition – the change from high *Birth rates* and *Death rates* to low birth rates and death rates.

Demographic transition model – diagram which shows the relationship between birth and *Death rates* and how changes in these affect the total population.

Demography – the study of population dynamics; demographers examine *Birth rates*, changing birth patterns, migration and changing patterns of death (among other things); undergirded by the study of changing economic, political, social and cultural processes that explain changes in population dynamics.

Densely populated – an area that is crowded.

Density – a measure of how close together people live in an area.

Dependency ratio – the ratio between those of working age and those of non-working age. This is calculated as:

$$\frac{\%\ \text{pop aged } 0-14 + \%\ \text{pop aged } 65+}{\%\ \text{of population aged } 15-65} \times 100$$

Dependency theory – a model of economic and social *Development* that explains global inequality regarding the historical exploitation of poor nations by rich ones.

Dependent person – either a dependent child or a person with a long-term sickness preventing them from working.

Dependent population – those who rely on the working population for support (e.g., the young and the elderly).

Depopulation – the decline or reduction of population in an area.

Deposition – the laying down of material carried by rivers, sea, ice or wind.

Deposition landforms – landscape features made up of material that has been deposited by rivers, sea, ice or wind.

Deprivation – the degree to which an individual or an area is deprived of services and *Amenities*; there are many different types and levels of deprivation, including poor and overcrowded housing, inadequate diet, inadequate income and lack of opportunity for employment.

Derelict land – wasteland with decaying houses and closed-down industry; typical of *Inner-city* areas in MEDCs.

Derelict – abandoned buildings and wasteland.

Desertification – the process of desert expansion into neighboring steppes as a result of human degradation of fragile semi-arid *Environments*.

Detached house – a house standing alone (not joined to another); typical of the wealthy suburb zone of a *City*; see *Burgess*.

De-urbanization – the process in MEDCs by which an increasingly smaller percentage of a country's population lives in towns and cities, brought about by urban-to-rural migration; see *Counter-urbanization* and *Urban-rural shift*.

Development – the process by which a society goes about realizing its potential; contrast *Underdevelopment*; see *See-saw motion of capital* and *Uneven development*.

Development areas – areas of high unemployment in the UK; the government tries to encourage industries to move to these areas by offering incentives, such as labor subsidies, purpose-built, rent-free factory sites, tax-free periods of up to 10 years, grants for machinery and equipment, excellent *Communications* (freeway) and retraining schemes to provide a skilled workforce.

Devolution – in which a region receives greater autonomy from the central government; may be initiated by the central government as a means toward *Decentralization* or demanded by a region's inhabitants desiring local rule; such processes may be peaceful or accompanied by violence.

Dialect – local or regional characteristics of a language.

Diaspora – a forced scattering or dispersion of a people (e.g., the Romans forced the Jews into a diaspora following a failed uprising in the first century C. E.).

Diffusion – the spread of a *Culture* element or some other phenomena.

Disability – according to the social model of disability, the disadvantage a person faces because of an impairment.

Dispersed population distribution – the opposite of a concentrated *Distribution*; the population may be spread evenly over a *Fertile* farming area rather than concentrated in an urban center; tends to be of low *Density*.

Dispersed settlement pattern – where buildings in a settlement are not clustered around a particular point but are scattered randomly; see *Linear settlement* and *Nucleated settlement pattern*.

Distance – the degree of spatial separation between *Places*; may be absolute, such as an inch or a mile, or relative, such as travel time or perceptual distance.

Distribution – the frequency or occurrence of something.

Distribution (of a population) – where people are found and where they are not found.

Divided capital – a capital *City* that shares typical *Functions* with other cities in the state (e.g., La Paz and Sucre in Bolivia and Bloemfontein, Cape Town and Pretoria in South Africa).

Division of labor – the ways in which tasks are divided among workers; geographers are particularly interested in spatial divisions of labor; in general, divisions of labor can be seen at the global scale (as between first and third world countries), the mesoscale (as between minority and majority cultures in a region) or the micro-scale (as between management and assembly workers, or between different workers in a factory assigned different tasks).

Dominance behavior – the tendency for dominant cultural groups to settle in the most desirable regions, creating identifiable spatial patterns across states and regions.

Domino theory – a theory promoted during the Cold War; suggested that the fall of any state to communist forces would automatically lead to pressure and the eventual fall of neighboring countries; although widely discredited, the concept remains a subject of discussion, most recently regarding the potential for Islamic extremism to bring about the fall of governments in the Islamic world.

Dormitory settlement – one where many commuters "sleep" overnight but travel to work elsewhere during the day.

Doubling time – the time it takes a population to double in size from any given numerical point.

Dowry death – in the context of arranged marriages in India, disputes over the price to be paid by the family of the bride to the father of the groom (the dowry) have, in some cases, led to the death of the bride.

Drought – a long spell of dry weather resulting in a serious water shortage.

Dry-point site – a settlement site on dry land surrounded by low, wet ground; good for defense.

E

Earthquake – a movement or tremor of the Earth's surface.

Ecology – the study of the mutual relations between organisms and their *Environment*.

Economics – the production and management of material wealth; geographers are especially interested in the spatial aspects of economic systems, including patterns of production, *Distribution*, and *Consumption* and in how differing economic processes work in and through *Places* and spaces.

Economic activity – industry, jobs, earning a living and producing wealth.

Economic base – a wide economic base is typical of MEDCs where many industries contribute to generating wealth; a narrow economic base is typical of LEDCs where only a few industries contribute.

Economic development – the generating of wealth through the *Development* of industry.

Economic imperialism – a variety of imperialism that does not rely on military conquest; instead, it seeks to make a country dependent on an imperial state through a variety of economic means.

Economic infrastructure – transport networks (e.g., gas, electricity, water grids, sewage systems).

Economic migrant – person leaving their native country to seek better economic opportunities (jobs) and settle temporarily in another country.

Economic union – complete economic integration that goes beyond a common market; members share common economic and banking policies, use a common currency and establish common systems for banking, insurance, taxes, corporate regulations and so on.

Economies of scale – savings made as a result of large-scale production through buying in bulk, *Division of labor*, etc.

ECOWAS – the Economic Community of West African States; the primary supranational organization for economic integration in West Africa.

Ecumene – derived from the Greek word *oikoumene,* meaning the inhabited world; used to refer to the habitable portions of the Earth's surface where permanent human settlements have arisen; states consider their ecumene to be the portion of their territory that contributes to its economic viability and where the government *Functions* effectively.

Edge city – a satellite *City* typically found near the *Periphery* of a large metropolitan area; often beginning as suburban communities, they serve as magnets for businesses seeking to escape the high cost of operating in the metropolitan area.

Electoral geography – a subfield of political geography that studies the spatial patterns of voting and representation; includes the organization of campaigns, the conduct of the election itself and the results of the election.

Electronic ghetto – Mike Davis uses this term to describe areas of cities structurally excluded from the so-called "information revolution;" the *Places* that have little or no access to computer networks, high-quality fiber optic phone lines, etc.; compare with *Information city*.

Elongated state – a state whose territory is long and narrow in shape (e.g., Chile).

Embargo – a form of economic sanction that prohibits some or all imports from a country, group of countries or region; its counterpart is a *Boycott*.

Emigrant – someone who leaves an area to live elsewhere.

Emigration – movement out of a *Place*; compare with *Immigration*.

Empire – a political entity that groups many regions or peoples under one supreme ruling group.

Employment structure – see the *Occupational structure*.

Enclave – a territory whose geographical boundaries lie entirely within the boundaries of another territory (e.g., Lesotho is an independent country that is an enclave within South Africa); see *Exclave*.

Energy – the power to do something; to give off heat.

Enfranchisement – to admit to citizenship; the right to vote.

Enterprise zones – small, run-down *Inner-city* areas and other areas of industrial decline with high unemployment in the UK where financial incentives are available to encourage investment and renewal; the government gives tax concessions to firms, grants for buildings and machinery, removes various planning restrictions and improves *Communications* and infrastructure (e.g., *London Docklands*).

Entrepôt – a *Place*, usually a port *City*, where goods are imported, stored and transshipped; a break-of-bulk point.

Environment – the natural or physical surroundings where people, plants, and animals live.

Environmental determinism – the idea that the Physical Environment controls human behavior.

Era of bipolarity – a name given to the Cold War era to indicate that the geopolitical system was dominated by a "tug-of-war" between two, fairly-equally matched "superpowers;" states in the global system were attracted to (or forced to) one or the other of these two poles like iron to a magnet.

Erosion – the wearing away and removal of rock, soil, etc. by rivers, sea, ice, and wind.

Erosion landforms – landscape features resulting from the wearing away of rock.

Ethnic cleansing – the systematic killing or extermination of an entire people or nation; a term used in the former Yugoslavia whereby dominant *Ethnic groups* "cleansed" their communities of minorities by expulsion or genocide.

Ethnic conflict – a struggle caused by ethnicities interacting.

Ethnic conclave – a gathering of an *Ethnic group*.

Ethnic group – a group which is defined by race, religion, nationality or culture.

Ethnic homeland – a sizable area inhabited by an ethnic majority that exhibits a strong sense of attachment to the region.

Ethnic nationalism – whereby people feel a sense of oneness based on *Ethnicity*, frequently due to a common language.

Ethnic neighborhood – a neighborhood, typically situated in a larger metropolitan *City* and constructed by or comprised of a local *Culture*, in which a local culture can practice its customs.

Ethnic religion – a religion that is particular to one culturally distinct group of people.

Ethnicity – the real or perceived commonalities within a group of people that differentiates it from other groups.

Ethnocentrism – conviction of the evident superiority of one's *Ethnic group*.

European Communities (EC) – the forerunner of the *European Union*; established in 1967 with the merger of the European Coal and Steel Community, European Economic Community and Euratom (the European Atomic Energy Community).

European Free Trade Association (EFTA) – This is the supranational organization that was established in 1960 as an alternative to the European Economic Community. Many of its former members are now part of the EU.

European Union (EU) – one of the world's most advanced supranational organizations; composed of 25 European states that share common economic interests and are slowly moving toward greater political cooperation; four additional states, including Turkey, are candidates for future membership.

Exchange-value – the value of a *Commodity* realized when that commodity is exchanged for other commodities (including money); compare with *Use-value*.

Exclave – a bounded (non-island) portion of territory that is part of a larger state but is non-contiguous (physically separated) (e.g., Cabinda (Angola), Kaliningrad (Russia), Ocussi (Timor-Leste)); see *Enclave*.

Exclusive economic zone (EEZ) – a zone extending seaward from the territorial sea to a maximum *Distance* of 200 nautical miles from a coastal state's baselines; the coastal state enjoys sovereign rights to the living and non-living resources of the seabed, subsoil, and superjacent waters.

Expansion diffusion – a form of *Diffusion* in which the cultural component spreads outward to new *Places* while remaining strong in its original hearth; contrast with *Relocation diffusion*.

Exports – goods sold abroad.

Extensive agriculture – crop or livestock growing which involves relatively large amounts of land and relatively small amounts of labor (or other *Energy*); contrast with *Intensive agriculture*.

Extinct – no longer be found living on the planet.

Extraterritoriality – suggests that the property of one state that lies within the *Boundaries* of another actually forms an extension of the first state; in modern times, the idea is associated with embassies and consulates as well as international law applying to diplomatic personnel; embassies and consulates can, therefore, be viewed as micro-scale examples of *Enclaves* and *Exclaves*; during the latter stages of the colonial era, the major imperial powers went so far as to exercise civil and criminal jurisdiction in dominated countries such as China and Morocco.

F

Facilities – services that are people feel are essential, such as toilets, heating, telephones, etc.; see *Amenities*.

Factories – *Places* where things are made from natural resources and raw materials.

Family life cycle model – based on the movements of people within a *City* seeking a better home as their circumstances (both financial and social) change over time.

Family planning – using *Contraception* to control the size of your family.

Family status – a person's family status reflects age, whether or not the person is married and whether or not the person has children.

Family ties – the lack of family ties (no wife or children) encourages young males to migrate from LEDCs to MEDCs or from rural to urban areas to seek a better life; the young (20-35) are also best-suited physically to heavy unskilled/semi-skilled work; see *Guest-worker*.

Fast world – a term that describes those *Places* exhibiting a high degree of *Connectivity* with other places and which are marked by good telecommunications service, a high degree of inward investment and ease of transportation to the rest of the world; contrast with the *Slow world*.

Favela – a Brazilian term for an informal, shanty-type settlement; see *Barrio*.

Federal state – a state that utilizes a central government to represent the common interests of all its civil divisions, but which allows those civil divisions substantial freedom to manage their local affairs; see *Confederation*.

Feedback – the reinvestment of some of the profits into new inputs within the factory system.

Fertile – land or soil where crops can be grown successfully.

Fertile age group – the childbearing years of women, normally 18-45 years of age.

Feudalism – a pre-capitalist system of rule in which a hierarchy of ruling classes distributed land to subordinates in return for various rents and services; local peasants remained tied to the land and worked as serfs under the direction of the lords.

Filtering – the process whereby middle- and upper-income groups leave their houses and move to more expensive ones, decreasing the value of real estate in their old neighborhoods and making the houses available to lower income groups; the assumption that the filtering process operates efficiently in the U.S. is a major tenet of American housing policy; also important for understanding the *Concentric zone model*; contrast with *Gentrification*; see *Social leapfrogging*.

First-order civil division – the highest level of civil division short of the state (e.g., the state in the United States, the province in Canada).

Fixed industry – one which is tied to a particular location.

Floodplain – the flat area at the bottom of a valley which is often flooded.

Food mountains and lakes – surplus supplies of farm products that are stored.

Folk culture – cultural traits such as dress modes, dwellings, traditions and institutions of usually small, traditional communities.

Folklore – consists of legends, music, oral history, proverbs, jokes, popular beliefs and customs that are the traditions of that culture, subculture or group.

Folkways – any informal norms, virtues or values characterized by being followed through imitation and mild social pressure but not strictly enforced or put into law.

Footloose industries – those industries which are free to locate almost anywhere; economic activities not bound by site factors to locate in any particular *Place*; economic activities (even including *Agriculture*) are becoming increasingly footloose as transportation and communication costs fall.

Forced Migration – a migration that occurs involuntarily due to war, famine, oppression or other factors not under the control of individuals; almost always a result of push factors; see *Voluntary migration*.

Ford – a crossing where the river is shallow.

Fordism – a system of manufacturing named after Henry Ford that involves large-scale mass-production of commodities for national and global markets, detailed *Division of labor*, de-skilling of workers and repetitive tasks; in the U.S., an "era of Fordism" can be recognized from roughly the turn of the twentieth century until the mid-1970s; often associated with industrialization, with firms showing high degrees of vertical integration; many analysts argue that since the 1970s the U.S. has entered an era of *Post-Fordism*.

Formal employment – where people work to receive a regular wage and are assured certain rights (e.g., paid holidays, sick leave) and wages are taxed.

Formal region – a region delineated by one or more identifiable trait which sets it apart from other regions (e.g., a region defined by language or *Dialect*); compare with *Functional region* and *Perceptual region*.

Formal sector – the employment sector comprising "proper" jobs that are usually permanent, with set hours of work, agreed on levels of pay and sometimes pensions and social security rights.

Forward capital – an introduced capital that is created by a state to spur *Economic development* in relatively underdeveloped regions or to assert political control in a contested region (e.g., Brasília, Islamabad).

Fossil fuels – fuels from the remains of plants or ancient life.

Fragmented state – a state that is composed of two or more non-contiguous segments; segments may be islands, such as the Philippines, a mix of islands and mainland territory, such as Malaysia, or separate portions of mainland territory, such as Angola and Cabinda; in the last case, the smaller segment also qualifies as an *Exclave*.

Forward-thrust capital – a capital *City* deliberately sited in a state's *Frontier* zone.

Free city – a special class of international territory in which a separate regime is established for a disputed *City* and its hinterland, creating city-states that lack sovereignty (e.g., Tangier, which was jointly ruled by Britain and France for three decades before its return to Morocco in 1956).

Free Trade Agreement of the Americas (FTAA) – supranational arrangement that sought to eliminate all trade *Barriers* among all the countries in the Americas from Point Barrow to Tierra del Fuego; Cuba was the only potential member that was excluded from the agreement; the committee missed the deadline for the FTAA to become official on December 2005, and it has not been revived since.

Free trade area – an economic arrangement in which two or more countries agree to eliminate tariffs and other *Barriers* to trade between or among them so that goods flow freely across their mutual *Boundaries*.

Frontier – a zone separating two states in which neither state exercises political control (e.g., Brazil's vast Amazonian region, which has only been partially integrated into the *Ecumene*).

Frontier (border) – the *Boundary* around a country.

Functional boundary dispute – disagreement between neighboring states over policies to be applied to their common border; often induced by differing customs regulations, movement of nomadic groups or illegal immigration or *Emigration*.

Functional region – delineated by a process or processes occurring in it; has a central node around which processes are organized and into and out of which all processes flow (e.g., a newspaper delivery area delineates a functional region as all editorial information flows into a node (the editorial and publication offices in a *City*) and newspapers flow out to the surrounding hinterland); compare with *Formal region* and *Perceptual region*.

Functional (nodal) region – a group of *Places* linked together by some *Function's* influence on them.

Function of a settlement – what the settlement does to "earn its living" (e.g., market town, mining town, administrative center, tourist resort, etc.).

Function – the reason for something to be somewhere; its use or purpose such as a port, market, industry or tourism.

Fundamentalism – the interpretation of every word in a sacred text as literal truth.

Fundamentalist – one who subscribes to a traditional or literal interpretation of religious texts, sometimes, but not always, promoting it as part of religion-based political activism.

G

Gap – a low point along a line of hills or mountains through which roads and railways can pass through.

Gap town – a town located at a *Gap* between hills, providing a good *Defensive site* and route center that led to a trade and market *Function*.

Gateway region – a concept developed by Saul Cohen that certain transitional zones offer a geopolitical mechanism for restoring the balance between continental and maritime powers (e.g., Eastern Europe).

GATT – the General Agreement on Tariffs and Trade; a post-World War II network of rules and over 200 bilateral trade agreements; the forerunner of the World Trade Organization (WTO).

Gender – social differences between men and women, rather than the anatomical, biological differences between the sexes.

Gender gap – a measurable difference between the behaviors of men and women.

Genetic boundary types – classification of *Boundaries* based on when they were established in relation to the region's settlement history.

Genotype – the genetic make-up of an organism, as opposed to that organism's physical; contrast with *Phenotype*.

Gentrification – a process whereby lower-income housing (or other buildings) are renovated for middle- and upper-income people and businesses; the displacing of lower-income people through eviction, rising real estate values or increased taxes; contrast with *Filtering*.

Geoeconomic power – global power based on economic rather than political or military might; many commentators suggest that after the *"Era of bipolarity"* geo-economic power will be more important than geopolitical power in determining the *Functioning* of the global system; see *Geopolitics*.

Geographic information systems – a computer program that stores geographic data and produces maps to show those data.

Geographic structure – often called "spatial structure;" refers to the modes in which space is organized in any given society.

Geography – literally, "earth-writing," or earth-describing; most broadly, the study of the changing nature of the Earth's surface and the humans, plants, and animals that live on it; see *Social reproduction*.

Geomancy (feng shui) – the Chinese art and science of the placement and orientation of tombs, dwellings, buildings, and cities.

Geometric boundaries – *Boundaries* of convenience drawn along the lines of latitude or longitude without consideration for cultural or ethnic differences in an area.

Geopolitical theory – the theory that states are equivalent to living organisms in their hunger for land and, like organisms, want to grow larger by acquiring more nourishment in the form of land.

Geopolitics – the study of states in the context of global-spatial phenomena and the attempt to understand both the bases of state power and the nature of states' interactions with one another.

Geopolitik – a distorted version of geopolitics created during the interwar period and used to justify Nazi expansionism based on the quest for *Lebensraum*.

Geostationary orbit – a geosynchronous orbit that allows a satellite to remain constantly above a particular point along the equator; satellites must remain at an altitude of approximately 35,787 kilometers to maintain such an orbit.

Geostrategy – a geopolitical approach that focuses on global patterns of state *Development* rather than linkages between individual states; many of its proponents served in the military and were interested in geopolitical issues such as sea power, air defense networks and the balance of power between Cold War adversaries.

Geosynchronous – an orbit in which a satellite completes a revolution about the planet in the same period as the Earth rotates on its axis.

Gerrymandering – the redrawing of electoral district *Boundaries* to produce unusual, convoluted shapes designed to favor a particular political party or group.

Ghetto – a forced or voluntarily segregated residential area housing a racial, ethnic or religious minority; the term comes from the district of Geto in medieval Venice, which was reserved for Jews

Global commons – parts of the *Environment* available to everyone but for which no single individual has responsibility (e.g., atmosphere, fresh water, forests, wildlife, ocean fisheries).

Global economy – industrial location is no longer linked to one specific country; choices of location are global and depend on strategies to sell the maximum number of products with the lowest costs possible; see *Overseas competition*.

Global-local continuum – the notion that what happens at the global scale has a direct effect on what happens at the local scale and vice-versa.

Global warming – a general warming trend around the world that is believed to be the result of human impacts rather than natural climatic fluctuations.

Globalization – the increasing interconnection of *Places* culturally and economically as the result of changes in the location of production (the new international *Division of labor*), the emergence of global markets, new *Communications* and transportation technologies, and the growth of homogenous *Consumer* markets spanning the globe; trend where people are becoming more interconnected and interdependent.

Good offices – the simplest form of third-party participation provided by a state assisting with conflict resolution; the state expedites *Bilateral negotiations* by performing such services for the disputants as providing a neutral site for the negotiations, supplying interpreters, office space, secretarial services and the like, transmitting messages between the parties, doing basic research and providing factual information to the parties and working to maintain a relaxed atmosphere conducive to successful negotiations.

Goods – things made by people to sell in a market.

Government disincentives (controls) – include *Greenbelt* and *Industrial development certificates*.

Government incentives – include *Grants*, *Labor subsidies*, *Tax-free periods*, *Rent-free periods*, *Removal of planning controls*, improvements in *Infrastructure* and *Communications*, *Purpose-built factories*, *Greenfield sites*, worker *Retraining* schemes, and *New towns*.

Government policy – aims at attracting labor-intensive industries (e.g., assembly plants) to areas of high unemployment; the UK has been called "Taiwan of Europe," with Japanese transnational corporations locating their branch plants in areas with the cheapest labor, taking advantage of government grants; see *Government disincentives* and *Government incentives*.

Gradient – the slope of the land.

Grants – money paid to an industry towards the cost of new machinery, training, etc.; given in *Development areas* to attract new industry.

Greenbelt – an area around a *City*, composed mostly of parkland and farmland, in which *Development* is strictly controlled; prevents the outward growth of the city, preserves countryside for farming, wildlife and recreation and often prevents two or more cities from merging to form one huge urban area.

Greenfield land – a term used to describe a piece of undeveloped rural land, either currently used for *Agriculture* or just left to nature.

Greenfield site – an industrial site often located on the edge of town, previously used for farming or other rural activity.

Greenhouse effect – a condition whereby carbon dioxide, methane, ozone and other "greenhouse gases" in the atmosphere insulate the lower levels of the atmosphere, reducing the amount of thermal *Energy* that radiates into outer space; without it, Earth would have an average temperature below freezing; excessive amounts, however, contribute to global warming.

Grid – a grid is a pattern of squares on a map which serves to fix your position; coordinates will provide numbers that allow you to find a horizontal line and also a vertical line and follow them to the point of intersection, placing you at the bottom left-hand corner (southwest) of a particular grid.

Grid references – any location in the United Kingdom can be described in terms of its *Distance* from the origin (0,0), which lies to the west of the Isles of Scilly; always presented in terms of "eastings" (distance east from the origin) and "northings" (distance north from the origin); increasing easting numbers indicate you are heading east; decreasing indicates you are heading west; increasing northing numbers indicate you are heading north; decreasing indicates you are heading south.

Gross Domestic Product (GDP) – the annual total value of all goods and services produced by a country in a year (but not including income from overseas); contrast with *Gross National Product*.

Gross National Product (GNP) – the annual total value of all goods and services produced in a country, plus income received from overseas; contrast with *Gross Domestic Product*.

Gross National Product (GNP) per capita – the total value of goods produced and services provided by a country in a year, divided by the total number of people living in that country.

Group of Three – also known as the G-3; a supranational organization composed of Colombia, Venezuela, and México that formed a free trade zone and is working to abolish internal tariffs.

Group of 77 – named for the original 75 developing countries (plus two that joined later) that were instrumental in establishing *UNCTAD* in 1964; now has 134 members and lobbies for improved economic conditions in the developing world.

Growth rate – in the study of population, the annual percentage rate at which population grows; also called the rate of natural increase because this statistic excludes migration.

Guerrilla warfare – a method of waging war in which small, irregular units rely on mobility and surprise to conduct hit-and-run attacks against often numerically superior adversaries; they typically suffer from shortages of weapons and supplies and often lack uniforms or opt for civilian clothing which allows them to hide within the general population.

Guest-worker migration – people leaving their country to work in another land but not to settle; associated with unskilled/semi-skilled labor.

H

Hajj – the Muslim *Pilgrimage* to Mecca, the birthplace of Muhammad.

Hague Court of Arbitration – officially known as the Permanent Court of Arbitration; established in 1899 as part of the Convention for the Pacific Settlement of International Disputes; provided the first mechanism for the peaceful resolution of disputes between states and remains one of the most important international judicial bodies.

Headlink – the focal region, often the capital, from which *Development* progresses linearly, like links in a chain; the primary link in the development chain.

Heartland – the Eurasian *Core area* that Halford Mackinder cited as a pivotal area where a large land-based power could emerge that was protected from rival maritime powers; whoever controlled the Heartland would eventually control the world.

Heavy industry – one with heavy/bulky raw materials and heavy/bulky finished products (e.g., iron, steel); tend to be very polluting.

Hectare – an area equivalent to 2.471 acres.

Heuristic – a device for teaching that aids or guides discovery; does not answer a question but rather helps create a means for answering a question.

Hierarchy – a ranking of settlements or shopping centers according to their population size or the number of services they provide.

Hierarchical diffusion – a form of *Expansion diffusion* in which an innovation (or another phenomenon) spreads over space from large *Places* to progressively smaller ones, skipping the spaces in between; contrast with *Contagious diffusion*.

High birth rate – many babies born for each 1,000 of the population.

High-order goods/services – a good or service, usually expensive, that people buy only occasionally (e.g., furniture, computers, jewelry); usually located in larger towns and cities with a large market area and are *Accessible* to large numbers of people.

High seas – all of the Earth's waters that are not classified as internal waters, territorial seas, contiguous zones, *Exclusive economic zones* or *Archipelagic waters*.

High-tech agglomerations – by locating near each other, high-tech firms can exchange ideas and information, share training services and *Amenities* such as calibration laboratories and research *Facilities* and have access to a pool of highly-skilled labor; see *Business Parks*.

High-tech industries – industries using advanced machines and skilled people (e.g., computers and electronics).

Hinduism – religion; unique in that it does not have a single founder, a single theology or agreement on its origins.

Hinterland – a region or market area composed of smaller towns and rural areas surrounding an urban center or *Core area*; the area surrounding a node or center (such as a *City*) and influenced by it; the area served by a port (its *Sphere of influence*). Singapore is one of the best contemporary examples.

Historic sites – important old settlements and buildings which are interesting to people.

Homelessness – the condition of being without a home.

Household – a person living alone or a group of people, not necessarily related, living at the same address with shared housekeeping; shared housekeeping involves sharing at least one meal a day or sharing a living room or sitting room.

Hoyt model – an urban land use model showing wedges (sectors) based upon main transport routes and social groupings.

Human development index – a social welfare index, adopted by the United Nations as a measure of *Development*, based upon life expectancy (health), adult literacy (education) and real GNP per capita (economic).

Human and economic location factors – include labor supply, *Capital* (money), markets, transport, government policy, *Economies of scale*, improved technology, recreation/*Environment*.

Human features/activities – the actions and results of humans, especially where and how people live.

Human geography – a branch of geography that focuses on the study of patterns and processes that shape human interaction with the *Built Environment*, with particular reference to the causes and consequences of the spatial *Distribution* of human activity on the Earth's surface.

Hydraulic civilization – a civilization based on irrigation agriculture that arose along the banks of a river due to the presence of reliable water resources and *Fertile* soils (e.g., ancient Egypt, Mesopotamia).

Hydro-electric power – *Energy* obtained from using the power of water.

Hypermarket – a giant shopping center containing very large supermarkets and other smaller shops found in an out-of-*City* location, close to a freeway junction; benefits from cheap land and the new trend to shopping by car, with large parking lots to cater for this; prices are kept low by the supermarket buying in bulk, which enables it to negotiate the lowest possible prices from its suppliers.

I

Iconography – the promotion of national images as part of the process of nation-building.

Ideology – a partial truth that benefits a particular group or class of people; a suite of ideas fostered by a group which colors perceptions of the social order and provides a distorted vision of the true nature of social, political, economic or other conditions.

Imagined community – a term coined by political theorist Benedict Anderson to describe the way, through media and other large-scale activities, people imagine for themselves a shared sense of history and *Culture* in which their commonalities (across a relatively expansive space) are greater than their differences; see *Nation*.

Immigrant – someone who moves into an area from elsewhere.

Immigration – movement into a *Place*; compare with *Emigration*.

Impairment – the loss of *Function* in a limb or organ; compare with *Disability*.

Imperialism – an unequal relationship usually between states in which a dominant state seeks to control the economic and political activities of a subordinate state (or states) in order to reap economic and geopolitical benefits; similar to *Colonialism* but differs in that imperialism does not necessitate a military presence or a colonial government in the subordinate territory.

Impermeable – a rock that will not let groundwater pass through it (e.g., clay).

Imports – goods bought from abroad.

Import substitution – when a country (LEDC) tries to produce all its goods and services to limit imports.

Income – what a person or country earns or gains in money from working, selling or trading.

Independent invention – when many hearths invent similar innovations without knowing about each other.

Indigenous – Native or belonging to a particular region.

Indigenous people – descended from the original inhabitants of a region; generally, not used to refer to a dominant *Ethnic group* within a particular state, even if they are the original inhabitants.

Indirect rule – the principal colonial policy of the British; relied on treaties with local ruling elites who governed in the name of the British crown.

Indo-European language – a family of several hundred related languages and *Dialects*.

Industrialization – the *Development* of industry such as manufacturing into a major facet of a region or national economy, replacing small-scale production for local markets with large-scale mechanized production for national or global markets; contrast *Deindustrialization*; see *Fordism*.

Industrialized – using machines and power (*Energy*) on a large scale to make things.

Industrial classification – the categorization of industry into primary, secondary, tertiary and quaternary sectors.

Industrial development certificates – issued by the UK government to control where industry can locate; difficult to obtain for firms wishing to locate in South East England; see *Core region*.

Industrial estate – an area of land planned and zoned for industry, usually with good access to the motorway network.

Industrial inertia – the survival of an industry in an area even though the initial advantages of the location are no longer relevant (e.g., the survival of the steelworks in Sheffield is due to the prestige of Sheffield cutlery).

Industrial Revolution – the growth and *Development* of manufacturing industry and the factory system which began in the U.K. in the eighteenth century.

Industry – a general term for working and making money.

Infant mortality – the number of babies dying before their first birthday per 1,000 live births.

Infanticide – the murder of infants.

Infertile – poor soil or land in which crops won't grow well.

Informal sector – casual, irregular work (e.g., street selling); particularly strong in LEDCs and made up of work done without the official knowledge of the government and without paying taxes.

Informal work – jobs people have set up for themselves, such as shoe shining; require little *Capital* to set up, few skills, are labor intensive, small-scale and can often be done from home.

Information city – a *City* which acts as a focus for information, especially via high-technology; a large percentage of the workforce is engaged in high-tech communication or services that rely on a steady flow of information; compare with the *Electronic ghetto*.

Information Technology (IT) – the exchange of ideas and information.

Infrastructure – the *Facilities* which provide the essential framework for industry (e.g., roads, power supply, sewerage).

Inner city – the part of the urban area surrounding the CBD; often contains older housing and industry, in a state of poor repair and dereliction; see *Urban redevelopment* and *Urban renewal*.

Innocent passage – the freedom of foreign vessels, including warships, to pass through the territorial waters of another country while in transit provided that no threat be made to the peace, good order or security of the state controlling those waters.

Innovation adoption – the *Diffusion* of new ideas.

Interfaith boundaries – *Boundaries* between the world's major faiths.

Inputs – the things needed to run a factory (e.g., capital, raw materials, power, labor).

Insurgency – a spatial process involving a deliberate, often lengthy, campaign of violence directed by dissident elements of society with the aim of installing new leadership, achieving regional autonomy or independence, modifying controversial policies or bringing about other changes to a state's political system.

Insurrection – dissident elements of society stage a spontaneous uprising aimed at enacting changes within a state's political system; see *Insurgency*.

Integration and disintegration – whereby states grow, integrating new territories in the process and decline as rival states or regions weaken or destroy the dominant state, causing its disintegration; the process may continue indefinitely in cases where states undergo alternating periods of growth and decline.

Intensive agriculture – crop or livestock growing that involves relatively small amounts of land and relatively high inputs of labor (or other forms of *Energy*); contrast with *Extensive agriculture*.

Intensive farming – farms which cover small areas but which use either many people or a lot of *Capital* (money); no land is wasted.

Internal cohesion – the condition of nations and states "hanging together" through political, economic or cultural rituals and processes (such as holidays, election rituals, national mythologies, etc.).

Internally displaced person (IDP) – used by the United Nations to describe people who are displaced by conflict or *Environmental* problems but have not crossed an international border; essentially refugees in their own country.

Internal waters – any bodies of fresh or salt water lying between the shore and the baseline used to begin measurement of a state's territorial sea; generally no right of innocent passage in a country's internal waters.

International law – a complex network of principles, treaties, judicial decisions, customs, practices, and writings of experts that are binding on states in their mutual relations.

International river – a river that traverses or borders two or more countries.

Internationalized river – a river that, by treaty or other formal arrangements, has been opened to navigation by vessels of states in addition to those of the riparian countries; may be international rivers or rivers lying entirely within a single country.

Introduced capital – a capital *City* that is a relatively recent creation; one that has been introduced as a replacement for an older, historical capital (e.g., Brasília, Tokyo).

Irredentism – the desire of a people to incorporate within their state all areas that have ever been part of the state and/or any areas that have become home to people of their nation; also appears in the actions of governments and peoples who demonstrate concern for the welfare of their ethnic kin in neighboring countries; assertion by the government of a country that a minority living outside its formal borders belongs to it historically and culturally.

Islam – religion; based on the teachings of Muhammad.

Islamism – Islamic political activism; believe that governments in predominantly Muslim countries should draw their inspiration from Islamic values, especially the *Shari'a* (Islamic law).

Island – a naturally formed area of land, surrounded by water, which is above water at high tide.

Isogloss – a geographic *Boundary* within which a particular linguistic feature occurs.

Isolated – difficult to reach; far from other *Places*.

Isotropic plain – an assumption often made in models (such as the Von Thünen model) that the world is a flat, featureless plain with a uniform *Distribution* of population, wealth, transportation costs, access to markets and so on.

Interconnections – reciprocal links.

Invisible trade – trade in products that cannot be "seen" (e.g., tourism, financial services, technological "know-how").

J

Jihad – an Arabic term that literally means "holy struggle;" according to Islamic teachings, the "greater *jihad*" is the task of becoming and remaining a devout Muslim who adheres to Islamic customs; the "lesser *jihad*" involves warfare against the enemies of Islam.

Job rotation – workers are skilled in a number of different jobs, and several people are capable of doing each job; ensures that each job can be covered in the case of absence; jobs can be regularly rotated to prevent a worker from becoming bored in a particular role.

Jainism – an Indian religion that prescribes a path of non-violence towards all living things.

Judaism – religion; roots in the teachings of Abraham, who is credited with uniting his people to worship only one god.

Judicial proceedings – formal adversary proceedings before a permanent court following established rules; typically, the last resort for parties willing to pursue third-party participation as a means to settle a dispute.

Just-in-time – a production system where *Components* are delivered just in time for assembly; saves transport and storage costs as well as prevents theft.

K

Kaizen – a Japanese concept meaning "continuous improvement;" requires workers thinking about improvements day-by-day and minute-by-minute.

Knowledge economy – the new economies based on the processing of knowledge and information using telecommunications.

L

Labor – most generally, work; indicates work that is socially organized; in capitalism, work performed for a wage and creating surplus value; stands in relation to *Capital* in that both capital and labor are necessary to engage in production, but it is labor that creates the surplus value (i.e., profit) that capital appropriates; compare with *Means of production*; see *Social reproduction* and *Exchange value*.

Labor-intensive – industries where labor costs are high compared to *Capital* costs (e.g., clothing).

Labor location – access to skilled labor is a very important factor in the location of modern industry today.

Labor surplus – more people than there are jobs in any given region or for any particular *Economic activity*; all other things being equal, a labor surplus will lower the value of labor and (potentially) increase the surplus value available to capital; Marx argued that overpopulation was in reality surplus population (i.e., local labor surpluses); see *Uneven development*.

Laissez-faire – the economic system that government intervention in or regulation of commerce should be kept to a minimum; literally, "let do."

Land-locked – countries with no access to a seaport; a particular problem for LEDCs (e.g., Zaire, Zambia) that are heavily reliant (60% and 98%) on the export of copper.

Land-locked developing country – a land-locked state that is also designated as a developing country by the United Nations.

Land tenure – the system of land control, management and/or ownership.

Landscape – the natural and built *Environment* perceived as a form or view; refers to both the actual, physical environment (including buildings, streets, etc.) and pictorial representations of it; see *Cultural landscape* and *Natural landscape*.

Landscapes of the dead – landscapes such as cemeteries that are only there because of the dead.

Language family – group of languages with a shared but fairly distant origin.

Language group – set of languages with a relatively recent common origin and many similar characteristics.

Latifundia – a large, privately-owned estate that was traditionally worked by slaves or hired workers in a quasi-feudal system that primarily benefited the landowning family or corporation.

L.D.D.C. – London Docklands Development Corporation; given the task by the government of clearing large areas of *Derelict land* in London Docks and selling the sites to property developers; also involved in improvements in infrastructure to attract new industry.

League – an association or alliance of states or other political entities for the common defense, commerce or other purposes.

League of Nations – a supranational organization, established after World War I; although it failed to preserve peace, it did a lot of very important work and provided a point of departure for the establishment of the United Nations.

Lebensraum – a German term meaning "living space," the alleged need for which was cited by Nazi Germany as a reason for its campaign of *Conquest* during World War II.

Less developed – a poorer area where there are fewer communications, services and where people have lower living standards.

Life expectancy – the average number of years a person born in a particular country might be expected to live.

Light industry – manufacturing industry which has light raw materials/*Components* and finished products.

Limestone – a pale-colored rock that is permeable and stores water.

Linear settlement – a settlement which follows the line of something (e.g., a road or river).

Lingua franca – a language that is used for trade or general communication by people who speak other languages at home.

Linguistic diversity – the amount of variation of languages a *Place* has.

Literacy rate – the proportion of the total population able to read and write.

Living standards – how well people can live, linked to the amount of money they earn.

Location – where a *Place* is.

Locational boundary dispute – arises due to disagreement over the delimitation or demarcation of a *Boundary*.

Locational factors – things that affect where industry decides to set up — usually in the most profitable *Place*.

Logistics – the management and control of the flow of goods and services from the source of production to the market; involves knowledge, communication, transport, and warehousing.

London Docklands – a declining *Inner-city* area, designated an Enterprise Zone by the government to attract new industry and employment after the closure of the docks.

Longevity gap – the difference of average expected life spans between different groups of people, nations, races, etc.

Loose-knit settlement – a settlement with many *Gaps* between its buildings and little, if any, pattern; see *Dispersed settlement pattern*.

Low-order goods/services – a good or service, usually inexpensive, that people buy on a regular, often daily basis (e.g., newspapers, bread, milk); usually purchased from shops located in suburban or neighborhood centers close to where people live; see *Corner shop*.

Lunar space – the region of outer space extending from Earth (or terrain) space to encompass the moon's orbital path.

M

Machinery – used in industrial processes to produce the finished product for sale.

Mackinder's Heartland Theory – a geopolitical hypothesis, proposed by British geographer Halford Mackinder during the first two decades of the twentieth century, that any political power based in the heart of Eurasia could gain sufficient strength to dominate the world eventually; Mackinder further proposed that since Eastern Europe controlled access to the Eurasian interior, its ruler would command the vast "heartland" to the east.

Maghreb – literally "*Place* of the sunset" or "western place" in Arabic; the northwest region of Africa encompassing Morocco, Algeria, Tunisia, and western Libya; also offers an Arab example of relative direction.

Maladapted diffusion – *Diffusion* in which image takes precedence over practicality.

Malnutrition – ill-health caused by a diet deficiency, either in amount (quantity) or balance (quality).

Malthus, Thomas – (1766-1843) English clergyman, economist, and demographer who argued that if the population were not checked by moral restraint (negative checks), it would outstrip available resources (creating a condition of overpopulation) and be stopped by various positive checks like war, famine, disease.

Mandate – a system established by the League of Nations whereby major powers, notably France and Great Britain, assumed responsibility for administration of colonies and other territories that were previously ruled by powers defeated during World War I (they were divided into three categories based on their readiness for eventual independence; following World War II, the United Nations established a system of trusteeships to replace the mandates).

Map projection – a technique for providing two-dimensional representation on a map of the Earth's three-dimensional, spherical surface.

Map scale – the relationship between *Distance* on a map and distance in the real world between *Places* depicted on the map (e.g., one inch = 50 miles); a large-scale map shows greater detail but less area than a small-scale map, which shows larger areas in less detail.

Map symbol – any graphics device used to represent natural or artificial features on a map.

Maquiladora – a factory on the Mexican side of the U.S.-Mexican border which specializes in assembling *Components* shipped from the U.S. (or other markets); the finished product is also returned to the U.S. market; many but not all maquilas are subsidiaries of U.S. corporations; firms locate in the maquiladora zone to take advantage of low-cost labor and lax *Environmental* regulations while still having rapid access to the U.S.

Market – a *Place* where raw materials and goods are sold.

Market (economic) – where industrial products are bought and sold.

Market area – the area served by a particular settlement, shop or service; see *Sphere of influence*.

Market gardening – the growing of fruit, vegetables, and flowers.

Market location (for industry) – where transport costs for the finished product exceed the transport costs of the raw materials; transport costs are lowest if the raw materials are transported to the factory located at the market and processed there; today, since power (electricity) can be transported over long *Distances*, a market location is more important than a raw material (coal) location.

Market town – a town whose main *Function* is that of a shopping and service center for the surrounding region.

Marx, Karl – (1818-1883) German philosopher, economist and political revolutionary who provided an incisive analysis and critique of *Capitalism* to show how it necessarily involved the exploitation of a class of people (the workers) in order to grow and develop; in population studies, Marx argued against Malthus to suggest that the theory of overpopulation was incorrect; instead, Marx argued that capitalism continually created (and had to create) a condition of surplus population in order to survive as an economic system.

Material culture – the art, housing, clothing, sports, dances, foods, and other similar items constructed or created by a group of people.

Maternal mortality rate – **the** annual number of deaths of women from pregnancy-related causes per 100,000 live births.

Maps – a physical, a linguistic or virtual representation of spatial data; a graphical model of the world.

Meander – a bend in a river.

Means of production – the tools, machinery, land and so forth necessary in the production process; labor works on the means of production (but under *Capitalism* does not own them) to produce commodities which the owners of the means of production then sell to realize the surplus value workers have produced.

Mechanized – work done by machines.

Median-line principle – lines made to distribute waterways when states are within 200 miles of each other.

Mediation – a form of third-party participation in which the mediator studies the case in some detail, participates actively in negotiations and offers a formal proposal for the solution of the problem.

Medical Revolution – medical technology invented in Europe and North America that is diffused to the poorer countries of Latin America, Asia, and Africa; improved medical practices have eliminated many of the traditional causes of death in poorer countries and enabled more people to live longer and healthier lives.

Mediterranean climate – *Places* which have hot, dry summers and mild, wet winters.

Megacity – a *City* with a population greater than 10 million that has a high degree of centrality within the national economy; also usually *Primate cities*.

Megalopolis – a continuous stretch of urban settlement which results from towns, cities, and conurbations merging.

Mental map – a cognitive map based on one's perceptions and knowledge of a *Place*.

Mercantilism – an economic system that dominated the commerce of most European countries and their colonies during the sixteenth to eighteenth centuries; key elements of the policy included the acquisition of large quantities of gold and silver as well as maintaining a "favorable *Balance of trade*."

Mercosur – Southern common market; a supranational organization in the *Cono Sur* (Southern Cone) of South America that has established a *Customs union* and is working toward a *Common market* among its four full members (Argentina, Brazil, Paraguay, and Uruguay) and its two associate members (Bolivia and Chile).

Metaphor – a figure of speech that links two objects by speaking as if they were one, as in referring to the world as "spaceship earth" or "a lifeboat;" in geography, models are metaphors of the geographical world.

Metropolitan statistical district (MSD) – an urban area in the United States that serves as an integrated economic and social unit with a recognized large population nucleus; *County Boundaries* are often used, enclosing rural regions as well.

Microstates – the smallest independent states in the world; typically possess less than 1,000 square miles (e.g., Liechtenstein, Malta, Nauru, San Marino).

Migrant – someone who moves from one *Place* to another to live.

Migrant workers – people who are born in one country and travel to work in another.

Migration – the movement of individuals or groups from one *Place* to another; see *Immigration* and *Emigration*.

Millionaire city – a *City* with over one million inhabitants.

Military imperialism – the extension of political and military control by an imperial state over a territory; if the territory is inhabited, the indigenous peoples will be subjugated and ruled by the imperial state.

Minerals – found in rock; may be mined or quarried and then either melted down like iron ore (iron) or bauxite (aluminum) or used as a source of power (coal, oil).

Mini-state – the result of the breakdown of nation-states into smaller political units, as in the former Soviet Union or the former Yugoslavia; contrast with *Supra-state*.

Mining – the extraction or digging out of minerals from deep under the ground (e.g., coal, iron ore).

Ministates – very small states that are larger than microstates; generally have less than 10,000 square miles of territory (e.g., Brunei, Luxembourg).

Model – a theoretical representation of the real world in which detail and scale are simplified to help explain reality; see *Heuristic*, *Normative* and *Metaphor*.

Monolingual – only one language is spoken.

Monotheism – the belief in a single god.

Mormonism – comprises the religious, institutional and cultural elements of the most populous branch of the Latter Day Saint movement.

Morphology – the shape and structure of a thing; in human geography, often used to understand landscapes or cities.

Most-favored-nation – a clause in a trade treaty committing each party to grant to the other whatever tariff and other trade concessions had been granted or would be granted in the future to any third country; after World War II, it became the foundation for the entire *GATT* system.

Mouth – the end of a river where it flows into the sea.

Multilingual – people or societies that commonly use three or more languages in their daily affairs.

Multinational state – a state that is home to multiple nationalities; in some cases, such as Indonesia, the number of nationalities or *Ethnic groups* may number in the hundreds.

Multiplier effects – the phenomenon whereby a job is created in one sector of the economy, it leads to the creation of jobs in other economic sectors; the "snowballing" of *Economic activity* (e.g., if new jobs are created, people who take them have money to spend in the shops, which means that more shop workers are needed; the shop workers pay their taxes and spend their new-found money, creating yet more jobs in industries as diverse as transport and education); contrast with *Negative multiplier effects*.

Municipality – the smallest general-purpose administrative unit in the United States and many other countries.

N

NAFTA – the North American Free Trade Agreement; a set of agreements between Mexico, the United States and Canada breaking down *Barriers* to the movement of *Capital* and commodities between these three nation-states; went into effect on January 1, 1994.

Narcoterrorism – the use of terrorist tactics by criminal groups to eliminate or intimidate rival gangs, military and police forces, government officials and others who might interfere with narcotics trafficking.

Nation – a people bound together by a shared sense of history and *Culture* and rooted in a particular territory; built by constructing successful imagined communities; see *Nation-state*, *Nationalism*, and *State*.

National iconography – figural representations, individual or symbolic, religious or secular; more broadly, the art of representation by pictures or images, which may or may not have a symbolic as well as an apparent or superficial meaning.

Nationalism – 1) a feeling of belonging to a nation; 2) an ideology that asserts the primacy of national feeling over other means for organizing societies; as an ideology, nationalism has provided strong fuel both for particular groups seeking to assert power over territory and to oppress groups within "their" territory that they perceive as different from themselves; often expressed as a desire for national control over a state.

Nation building – the process of fostering *Centripetal forces* among diverse cultural groups inhabiting a state; the drive for unity normally focuses on building a sense of civic nationalism as a substitute for ethnic and religious nationalism which often prevails in countries with superimposed *Boundaries*.

Nation-state – a state that is overwhelmingly composed of people of one nation; the recognized *Boundaries* of the nation are closely overlapped by the official boundaries of the state; very few countries in the world meet this standard; two examples are Iceland and Japan; see *Nationalism*.

NATO – the North Atlantic Treaty Organization; the premier military alliance among the developed countries of Europe and North America; formed during the early stages of the Cold War and is now assuming a greater role in military operations outside of Europe.

Natural boundaries – a *Boundary* line based on recognizable physiographic features, such as mountains or rivers.

Natural harbor – a safe *Place* for ships where the shape of the coastline provides shelter from the wind and waves.

Natural increase or decrease – the difference between the *Birth rate* and the *Death rate*; additional effects of migration are not included; also known as natural population change; see *Growth rate*.

Natural landscape – the surface of the Earth as modified by natural physical processes; see *Nature*; contrast with *Cultural landscape*.

Natural resources – raw materials which are obtained from the *Environment* (e.g., water, coal, *Fertile* soil).

Natural routes – river valleys and flat areas that were essential transport routes in the days before the railway, car or truck.

Nature – that which is characterized by the absence of human modification or production; that which is not culture; "human nature" indicates that people are conceived of as both within and apart from "nature;" like culture, one of the most complex words in the English language.

Nautical mile – based on one minute of latitude which is 1/60 of one degree of arc on the Earth's surface; because the Earth is an oblate spheroid whose arcs are not quite uniform, an international agreement set the *Distance* at 6,076.12 feet or about 1.15 statute miles (1.852 kilometers).

Negative checks – sometimes called "moral checks;" for Thomas Malthus were those factors (specifically abstinence and the delaying of marriage) which through individual moral choice curbed population growth and stemmed the threat of overpopulation; for Neo-Malthusians, a wider range of negative checks are advocated, such as artificial birth control and/or abortion; contrast with *Positive checks*.

Negative Multiplier Effect – a phenomenon in which the loss of jobs in one economic sector leads to further job loss in other economic sectors (e.g., when the elimination of university staff positions leads to less money spent in local bars, stores, churches or real estate offices, leading to layoffs in those sectors and less money being paid in taxes, leading to the erosion of jobs for road workers, assessors, *County* clerks, police personnel and so forth); can have profound consequences for local and regional economies; contrast with *Multiplier effect*.

Neighborhood unit – the basic building unit for planned new towns, designed to provide people with a safe, traffic-free *Environment* and access to all frequently-needed services, such as primary schools, shops, and clinics, within walking *Distance*.

Neocolonialism – economic and political strategies by which powerful states in *Core* economies indirectly maintain or extend their influence over other areas or people; the *de facto* continuation of colonial status for colonies that have received independence but whose economic systems (and consequently their political policies as well) remain strongly influenced by the former ruling state; *Economic imperialism* continues after independence has been achieved, and the rich-poor *Gap* is exacerbated rather than eliminated.

Neoimperialism – imperialism that is waged by countries that are themselves recent victims of imperialism (e.g., Morocco, India, Vietnam, Indonesia).

Neo-Malthusian – a contemporary stance that that builds off of Malthus's ideas about overpopulation to argue that world population is in a state of crisis; generally agreeing that a wider range of negative checks on population growth than Malthus advocated should be implemented.

Net migration – the difference between the number of *Emigrants* and the number of immigrants.

Neutral zone – territories that serve as buffer zones between states instead of using distinct *Boundaries*; in some cases, no state has sovereignty over the territory.

New town – a well-planned, self-contained settlement complete with housing, employment, and services.

New commonwealth – the more recent members of Britain's Commonwealth (ex-colonies, now independent), including countries such as India, Pakistan and the West Indian islands.

Newly industrializing country (NIC) – LEDCs which are developing manufacturing industries, usually with the help of transnational corporations attracted by *Cheap labor* and *Government incentives* (e.g., South Korea, Hong Kong, Taiwan, Malaysia, Brazil, India).

New International Economic Order – a 1974 UN resolution sponsored by developing countries that stated that developed countries had a responsibility to share the wealth with less developed countries and that this should be the basis for international relations.

Non-aligned movement (NAM) – formed in 1955 by developing countries wishing to adopt a neutralist policy during the Cold War, it now serves as a forum for developing countries seeking to improve the North-South trade imbalance.

Non-governmental organization (NGO) – national or transnational organizations that are primarily composed of private *Citizens* who act in consultation with the United Nations and other national and supranational entities (e.g., private relief agencies, religious institutions, philanthropic foundations, *Environmental* groups, and other organizations).

Non-material culture – the beliefs, practices, aesthetics, and values of a group of people.

Non-renewable resources – resources that can only be used once (e.g., coal, oil).

Normative – implying or establishing a norm; a normative model is one that describes not just how the world is but also suggests how the world should be.

Nucleated settlement pattern – a settlement where buildings are clustered around a particular point.

O

Occupation – the control of territory by a foreign military force; only exists in those portions of territory where authority has been established and can be exercised.

Occupational structure – the balance between the different sectors of a country's workforce (e.g., primary, secondary, tertiary, quaternary); see table below:

MEDC	NIC	LEDC
Mainly tertiary	Mainly secondary	Mainly primary

OECD – Organization for Economic Cooperation and Development; a supranational organization established in 1961 as a continuation of the successful Marshall Plan of the post-World War II era; its membership is primarily composed of the most developed countries; seeks to expand world trade and serve as a conduit for *Development* aid to the world's poorer countries.

Official language – in multilingual countries, the language selected to promote internal cohesion; usually the language of the courts and government.

OPEC – Organization of the Petroleum Exporting Countries; a supranational organization that acts as a cartel for oil-producing countries from around the world; its power was greatest during the 1970s and 1980s; since then, it has lost power due to internal disputes and rising production among non-OPEC countries.

Open-cast mine – a large quarry where a large pit is excavated on the Earth's surface to remove rock.

Operational boundary dispute – arises due to a conflict about the *Administration of a boundary*.

Orbit – a relatively stable path of a natural or artificial object around a larger celestial body in which the gravitational pull of the larger body and the centrifugal force of the object are in equilibrium.

Ordnance Survey – the official government organization for producing maps of the UK.

Ore – a rock containing minerals useful to people (e.g., iron ore, gold ore).

Organic state theory – Friedrich Ratzel's theory of state formation and *Development* that equated the state to a living organism that needed to expand through territorial growth or risk decay and death; growth was typically measured in stages of youth, maturity and old age, with possible rejuvenation.

Organization of American States (OAS) – the foremost supranational organization for the Americas.

Out-of-town shopping center – a large group of shops built either on a site on the edge of the urban area or the site of a former large industrial area; usually have large parking lots, a pedestrian-friendly, air-conditioned *Environment* and over 100 shops.

Outputs – products from a factory system; includes pollution and waste.

Overheads – costs which do not vary with output; includes rent, wages, electricity, etc.

Overpopulation – a condition where the number of people in an area exceeds the resources available to support that population; most closely associated with Malthus and Neo-Malthusians and strongly critiqued by Marx, who favored the idea of surplus population.

Overseas competition – NICs have the advantage of cheap labor, expanding national markets and the newest technology; led to a global shift of manufacturing industry towards Southeast Asia.

Overspill town – a town that expanded by taking people who were forced to move out of cities as a result of slum clearance and redevelopment schemes.

Over-urbanization – problems experienced by most LEDC cities (e.g., Bombay) where too many people are migrating to the *City*, resulting in housing shortages, poor housing conditions, lack of sanitation and piped water, illness, crime, traffic congestion, pollution, over-stretched services, unemployment, underemployment, etc.

Owner-occupied – a house lived in by its owner, as opposed to renting; see *Tenant*.

P

Pandemic – a disease that occurs over a wide geographic area and affects a very high proportion of the population.

Partition – the separation of a country or territory into two or more separate entities, often as part of an effort to resolve the conflict between competing nations.

Pastoralism – an economy based on the herding of animals.

Paternalism – the primary colonial policy of Belgium whereby colonial authorities retained decision-making power with little effort to prepare the colonial peoples for eventual self-rule.

Patriarchy – a condition in which *Gender* relations are characterized by the dominance of men over women or masculinity over femininity; a relationship supported and socially reproduced through institutions and cultures.

Pattern – a consistent or characteristic arrangement.

Peace enforcement – the most dangerous of *Peace operations*; designed to use military intervention to force an end to hostilities.

Peace operations – encompasses three major operations: *Peace enforcement, Peacekeeping,* and *Peacemaking*.

Peacekeeping – the deployment of military and/or civilian forces from one or more countries or a recognized intergovernmental organization (IGO) into a zone of conflict with the consent of the parties involved in the conflict; such forces are typically deployed after a ceasefire has been arranged; the personnel monitor situations and serve as a buffer between opposing parties.

Peacemaking – the use of a diplomatic activity, and perhaps military force, to persuade combatants to accept a ceasefire.

Peak – the top or summit of a hill or mountain.

Peak Land Value Intersection (PLVI) – that historical point in a *City* with the greatest access to and from all other points in the city and the hinterland, where land values are the highest; serves as the center of the *Concentric zone model* of the city; in a real city it is usually located where the tallest buildings (and thus the densest land uses) are located.

Peninsula – a narrow piece of land jutting out into the sea.

Pensionable age – a person of pensionable age is a man aged 65 or over or a woman aged 60 or over.

Perceptual region – a region perceived to exist, usually in the collective imagining of people at large, and possessing an identifiable nickname (i.e., "the Midwest"), but which may not be either formally or functionally coherent as a region; sometimes called a "vernacular region;" compare with *Formal region* and *Functional region*.

Perforated state – a state that surrounds the territory of another state (e.g., South Africa, which is perforated by Lesotho).

Peripheral region – an area on the fringe of *Economic activity*; a poor region of a country (e.g., South Wales).

Permanent capital – a capital *City* that has served as such for centuries, often spanning distinct historical periods (e.g., Athens, London, Paris).

Permeable – a rock that will allow water to pass through it, such as limestone.

Personal space – an envelope of territory surrounding people that they perceive as an extension of themselves; *Distances* vary among cultures and in regard to space in front of, beside and behind people.

Phenotype – the physical appearance of an organism; compare with *Genotype*.

Permeable barriers – a feature or condition which partially prevents, slows or transforms *Diffusion*; compare with *Absolute barrier*.

Physical factors affecting location of industry – include raw materials, *Energy* (power supply), natural routes, site, and land.

Physical features/activities – these are the result of natural forces which shape the Earth and affect the atmosphere.

Physical geography – the study of the physical features of the earth's surface.

Physical reproduction – the ability to physically "return" tomorrow as healthy as one is today (i.e., to have enough food, shelter, clothing, rest and so forth so as to maintain one's health); alternatively, the act of producing an adequate physical substitute for oneself (i.e., making babies); only possible if a society has an adequate and stable system of social reproduction.

Physiographic boundary – a *Boundary* based on physical features such as mountains or rivers.

Physiological density – the number of people per unit area of arable (farmable) land; compare with *Agricultural density* and *Arithmetic density*.

Pidgin – when two or more languages are combined in a simplified structure and vocabulary.

Pilgrimage – a journey to a specific location that is associated with someone or something well known or respected, usually religious in motivation.

Pioneer boundary – a *Boundary* that is drawn through essentially unoccupied territory.

Piracy – the act of boarding any vessel in international waters with the intent to commit theft or other crime and with the capability to use force in furtherance of the act.

Place – a portion of geographical space occupied by a person or thing and given meaning; constructed out of interconnected processes operating at all scales but which come together in a unique configuration in a particular location.

Placelessness – the loss of uniqueness of *Place* in the *Cultural landscape* so that one place looks much like another.

Plain – a low flat area.

Plan – a detailed map of a small area.

Planning – attempting to carry out a program of work, such as building a new town or protecting historic buildings, by following an agreed set of guidelines, design or plan.

Plateau – a high flat area.

Plural society – a society that contains various cultural groups.

Political map – a map which shows countries, their borders, and main cities.

Political system – a set of related political objects (parts) and their attributes (properties) that are arranged as the end product of the processes by which people organize themselves politically in their particular social and physical *Environments* and response to outside political systems (from Cohen and Rosenthal).

Politics – the exercise of power, often but not always through formal institutions (such as governments).

Pollution – noise, dirt and other harmful substances produced by people and machines which spoil an area.

Political culture – in geography, the idea that regions have relatively homogenous, stable and long-lasting attitudes toward the nature of government and politics and that these regional attitudes often differ in predictable ways from the attitudes of other regions.

Political geography – a subdivision of human geography focused on the nature and implications of the evolving spatial organization of political governance and formal political practice on Earth's surface.

Polytheism – belief in multiple gods.

Popular culture – cultural traits such as dress, diet, and music that identify and are part of today's changeable, urban-based, media-influenced western societies.

Population – the number of people in a given area.

Population change – births - deaths + in-migration - out-migration = population change.

Population density – **the** number of people per square kilometer

Population distribution – how people are spread out over an area.

Population explosion – a sudden rapid rise in the number of people.

Population growth – the increase in the number of people in an area.

Population growth rate – a measure of how quickly the number of people in an area increases.

Population pyramid – a graphic model that depicts the age and sex structure of a population in a particular area.

Port – a settlement site located where ships could be anchored in safety, sheltered from the sea; large ports tend to be route centers serving a hinterland.

Position – where a *Place* is.

Positional boundary dispute – disagreement about the actual location of a *Boundary*.

Positive checks – for Malthus and Neo-Malthusians, those checks on population growth that ensue during a crisis of overpopulation; might include, war, famine, disease, revolution and so forth; contrast with *Negative checks*.

Possibilism – the idea that the natural *Environment* places limits on the set of choices available to people.

Post-Fordism – in contrast to *Fordism*, smaller-scale, more flexible and individualized production and the vertical disintegration of firms; may be a greater emphasis on workers' abilities to perform a number of tasks, rather than the single, rote sort of work demanded by large-scale assembly lines; in the U.S., often associated with the *Deindustrialization* of *Places* and regions.

Post-industrial economy – the economies of economically developed countries where most employment is in service industries.

Poverty – when people are poor, have no savings, own very little and often have low living standards.

Power – 1) the real or presumed ability of a person, group or institution to exert force or influence, to make others do their bidding; 2) *Energy* needed to work machines and to produce electricity.

Prescription – acquisition of territory based on one country's occupation for many years, without objection, of land that was initially claimed by another state.

Prestige – the image of a company, gained from its headquarters address (e.g., Oxford Street, London) or its traditional high-quality manufacturing location (e.g., Sheffield for steel); see *Industrial inertia*.

Primary activity – collecting and using natural resources (e.g., farming, fishing, forestry, mining).

Primary industry – industry engaged in withdrawing resources directly from the earth, such as mining, tree-cutting, farming or fishing; compare with *Secondary industry, Tertiary industry,* and *Quaternary industry*.

Primary product dependency – see *Single product dependency*.

Primate city – a *City* that is disproportionately large, typically at least twice as large as the second-largest city in a country; often, although not necessarily, the national capital; tends to attract people from throughout the country, offering a representative sample of all of the country's various cultural groups.

Private space – space owned or controlled by an individual or group and available to members of the "public" only by permission of the owner or controller; contrast with *Public space*.

Privatization – the sale or transfer of public assets (including space) to private interests; the privatization of public space is an important issue because it changes the social rules for the use of that space.

Probabilism – the belief that the *Environment* influences but does not determine the manner in which societies evolve.

Processes – the activities that take place within a factory (e.g., rolling out steel).

Producer services – services for manufacturing and other tertiary industries (e.g., advertising, legal services, management consultancy, market research).

Production – the process of making something; in general, the term is used to indicate the whole of economic activities in a given region or country, but it should be remembered that processes of production are complex and include spatial divisions of labor; only possible if there is successful social reproduction in a given society.

Professional occupations – employers, managers and professional workers whose occupations normally require a university degree or other highly selective qualification, such as doctors, civil engineers, etc.

Profits – money left over when wages, interest, rent, raw materials, and other costs have been paid by businesses; the financial reward for taking risks.

Proletarianization – the process by which people lose control over their "means of subsistence" (the land on which they subsist) and are forced into a relationship of wage labor vis-a-vis capital.

Propaganda map – designed to promote a state or other entity's objectives.

Prorupt state – also known as a protruded state; a state that features an elongated portion of territory extending from the main body of territory; India is a good example, especially regarding Jammu and Kashmir in the north and its states along its border with Myanmar; Thailand offers another excellent example.

Proselytic religion – a universalizing religion, which attempts to be global, to appeal to all people, wherever they may live in the world, not just those of one *Culture* or location.

Prosperous – when people are rich and well-off.

Protectorate – a territory in which indigenous leaders have requested the intervention of an imperial state to prevent colonization by the same or another imperial country; in practice, however, some territories had protectorate status forced upon them.

Protolanguage – an assumed, reconstructed or recorded ancestral language.

Public – refers to private *Citizens* freely coming together in a public space to deliberate on important political issues of the day; the idea of "the public" is an important aspect of American political ideology.

Public space – space either made available by government or private groups (or not well-controlled in the first place) for the use and pleasure of "the public" (e.g., for political discussion and demonstrations or leisure and amusement); how public space is socially defined and the uses of it that are deemed appropriate in any given time or *Place* are important issues for understanding the workings of politics in any society.

Pull factors – in studies of migration, those factors that encourage immigration to a *Place*; the perception of various pull factors is usually more important to individuals or groups contemplating migration than is the actuality of those factors; contrast with *Push factors*.

Punjab – the "land of five rivers;" the *Core area* of Pakistan which extends into neighboring India.

Push factors – in studies of migration, those negative characteristics of a *Place* that encourage *Emigration* out of that place; contrast with *Pull factors*.

Q

Quality of life – an idea which is difficult to define because it means different things to different people; things which make for a good quality of life might include high income, good health, good housing, basic home *Amenities*, pleasant surroundings, recreational open space, good local shops, a secure job, etc.

Quality of life index – a single number or score used to place different countries in rank order based on their quality of life; various indicators are included (e.g., GNP per person, calorie intake, life expectancy, access to health care, number of doctors per 100,000).

Quarry – a large pit dug to obtain a mineral from the ground. Rocks and ore are quarried.

Quaternary industry – *Economic activity* generally referred to as "research and *Development*" or "brain work," such as software writing, architectural design, or consulting; often the most *Footloose* of all economic activities; compare with *Primary industry*, *Secondary industry,* and *Tertiary industry*.

R

Race – a categorization of humans based on skin color and other physical characteristics.

Racial prejudice – thinking unpleasant things about people because of the color of their skin and/or their *Ethnic group* without knowing them.

Racism – unfair, ridiculing or threatening behavior toward someone because of their particular racial group.

Raison d'être – reason for existing.

Range – the *Distance* that interested consumers, on average, will travel to obtain a given good or service; whereas the range of a carton of milk might be quite small (people are not willing to travel more than a mile or two to get it), the range of a concert grand piano might be very large (perhaps global, since those wishing and able to spend $150,000 on a piano might be willing to travel anywhere to purchase it); the idea of range is an essential concept in *Central place theory*; compare with *Threshold*.

Range of a good – the maximum *Distance* that people are prepared to travel for a specific service.

Rational economic beings – an assumption made in many models, particularly economic ones, that people rationally weigh the costs and benefits of any action and always seek to maximize the benefits and minimize the costs in any given situation.

Raw materials – items from which more complex items are made (e.g., steel is made using coal, iron, and limestone; coal, iron and limestone are raw materials).

Raw material location – the bulkier and heavier these are to transport, the nearer the factory should be located to the raw materials; with the decline of traditional heavy industry, the three main factors deciding industrial location today are the nearness to a large market, the availability of skilled labor and government policies.

Reapportionment – the process by which representative districts are switched according to population shifts so that each district encompasses approximately the same number of people.

Rebellion – an effort by elements of society to overthrow an incumbent government with the objective of replacing the leadership while leaving the system of government unchanged.

Recreation – leisure activities; what people do in their non-working time.

Recycling – turning waste into something which is usable again.

Redevelop – to knock everything down and start all over again.

Redevelopment – the rebuilding of parts of a *City*; sometimes large areas are completely demolished before being rebuilt; sometimes all or some of the old buildings are retained but modernized to combine what are perceived to be the best features of the old and the new.

Redistricting – a process in which individual states within the United States periodically redraw their various electoral districts to account for changes in population size and *Distribution*.

Refugee – a term used by the United Nations to describe people who are displaced by persecution, conflict or *Environmental* problems and have been forced to flee across international *Boundaries*.

Region – an area in which people, *Places* or processes possess a common characteristic or characteristics that make it distinct from other areas; the things within the *Boundaries* of the region have more in common with each other than they do with things outside the region; both an intellectual device for ordering the chaotic world and a real thing created through processes analogous to those that create place; see *Formal region, Functional region, Perceptual region* and *Regionalization*.

Regional state – a unitary state in which autonomy has been granted to regions within them, generally regions of ethnic distinctiveness or remoteness from the *Core area*; as such, these states tend to lie in the middle ground between unitary and *Federal states*.

Regionalism – a feeling of collective identity based on a population's politico-territorial identification within a state or across state *Boundaries*.

Regionalization – either the process by which areas are categorized into regions by an analyst or the actual construction of regions by economic, political and social processes working over and through space and time and at all scales (as in the creation of the "sunbelt" as a region of the U.S. possessing certain real economic-cultural characteristics that set it apart from the "rustbelt").

Relative deprivation – a concept suggesting that people are likely to engage in political violence against a government when their standard of living fails to meet their expectations.

Relative direction – one region typically named by people from another region based on the direction they would take to reach it; for instance, the people in the eastern United States gave the Midwest its name to distinguish it from the Far West; people in California, however, would travel east to reach the Midwest; other examples include the Near East, Middle East, and the Far East, based on European and North American perspectives.

Relative distance – *Distance* as measured by non-absolute criteria, such as travel time or psychological factors; the construction of an interstate highway through an area of rugged terrain can drastically shorten relative distance even though there are only minor changes to the absolute distance.

Relative location – one *Place's* location based on its *Distance* and direction from another known location (e.g., Flint, Michigan is approximately 50 miles northwest of Detroit).

Relic boundaries – old political *Boundaries* that no longer exist as international borders but that have left an enduring mark on the local cultural or *Environmental* geography (e.g., Hadrian's Wall, the former boundaries between East and West Germany, North and South Vietnam, North and South Yemen).

Reservoir – a manmade lake that is used to store water supplies, often behind a dam.

Reincarnation – the idea that after this life you will come back in another life either as a plant, an animal or a human.

Relative location – the location of something in relation to something else.

Relief – the shape of the land surface and its height.

Religious fundamentalism – **a** religious movement whose objectives are to return to the foundations of the faith and to influence state policy.

Religious extremism – *Religious fundamentalism* carried to the point of violence.

Religious nationalism – a sense of nationalism based on a shared religion (e.g., the rise of Jewish nationalism led to the creation of the modern state of Israel).

Religious toponyms – the origin and meaning of the names of religions.

Relocation diffusion – a form of *Diffusion* that involves the actual movement of the original adopters from their point of origin to a new *Place*.

Remote sensing – **the** technique of obtaining information about objects through the study of data collected by special instruments that are not in physical contact with the objects being analyzed.

Rent gap – the discrepancy between actual and potential rent (as predicted by *Bid-rent curves*) in a particular location; in the *Concentric zone model* of the *City*, often found in the ring just outside the *Central business district*; in real cities, often located in *Inner-city* areas neighboring areas of rising land values; an important inducement to *Gentrification*.

Repatriation – a government policy of returning immigrants to their country of origin.

Representation – a technical term that refers to the depiction of a *Place* or process; the representation of places and landscapes is often as important as their actuality.

Representative fraction – the numerical relationship between *Distance* on a map and corresponding distance in the real world; normally expressed with 1 in the numerator such as 1:25,000, meaning that one inch on a map equals 25,000 inches on the ground.

Reprisal – the most severe of the three modes of redress short of war in which aggrieved party resorts to a form of retaliation far more than the acts complained of.

Research and development (R&D) – the branch of a manufacturing firm concerned with the design and *Development* of new products; employs highly skilled workers and is often located close to the company HQ.

Residential – a housing area where people live.

Residential preference – where people would like to live.

Resistant rock – a hard rock which resists being worn down and stands out as hills.

Resources – things which can be useful to people; they may be natural like coal and iron ore or of other value like money and skilled workers.

Resource boundary dispute – (allocational) disagreement over the control or use of shared resources, such as *Boundary* rivers or jointly-claimed fishing grounds.

Resource mobilization – the idea that civil unrest occurs when people have both the willingness and the ability to mobilize; democratic societies typically see less political violence because peaceful protests are tolerated, while excessively repressive regimes stifle unrest at the first sign; revolutionary activity and other forms of political violence are expected to occur in those countries that are neither democratic enough to absorb protests, nor repressive enough to crush them altogether.

Retail park – an out-of-town shopping center with a few large warehouse-type stores selling electrical goods, carpets, D.I.Y. goods, building supplies, etc.

Retailing – the sale of goods, usually in shops, to the general public.

Retaliation – one of three modes of redress short of war; typically involves actions such as recall of an ambassador, closure of an embassy, economic sanctions or a small-scale military operation.

Retorsion – the mildest of the three modes of redress short of war; involves a response to acts that are unfriendly, but not illegal, such as the imposition of special tariffs, immigration restrictions, currency controls and so on; the complainant typically responds in kind.

Retraining schemes – government-funded schemes to retrain unemployed workers in *Declining areas* in the new skills required by high-tech *Assembly industries* attracted by *Government incentives*.

Returnee – a term used by the United Nations to designate a former refugee who has returned to their country of origin.

Re-urbanization – the process whereby towns and cities in MEDCs which have been experiencing a loss of population can reverse the decline and begin to grow again; some form of redevelopment is often required.

Revolution – a form of political violence in which dissident elements of society seek to overthrow an existing government and replace it with new leaders and a new system of government; encompasses the process of revolutionary violence as well as the outcome, if successful, of revolutionary change.

Ribbon development – when housing grows out from a town along the main road.

Rimland – the maritime *Periphery* of Eurasia that was vulnerable to both land and sea power; according to Nicholas Spykman, the country that controlled the rimland would also control the destiny of the world.

Rimland Theory – Nicholas Spykman's theory that the domination of the coastal fringes of Eurasia would provide the base for world conquest.

Ring-road – a *By-pass* that provides a route around the CBD.

Riparian – along the bank of a water body; a riparian state is one through or along which a river flows (e.g., Israel is a riparian state along the Jordan River, and Egypt is one of the riparian states of the Nile River); also used as a synonym for the adjective "littoral," which indicates a state that abuts a lake or the sea.

River basin – the territory encompassing an entire drainage basin of a river system including the tributary rivers that join the main channel and the distributaries that often form *Deltas*.

Route center – a settlement located at the meeting point of several roads/railways; the meeting point of two or more river valleys (which provide good road and rail routes through high land), is often the location of a route-center settlement; bridging points, ports and *Gap towns* are also natural route centers.

Rural – not urban (i.e., the countryside).

Rural-to-urban migration – the movement of people from the countryside to the towns and cities.

Rural depopulation – people leaving the countryside usually to live in towns (i.e., rural-to-urban migration).

Rural population structure – young males move to urban areas due to push-pull factors; creates a characteristic indentation in the 20-35 age group population structure.

Rural-urban fringe – a zone of transition between the built-up area and the countryside, where there is often competition for land use; a zone of mixed land uses, from shopping malls and golf courses to farmland and motorways.

S

SAARC – the South Asian Association for Regional Cooperation; a supranational organization working toward closer economic integration in South Asia; so far, however, political strife between India and Pakistan has largely thwarted its progress.

Sacred space – a *Place* or space that people infuse with religious meaning.

SADC – the Southern African Development Community; a supranational organization working toward closer economic integration among southern African countries; its membership overlaps with that of *COMESA,* which has produced conflicting objectives for some members.

Satellite nation – a country that is dominated by a more powerful nation.

Scale – the size or extent of a given process; typically, geographers refer to processes occurring at local, regional, national or global scales; to understand *Places*, it is often necessary to understand how different processes working at different scales come together in a specific location, thereby creating, out of a set of general processes, a unique outcome.

Scenery – the appearance or view across the natural landscape.

Scenic – attractive and interesting view of the landscape.

Science parks – an area of land, often located near university sites, where high-tech industries are located; scientific research and *Commercial Development* are carried out in cooperation with the university.

Scenic – attractive and interesting view of the landscape.

Screwdriver industries – industries based on the routine assembly of products manufactured elsewhere (e.g., Sony, South Wales).

Seam – see *Coal seam*.

Seasonal jobs – employment that lasts for only part of the year.

Secession – the withdrawal of a people and their territory from a state to establish an independent state of their own.

Secondary activities – where natural resources are made or manufactured in *Factories* into goods.

Secondary industry – the manufacturing of goods using the raw materials from primary industry; *Economic activity* designed to make things; manufacturing; take raw materials (from primary industries) and already manufactured items (from other secondary industries) and assembles them into commodities; see *Primary industry*, *Tertiary industry* and *Quaternary industry*.

Secondary industry second homes – homes purchased by *City* dwellers in country villages or areas of usually great natural beauty for holiday or weekend use only; these create problems for local communities since house prices in the area of second homes rise out of the reach of young people, and shops, schools, and bus services are forced to close due to lack of customers; the newcomers also bring unwanted social changes to the villages.

Sector model – see *Hoyt model*.

Secularism – the idea that ethical and moral standards should be formulated and adhered to for life on earth, not to accommodate the prescriptions of a deity and promises of a comfortable afterlife.

See-saw motion of capital – a theory that holds that capitalists shift *Capital* from one *Place* to another, depending on labor and other costs, leading to *Development* in places of active investment and underdevelopment in places of disinvestment; this process can be visualized as a see-saw in which resources, capital and so forth from one seat are continually lifted out and placed on the other seat until such time as diminishing returns on the investment side lead to a shift back toward the seat that has been disinvested, thereby tipping the see-saw back the other way; see *Uneven development*.

Segregation – the separation of ethnic, racial, religious or other groups into different districts within a *City*.

Sequent occupancy – **the** theory that a *Place* is occupied by different groups of people, each group leaving an imprint on the place from which the next group learns.

Self-determination – a concept that ethnicities have the right to govern themselves.

Self-help housing schemes – groups of people, especially in LEDCs, are encouraged to build their own homes, using materials provided by the local authority.

Semi-detached house – a house joined to one other; common in the middle-class suburb zones of a *City* in the MEDCs.

Semi-skilled occupations – involve skills that are quickly learned (e.g., bus conductors, laborers, kitchen hands, cleaners).

Services – these are used by people and include shops, schools, buses, and hospitals.

Service industry – this is an industry where a service is provided; includes cleaners, shop, and office workers, police, doctors and train drivers.

Settlement – where people choose to live.

Settlement function – the main activity of a *Place*, usually economic (e.g., tourist resort) or social (e.g., dormitory town).

Settlement hierarchy – settlements ordered by their size: hamlets, villages, towns, cities, conurbations.

Settlement pattern – the shape and spacing of individual settlements, usually dispersed, nucleated or linear.

Sex ratio – the number of males per 100 females in the population.

Shamanism – community faith in traditional societies in which people follow their shaman.

Shantytown – an area of poor-quality housing, lacking in *Amenities* such as water supply, sewerage, and electricity, which often develops spontaneously and illegally (as a squatter settlement) in a *City* in an LEDC.

Shari'a – Islamic law.

Sharia law – the system of Islamic law, based on varying degrees of interpretation of the Qur'an.

Shatter belt – a region caught between stronger, colliding external cultural-political forces; although it may serve as a buffer zone, it is under persistent stress leading to the creation, fragmentation, and demise of national *Boundaries* and entities brought about by aggressive rivals (e.g., the Balkans).

Shatter zone – see *Shatter belt*.

Sheltered site – a *Place* shielded or protected from stormy weather because it is low-lying or behind a hill.

Shia (Shi'ite) – branch of Islam; Persian variation; belief in the infallibility and divine right to authority of the Imams, descendants of Ali.

Shifting cultivation – see *Swidden*.

Shintoism – religion; located in Japan and related to Buddhism; focuses, particularly on nature and ancestor worship.

Shopping mall – a modern, very large out-of-town shopping center at a freeway junction location that provides a family outing "experience;" offers a range of entertainment besides a large number of shops in an air-conditioned enclosed area of up to half a square kilometer.

SICA – the *Sistema de Integración Económica Centroamericana* (Central American Economic Integration System); a Central American/Caribbean supranational organization dedicated to pursuing greater economic and political unity among the seven states of Guatemala, Honduras, El Salvador, Nicaragua, Costa Rica, Panama and the Dominican Republic; previously went by the name Central American Common Market (CACM) until December 1991.

Sikhism – religion; began in northern India; the principal belief is that faith in Vahiguru emphasizes faith in God.

Silicon Glen – a high-tech zone in Scotland.

Silicon Valley – a high-tech zone in California.

Silt – soil left behind after a river flood.

Single product economy – a country (usually LEDC) which relies on one, or a very small number, of products (usually raw materials) for its export earnings (e.g., Zambia, copper makes up 98% of its *Exports*; Uganda, 95% coffee beans).

Site – the absolute, physical location of a *Place* or thing; can be measured precisely (as with latitude and longitude) or accurately described regarding its physical characteristics; contrast with *Situation*.

Site and service schemes – a method of encouraging housing improvement in poor areas of cities in LEDCs; the government provides the land for a new *Development* and installs services such as water and electricity; local people can then obtain a plot in the scheme for low rent and build their own houses.

Site and situation – a basic geographic concept related to the importance of location; site refers to the internal physical and cultural attributes of a *Place*; situation refers to the external linkages that give a site its relative importance (e.g., New Orleans, which lies along the Mississippi River *Delta* (site), giving it the role of gateway to the Mississippi River and its tributaries (situation)).

Situation – the location of a *Place* relative to other places and human activities. Situations change over time in ways that sites do not; cannot be measured precisely; the location of a settlement in relation to places (physical and human) surrounding it (e.g., roads, rivers, land use, etc.); a settlement with a good situation is likely to grow to become a market town for the surrounding region.

Slash and burn agriculture – see Swidden.

Slope – the angle at which the land is tilted; can be gentle or steep.

Slow world – a term used to describe those *Places* exhibiting low degrees of *Connectivity* and marked by poor *Communications* with the rest of the world, little inward investment and a general state of under- or de-development; contrast with *Fast world*.

Slum – a house unfit for human habitation.

Social class – a person's social class reflects his or her wealth, income, education, status and power; a person's occupation is generally used to denote social class.

Social Darwinism – the application of Darwinian ideas about the natural world to the analysis of human societies (e.g., the organic theory of the state).

Social justice – the *Distribution* of burdens and benefits in society and the mechanisms by which this distribution comes about.

Social leap-frogging – the process by which those who can afford to do so move out of an area as it becomes older and more run down, to be replaced by less well-off people.

Social reproduction – the maintenance, day in and day out, of the formal and informal social institutions that make sexual reproduction in a given society possible; used to indicate that these institutions have to be constantly made and remade, supported and solidified.

Social space – space as it is perceived or used by social groups.

Socio-economic group – classification of people according to their occupation (e.g., professional, skilled, manual); occupation is related to income, wealth and education; the classification is shown below:

Group 1 Professional and managerial	Group 2 Intermediate	Group 3 Skilled (non-manual)	Group 4 Skilled manual	Group 5 Partly skilled	Group 6 Unskilled
e.g., employers, senior managers, architects, lawyers	e.g., teachers, nurses, social workers — all jobs requiring good qualifications	e.g., clerical workers, secretaries — jobs requiring training	e.g., supervisors, skilled workers, bus drivers, hair stylists	e.g., fitters, machine operators — jobs requiring some training	e.g., laborers — jobs requiring little training or experience

Soil erosion – the removal of soil by wind or water.

Solar space – the region of outer space beyond lunar space that encompasses the remainder of the solar system.

Source – the beginning of a river in the mountains.

Sovereignty – the ability of a state to govern its territory free from the control of other states.

Space – most simply, area; geographers distinguish "absolute" or abstract space, the sort of space that acts as a container for things, and "social" or "relative" space, the sort of space produced through social interaction; see *Spatiality* and *Place*.

Spacefaring – a capability to engage in manned or unmanned space travel.

Sparsely populated – an area that has few people living in it.

Spatial data – any information with a spatial component.

Spatial perception – the manner in which people perceive their surroundings.

Spatial perspective – the way geographers look at everything about space.

Special purpose district – civil divisions within the United States that are created for various tasks, such as to administer natural resources, provide *Energy*, manage school districts and utilities and numerous other *Functions*.

Spatial relationships – the way people, things and processes interact over and through space; akin to *Spatiality*.

Spatiality – the relationship between society and space; spatiality indicates the habitual and ingrained spatial behaviors that mark a people or society.

Sphere of influence – the area served by a settlement, shop or service.

Spontaneous settlement – a squatter settlement or shanty town containing self-built houses made of scrap materials such as corrugated iron and plastic; the settlement usually lacks piped water, an electricity supply and sewage disposal facilities; very common in cities in LEDCs and are illegal because the residents neither own the land on which the houses are built, nor have permission to build there.

Spring – where water flows out of the ground.

Squatter settlement – another name for a *Spontaneous settlement*.

Standard of living – how well-off a person or a country is.

State – a sovereign country with a permanent resident population, land territory, organized system of government, international recognition, economic system and circulation system of transportation and communications; also used for *First-order civil divisions* in the United States and several other countries.

State building – a constructive process that aims to create the institutions necessary for a state to be independent and self-governing.

Stateless nation – a nation that does not have a state of its own; also known as a non-state nation; most nations of the world fall into this category; contemporary examples include Kurds and Tibetans.

Stimulus diffusion – *Expansion diffusion* in which the innovative idea diffuses from its hearth outward, but its new adopters change the original idea.

Sterilization – a method of contraception; in men, an operation that prevents sperm from being released; in women, an operation that stops the production of eggs.

Strait – a narrow passage between two larger bodies of water; many straits are important to international navigation and are subject to special provisions whereby ships adhere to rules of transit passage rather than the more restrictive innocent passage (e.g., the Strait of Malacca).

Strategic minerals – minerals not widely available within a country that is regarded as essential to defense; typically subject to strict *Conservation* and control during wartime.

Structure (of a population) – the relative percentages of people of different age groups, usually shown on a population pyramid.

Structure of trade – the differing proportions of primary, secondary and tertiary products that make up a country's *Exports* and imports (e.g., LEDCs export low-value raw materials and commodities and import high-value machinery and *Consumer* goods from MEDCs); see *Single product economy*.

Subcontract – where a large company (e.g., Nike) arranges for its goods to be produced by another company.

Subsequent boundary – established after the area in question has been settled and that considers the cultural characteristics of the bounded area.

Subsidy – a grant of money made by the government to industries locating in *Development areas*; industries locating in South Wales receive a labor subsidy per worker, which encourages them to employ more people, reducing their costs and increasing profits.

Subsistence – growing just enough food for your own needs with nothing left over to sell.

Subsistence agriculture – crops and livestock are grown primarily for their local use-value (rather than *Exchange-value*); contrast with *Commercial agriculture*.

Suburb – residential and *Commercial* areas outside of *City* centers generally marked by relatively low *Population density* (compared to cities), segregated land uses and a reliance on personalized modes of transportation; historically suburbs have been dependent on *Core* cities, but that is less and less the case as all manner of economic activities have begun suburbanizing in the last half of this century.

Suburbanization – the *Development* of suburbs and the movement of people to them; the process of suburbanization has been the dominant mode of urban development in the U.S. at least since the turn of the twentieth century.

Suburbanized villages/towns – dormitory or commuter villages/towns with a residential population who sleep in the village/town but who travel to work in the nearby large urban area; the suburbanized village has increasingly adopted some of the characteristics (new housing estates, more services) of urban areas.

Sunbelt – a growth region of high-tech industry in the south and southwest of the USA.

Sunni – branch of Islam; orthodox/traditionalist; belief in the effectiveness of family and community in the solution of life's problems; accept traditions of Muhammad as authoritative.

Sunrise industries – high-tech industries.

Sunrise strip – a high-tech industrial zone following the route of the M4 westwards to South Wales.

Superimposed boundary – a political *Boundary* placed by powerful outsiders on a developed human landscape; usually ignores pre-existing cultural-spatial patterns, such as the border that now divides North and South Korea.

Supranationalism – a venture involving three or more states working toward common goals in cultural, economic, military, political and/or other fields; the most prominent example is the United Nations.

Supra-state – literally, larger than a state; an organization which takes on state *Functions* (such as taxation, regulation, etc.) but operates at a scale larger than the nation-state; contrast with *Mini-state*.

Surplus population – the number of people in excess of the "productive needs of society" (i.e., available jobs); Marx used this idea to argue against Malthus's notion of overpopulation, suggesting that under capitalism, increasing surplus value was only possible if the total cost of wages was less than the *Exchange-value* realized for goods produced; hence, Marx argued that surplus population was, in fact, a necessary condition of capitalist production; without a surplus population, wages would rise too high, and the system of surplus value extraction would be threatened; in short, Marx argued that *Capitalism* saw a certain level of unemployment as "good," and the system itself continually produced surplus population.

Surplus value – the value of goods above and beyond the costs of making those goods; in capitalism, according to Marx, surplus value is produced by labor, not by the owners of the means of production; his argument is roughly that wages are always some degree less than the total value of goods a worker produces; the difference between that value and the wages is the surplus value; the owner of the means of production, not the worker owns the surplus value produced under capitalism.

Survey systems – systems that are used to collect data.

Sustainable development – the goals of *Development* programs that are designed to stimulate economic growth, promote social equity and protect the *Environment*.

Swidden – a type of *Extensive agriculture* where a patch of forest is cut down and burned to release nutrients into the soil; the plot of land is then planted with a variety of crops which produce relatively high yields (with little input of labor) in the first years, but which steadily decline in yield over time as nutrients are used up; when a field is no longer sufficiently productive, it is abandoned to fallow, and the forest is allowed to re-colonize; in the meantime, as decline sets in on the first plot another patch is cleared, and the process begins again; ultimately, the rotation of cleared plots in this fashion leads back to the original plot, which ideally by this time is ready to be cut and burned all over again; also called *Slash and burn* and *Shifting cultivation*.

Syncretism – the *Development* of a new form of *Culture trait* by the fusion of two or more distinct parental elements.

System disequilibrium – a condition that can lead to political violence within a society due to rapid and perhaps unexpected changes (e.g., a newly-independent country that expands its educational system but cannot provide jobs for the new graduates may experience unrest due to the disequilibrium that ensues).

T

Taoism – religion; based upon Tao-te-ching, a book by Lao-Tsu which focuses on the proper form of political rule and the oneness of humanity and nature.

Tariffs – tax (customs duties) charged on imported goods (e.g., manufactured goods from LEDCs to the EU face a tariff of 30%; Japanese companies have located in the EU to avoid tariffs; these do not apply if 60% of the *Components* are made in Europe).

Technology – new ways of using resources and developing new equipment.

Teleworking – working from home using telecommunications.

Tenant – a person who rents their home from a private landlord or the local council.

Tenure – the way in which property is held; a house or apartment may be owned by the occupier or rented, either from the council or from a private landlord.

Tenement blocks – large residential blocks built in the *Inner cities* of the MEDCs during the Industrial Revolution to house workers in high *Density*, cramped and unhygienic conditions next to the *Factories*.

Terms of trade – the relationship between the average price of *Exports* and the average price of imports; always favor MEDCs at the expense of LEDCs; see *Structure of trade*.

Terraced house – a house within a (usually) long line of joined housing; typical of the *Inner-city* zone in the UK.

Terran space – the space above the Earth extending from the lowest range of low altitude orbits to just beyond the upper limits of high altitude orbits.

Territorial boundary dispute – disagreement between states over the control of the surface area.

Territorial dispute – a dispute involving possession of an entire region; islands are often the object of such disputes.

Territorial morphology – a state's physical shape; there are five basic shapes, which are compact, prorupted, elongated, fragmented and perforated.

Territoriality – a strong emotional attachment to one's territory that develops among members of tribes, nations and other peoples at varying geographic scales; often fosters a determination to defend the territory against any outside encroachment; although often compared to animal territoriality, many social scientists reject notions that it is a genetic trait.

Territorial sea – the zone of seawater immediately adjacent to a country's coast, held to be sovereign territory of the state but within which all vessels must be granted the right of innocent passage; most countries adhere to a 12-mile territorial sea drawn from the applicable baseline.

Terrorism – a form of warfare in which violence or the threat of violence is directed at multiple segments of societies, especially civilians, in pursuit of specific political objectives; also used by criminal groups to stifle opposition to illegal activities.

Tertiary industry – generally referred to as "services," this sector of *Economic activity* includes everything from retail and wholesale, transportation, utilities, government services, restaurants, entertainment, banking and insurance brokering; does not produce anything but involves work in the service sector of the economy; includes activities associated with commerce and *Distribution* (wholesaling and retailing) as well as banking, insurance, administration, transport, tourism, health, education and entertainment services.

Theocracy – a state whose government is under the control of a ruler who is deemed to be divinely guided, or of a group of religious leaders.

Third world – a term that originated with the non-aligned movement during the Cold War; denoted those countries that were part of neither the first world of industrialized, capitalist countries of the West nor the second world of communist countries; since then, it has often been applied to all developing countries.

Threshold – the number of potential customers necessary to support the sale of a particular good or service (e.g., it takes relatively few people in an area to support the sale of a carton of milk (because so many people buy milk and because they buy it so frequently), while it takes a huge number to support the sale of concert grand pianos (because so few people buy these, and they buy them so rarely); the idea of threshold is essential to *Central place theory*.

Threshold population – the minimum number of people required to support a particular good, shop or office (e.g., large stores such as Marks & Spencer have a threshold population of over 100,000, while shoe shops have a threshold population of about 25,000).

Time-space convergence – a process of decreasing the *Relative distance* between *Places* brought on as improved transportation systems and decreasing costs reduce travel time.

Town – an incorporated urban area that is larger than a village but smaller than a *City*.

Township – a subdivision of a *County* which, in the United States, is often divided into elements of 36 square miles each.

Trade deficit – where a country imports more goods than it *Exports*.

Trade surplus – where a country *Exports* more goods than it imports.

Trading blocs – groups of countries who join together for tax-free trading purposes (e.g., the EU).

Transculturation – occurs when two cultures of just about equal power or influence meet and exchange ideas or traits without the domination seen in *Acculturation* and *Assimilation*.

Traditional architecture – traditional building styles of different cultures, religions, and *Places*.

Traditional industries – old heavy industries located where cheap *Energy* (coal) and raw materials (e.g., iron ore) were found.

Transition zone – an area of spatial change where the peripheries of two adjacent realms or regions join; marked by a gradual shift (rather than a sharp break) in the characteristics that distinguish these neighboring geographic entities from one another; see *Zone in transition*.

Toponymy – the study of *Place* names of a region, or toponyms.

Topophilia – love of *Place*.

Total Fertility Rate (TFR) – the number of children that an average woman in a given society has over the course of her childbearing years.

Tourist attractions – *Places* where people travel for interest and pleasure.

Trade – the exchange of goods or services.

Transport – ways of moving people and goods from one *Place* to another.

Transportation – the movement of eroded material by rivers, sea, ice, and wind.

Trans-national corporation (TNC) – large companies which have branch plants throughout the world; their headquarters are often found in MEDCs.

Tribe – a subgroup of people who share unifying cultural characteristics; from a hierarchical standpoint, a tribe falls above the family or clan, but below the level of the nation.

Tributary – a small river which flows into the main river.

True North – the direction which points to the North Pole.

Twilight zone – the term applied to an *Inner-city* area as it begins to change into the *Zone of transition*.

U

UNCLOS – United Nations Convention on the Law of the Sea; a code of maritime law approved by the UN in 1982 that authorizes, among other provisions, territorial waters extending 12 nautical miles from shore and 200-nautical-mile-wide *Exclusive economic zones*.

UNCTAD – the United Nations Conference on Trade and Development; established in 1964, a UN body that provides a forum for developing countries to discuss and promote more favorable international trade arrangements.

Under-class – the new urban poor who are often ill, unemployed, homeless and unqualified.

Underdevelopment – the denial of *Development* to a region, often through a process of active disinvestment from that region or through the "mining" of that region's resources with little economic return to that region; leaves a *Place* with low levels of infrastructure, and the people marginal to the centers of geopolitical and geoeconomic power; the theory of uneven development and the idea of a see-saw motion of *Capital* assumes that underdevelopment in one area is a necessary component of development in another area.

Underemployment – the situation where people do not have full-time, continuous work and are usually only employed temporarily or seasonally (e.g., during the summer months in a hotel).

Unemployment rate – the number of people out of work for each 1,000 of the population.

Uneven development – the geographical expression of *Development* under capitalism, where development in one *Place* is interconnected with underdevelopment in another place; in general, this idea argues that differing areas develop (and under-develop) at differing rates, creating an uneven geographical surface across which *Capital* can move as it seeks the most advantageous location in terms of costs of labor, land, transportation and so forth; see *See-saw motion of capital*.

Unitary state – a state that is dominated by a central government that retains a monopoly on political power; best suited for states with a high degree of internal homogeneity and cohesiveness.

United Nations – established at the end of World War II; the world's principal supranational organization which addresses a multitude of issues concerning the international community

Universalizing – **a** belief system that espouses the idea that there is one true religion that is universal in scope.

Unskilled manual occupations – jobs that require no specific skills.

Urban – large area of houses, *Factories*, etc.

Urban restructuring – the transformation of urban areas through changing strategies of investment, urban renewal, *Gentrification*, changes in welfare or public housing policy and so forth.

Urbanism – a way of life associated with urban areas.

Urbanization – the process by which an increasing percentage of a country's population comes to live in towns and cities. Rapid urbanization is a feature of most LEDCs.

Urban diseconomies – the rising costs to industry as cities increase in size, due to the increasing cost of land and labor, traffic congestion, crime, etc.

Urban Fringe – see *Rural-urban fringe*.

Urban Hierarchy – see *Hierarchy*.

Urban population structure – young males move to urban areas due to push-pull factors; creates a characteristic population pyramid bulge in the 20-35 age range.

Urban redevelopment – the total clearance of parts of old *Inner-city* areas and starting afresh with new houses, especially high-rise apartments.

Urban renewal/regeneration – the improvement of old houses and the addition of *Amenities* in an attempt to bring new life to old *Inner-city* areas.

Urban-rural shift (population) – the movement of people out of towns in MEDCs to seek a better quality of life living in the countryside; some work from home using telecommunications technology; most travel into the *City* each day as commuters, contributing to the rush hour.

Urban-rural shift (industrial) – the movement of industry away from urban areas in recent years due to urban diseconomies, improvements in *Communications* (freeways) and telecommunications (internet/fax/computer links), *Counter-urbanization* (the move of the middle class workforce to small towns and villages) and planning policies (government incentives, new towns, green belts).

Urban sprawl – the unplanned, uncontrolled growth of urban areas into the surrounding countryside.

Use-value – the value in a *Commodity* realized when its owner consumes it; under capitalism, use-value is considerably less important than a commodity's *Exchange-value*.

V

Valley – an area of lowland with slopes either side; a river flows along the lowest part.

Vegetation – all kinds of plants, including shrubs and trees.

Vernacular – the commonly spoken language or *Dialect* of a particular people or *Place*.

Vernacular region – see *Perceptual region*.

Vertical disintegration – the process whereby vertically integrated firms are dismantled and in which there is a greater reliance on "out-sourcing" and sub-contracting in place of services and activities formerly provided by branches within the firm; see *Post-Fordism*.

Vertical integration – a system in which all or most sectors of a production process, from providing raw resources or other inputs and manufacturing to marketing, research, and design, are integrated into a single large firm; contrast with *Vertical disintegration*; see *Primary industry*, *Secondary industry*, *Tertiary industry*, *Quaternary industry* and *Fordism*.

Vineyard – where grapes are grown to make wine.

Virtual reality – the realistic simulation or modeling of *Places* or things using computers; sometimes used to refer to models or representations in general.

Volcano – a cone-shaped mountain made up from lava and ash.

Voluntary cession – the voluntary transfer of territory and its inhabitants from one country to another by agreement, with or without cash or other compensation; although now rare, it was once quite common for sovereign states to transfer territory in this manner.

Voluntary migration – migration by choice; the decision to migrate voluntarily may be influenced both by push factors and pull factors; see *Forced migration*.

Von Thünen model – describes patterns of *Commercial agriculture*; based on *Bid-rent curves*, this model seeks to show why more intensive agriculture is located closer to market centers while *Extensive agriculture* locates farther from those centers; makes a number of simplifying *Assumptions* — such as the assumption of an isotropic plain and rational economic beings — in order to show the importance of land and transportation costs to the geography of commercial agriculture.

W

Warsaw Pact – the 1955 treaty binding the Soviet Union and countries of eastern Europe in an alliance against the North Atlantic Treaty Organization.

Weapons of mass destruction (WMD) – nuclear, biological and chemical (NBC) weapons that are capable of creating very large numbers of casualties, often far removed from the initial point of detonation or dispersal; radiological weapons (dirty bombs) should also be included in this category.

Wet point site – a settlement location where the main advantage is a water supply in an otherwise dry area (e.g., at a spring where an impermeable clay valley meets the foot of permeable limestone or chalk hills).

Wildlife habitats – the homes of plant and animals.

Wholesaling – the sale of goods to retailers; wholesalers are not open to the general public.

Work – employment at a job or occupation; either formal or informal.

Working population – people in employment who have to support the *Dependent population*.

World city (global city) – a *City* that has a high degree of centrality in relation to the world economy; sites for transnational and national corporate headquarters, national and international government institutions and NGOs; major locations for producer services; New York, London and Tokyo are considered the three "top-tier" world cities.

World Trade Organization (WTO) – evolved out of *GATT*; has a permanent secretariat in Geneva; was established to develop a permanent set of rules for facilitating free trade, conducting trade negotiations, resolving trade disputes and enforcing trade regulations.

X

Xenophobia – fear, and hatred of foreigners or foreign influences.

Y

Youthful population – in the population structure of LEDCs, there is often a higher proportion of young people due to high *Birth rates* and a reduction in infant mortality due to better nutrition, education, and medical care; may create problems since the children need feeding, housing, education and eventually a job; medical care and education has to be paid for by taxing a proportionally small number of workers.

Youthful population structure – seen as a wide base on population pyramids that reflect high *Birth rates* in LEDCs.

Z

Zone in transition – the *Inner-city* area around the CBD; a zone of mixed land uses, ranging from car parks and *Derelict* buildings to slums, cafes and older houses, often converted to offices or industrial use.

Zone of peace – a region in which the neighboring countries agree to foster peaceful interaction and resist any efforts by countries from within or outside the region to resort to violence.

Zone of transition – according to the *Concentric zone model* of the *City*, just outside the *Central business district* and is distinguished by active disinvestment (and maybe later *Gentrification*) and land use one would not expect on land that should be relatively highly valued; where one is most likely to find a rent-*Gap*.

Zoning – where industry is separated from residential areas to avoid pollution, traffic *Congestion* etc.; zoned areas are a result of planning.

Zoroastrianism – religion; based on the teachings of the prophet Zoroaster; founded in the early part of the 5th century BCE.

Image Credits

Chapter 1

A small Anasazi dwelling lookout hole offers a view of the mountains of Colorado.
Anasazi Lookout Hole. Jeremy Cantelli. 2013. Flickr.

Sea stacks, such as this Australian one, are the result of countless years of erosion.
Latitudinous. Fraser Mummery. 2011. Flickr.

Precipitation map indicating the estimated rainfall in Puerto Rico and the U.S. Virgin Islands for an anticipated hurricane's passage.
Tropical Storm Bertha Puerto Rico rainfall. National Weather Service. 2014. Wikimedia Commons.

The Bottomley projection, created in 2003, is a less-commonly encountered map.
Bottomley projection SW. Strebe. 2012. Wikipedia.

Map indicating scheduled airline traffic
World airline route map. Jpatokal. 2009. Wikimedia Commons.

Scale model of Paris
My scale model of Paris. Nicholas Jones. 2010. Flickr.

Pyramid graph indicating the 2012 age demographics of Angola
Angola Population Pyramid. Pardee Center, International Futures. 2012. Wikimedia Commons.

The Ozarks: a cultural, architectural, linguistic and geographic region of the U.S.
Ozark Overview. Tosborn. 2006. Wikimedia Commons.

A dashboard-mounted GPS device used for motor vehicle navigation
GPS device. NDrive GPS. 2009. Flickr.

1854 London neighborhood cholera outbreak map
Cholera map. John Snow. 1854. Wikimedia Commons.

Chapter 2

Crowd of Parisian concertgoers
Crowd. James Cridland. 2007. Flickr.

Shaded area represents the boundary of Maryland's 3rd Congressional District, a prime example of gerrymandering.
Maryland's 3rd Congressional District. United States Department of the Interior. 2014. Wikimedia Commons.

2012 population pyramid for Malaysia
Population pyramid Malaysia. Pardee Center, International Futures. 2012. Wikipedia.

Parents pushing their young children in strollers
Babyboom. Norbert Niehusen. 2014. Flickr.

An Amazon Yanomami mother holding her child
Yanomami woman and child. Cmacauley. 1997. Wikimedia Commons.

A Filipino American stands next to his Californian produce stand, 1942
Fruit and vegetable stand on highway operated by Filipino. Dorothea Lange. 1942. Wikimedia Commons.

Saudi women are often regarded as possessing the least rights and autonomy in the world
Veiled Saudi women take photos. Tribes of the world. 2009. Flickr.

Mall food court containing numerous fast food businesses
Canal Walk food court. Henry M. Trotter. 2006. Wikimedia Commons.

Rural Chinese increasingly migrate to urban centers in hopes of securing jobs in more modern industry. Seagate Wuxi China factory tour. Robert Scoble. 2008. Flickr.

18th London cartoonists created the above satirical character Dirty Father Thames to critique the hazardous pollution of the Thames River.
Dirty Father Thames. Punch Magazine. 1848. Wikimedia Commons.

Chinese government sign translates "For a prosperous, powerful nation and a happy family, please practice family planning"
One child policy. Venus. 2006. Wikimedia Commons.

An Alabama billboard reflects the presence of religious tensions and intolerance in the area
Go to church. The Pug Father. 2008. Wikimedia Commons.

Indefinite military conscription, starvation wages and state acts of violence against the civilian population push many Eritreans (such as these refugees) out of their rapidly-depopulating nation.
Ethiopia hosting the most refugees in Africa. Humanitarian Aid and Civil Protection, European Commission. 2016. Flickr.

Syrian refugees in Slovenia largely endeavor to make their final destination Germany.
Syrian refugees and migrants pass through Slovenia. Robert Cotič. 2015. Wikimedia Commons.

A Haymarket strike promotion written in both English and German.
Haymarket newspaper. Chicago Historical Society. 1886. Wikimedia Commons.

Ad promoting the sale of tribal lands likely illegally seized.
Indian land for sale. United States Department of the Interior. 1911. Wikimedia Commons.

Kansas City Irish immigrants, c. 1909
Irish immigrants. Jeanne Boleyn. 1909. Wikimedia Commons.

Chapter 3

Indian practicing yoga on the banks of the Ganges River
Yoga before Ganges in the morning. Nakatani Yoshifumi. 2010. Flickr

A golf course and resort being constructed on the Arabian Peninsula
Golf course. Angus Fraser. 2008. Pixabay.

Shaded, scattered areas of the Republic of Ireland where Gaelic remains the predominantly-spoken language can benefit from the internets' ability to promote community cohesion
Official Gaeltacht regions in Ireland. Angr. 2006. Wikimedia Commons.

Most Commonly Spoken Language Other than English or Spanish.
http://www.slate.com/content/dam/slate/articles/arts/culturebox/2014/05/CBOX_BlattLanguage
_2.jpg.CROP.original-original.jpg

Languages in Europe.
Languages of Europe Map. 2014. Wikimedia Commons.

Religion in Europe
http://i.imgur.com/ejoCW5W.jpg

Spam musubi, a popular local Hawaii dish that evidences the American and Japanese cultural blending
Homemade Spam musubi. Arnold Gatilao. 2015. Flickr.

St. Louis Cathedral in New Orleans, the oldest cathedral in the United States
St. Louis Cathedral. Royalpt78. 2009. Wikimedia Commons.

Silk Road caravan traders
Caravan on the Silk Road. Cresques Abraham. c. 1380. Wikimedia Commons.

Depiction of the Norse god Odin meeting with a vǫlva (female shaman)
Odin and the Völva. Lorenz Frølich. 1895. Wikimedia Commons.

Illustrations from the manuscript Seventy-two Specimens of Castes in India
Seventy-two Specimens of Castes in India. Yale University. 1837. Wikimedia Commons.

Darunaman Mosque in Chiang Rai province
Chiang Rai mosque. Iceway12. 2009. Wikimedia Commons.

World Muslim population by percentage
Islam percent population in each nation world map. M. Tracy Hunter. 2014. Wikimedia Commons.

Buddhist monks gather in front of Angkor Wat in Cambodia
Buddhist monks in front of Angkor Wat. Sam Garza. 2006. Wikimedia Commons.

Batad Rice Terraces
Inside the Batad Rice Terraces. 2012. Wikimedia Commons.

Chapter 4

Modern-day Russian Federation (in black) with regions in white indicating lost territory after the fall of the Soviet Union; Crimea (striped) is currently contested between Russia and Ukraine.
Soviet Union – Russian SFSR. Shadowxfox. 2014. Wikimedia Commons.

Iraqi Kurdistan (in black) in May 2015, with territory controlled (dark and striped) and claimed (light striped) indicated
Iraqi Kurdistan in Iraq (de-facto and disputed hatched). Spesh531, TUBS. Wikimedia Commons.

Painting portraying the ratification of the Treaty of Münster, the primary agreement of the Peace of Westphalia ending the Thirty Years' War.
The Ratification of the Treaty of Münster, 15 May 1648. Gerard ter Borch. 1648. Wikimedia Commons.

Gran Colombia before splitting into Colombia, Ecuador, Panama and Venezuela and losing territory to Brazil and Britain.
Great Colombia. Keepcases. 2009. Wikimedia Commons.

World War II era German map indicating Lebensraum settler routes and destinations
Origins of German colonists resettled during the "Heim ins Reich" action to annexed Polish territories. German Federal Archives. c. 1939-1941. Wikimedia Commons.

Russian soldiers without insignia deployed to wrest control of Crimea away from Ukraine
Crimea soldier military green operation. Chief39. 2014. Pixabay.

View from the Chilean side, the Cristo Redentor pass marks the border with Argentina.
Switchbacks on the road up to Tunel del Cristo Redentor. Karora. 2008. Wikimedia Commons.

Map indicating the exclusive economic zones of the United States (dark shaded) and zones of other nations (light shaded)
Exclusive economic zones of the United States, including insular areas. B1mbo. 2011. Wikimedia Commons.

Map showing the many states that comprise India, the most populous federal state
India States and union territories map. Planemad. 2006. Wikimedia Commons.

Italy, completely two sovereign nations, both San Marino (indicated in magnification) and the Vatican City, is an example of a perforated state
San Marino in Europe. TUBS. 2011. Wikimedia Commons.

With a robust community of international persons and companies, Singapore is considered to very much be a global city of Asia.
Aerial view of the Civic District, Singapore River and Central Business District, Singapore. Jxcacsi. 2008. Wikimedia Commons.

Canada, Mexico and the United States are the member states of NAFTA.
NAFTA. Heraldry. 2009. Wikimedia Commons.

The Balkanization of Georgia can be seen in the breakaway.
regions of Abkhazia and South Ossetia
Georgia high detail. United Nations Cartographic Section. 2008. Wikimedia Commons.

Occupy Wall Street protesters gathered on day 60.
Day 60 Occupy Wall Street. David Shankbone. 2011. Wikimedia Commons.

A Canadian infantry column deployed during the surrender of FLQ members.
Liberation Cell Surrender. JillandJack. 2004. Wikipedia.

The Belgian national soccer team in 2013.
Belgium National Team vs USA. Erik Drost. 2013. Wikimedia Commons.

Chapter 5

In Madhya Pradesh, India, Paleolithic cave painting at the Bhimbetka rock shelters site depict early modern man hunting.
Bhimbetka rock painting. L. R. Burdak. 2005. Wikimedia Commons.

Modern boxed chocolates owe their existence to the processing discoveries of the Aztecs.
Box of chocolate. Petr Kratochvil. 2016. Publicdomainpictures.net.

C. 1310 depiction of English serfs harvesting crops under the supervision of a reeve
Reeve and serfs. Anonymous. c. 1310. Wikimedia Commons.

Indian farmer working the fields with an ox-driven plow
India farming. Ananth B. S. 2005. Wikimedia Commons.

Due to climate and growing season limitations, many regions must import a portion of their produce
Produce truck. David Arpi. 2007. Flickr.

Small dairy farm
Dairy farm with red barn in autumn. U.S. Department of Agriculture. 2016. Flickr.

Farmer using a McCormick Reaper in the Boise Valley, Idaho
Boise Valley wheat field. Anonymous. c. 1920. Wikimedia Commons.

Depiction of a traditional Iroquois longhouse
The Iroquois longhouse. Wilbur F. Gordy. 1913. Wikipedia.

Budapest was united into a single city in 1873
Budapest bridge landscape scenic outside river. Tpsdave. 2016. Pixabay.

Vendors and customers at a farmers' market in Boston, Massachusetts
Greater Boston – Boston, City Hall, farmers' market. Massachusetts Office of Travel and Tourism. 2013. Flickr.

An abandoned building in Kolmanskop, Namibia is increasingly claimed by advancing sands
Kolmanskop. Michiel van Balen. 2009. Flickr.

GMO Kenyan corn (maize) field
Kenyans examining insect-resistant transgenic Bt corn. Dave Hoisington. 2003. Wikimedia Commons.

Chickens allowed to move around in a free-range environment
Eggmobile and flock of chickens at Polyface Farm. Jessica Reeder. 2010. Wikimedia Commons.

Fish farm management in Shanghai
Managing fish harm, Jian De, Hangzhou, Shanghai. Ivan Walsh. 2009. Flickr.

Packaged red meats
Ground beef, pork and veal. U.S. Department of Agriculture. 2011. Flickr.

Female farmer working the field
A Kenyan farmer at work in the Mount Kenya region. Neil Palmer, International Center for Tropical Agriculture. 2010. Flickr.

Chapter 6

Early factory in the Kingdom of Saxony featuring machinery invented by Richard Hartmann
Hartmann machine hall. 1868. Wikimedia Commons

Children cotton mill workers
Interior of Magnolia Cotton Mill's spinning room. Lewis Hine. 1911. Wikimedia Commons

Boeing airplane factory in Everett, Washington
At Boeing's Everett factory near Seattle. Jetstar Airways. 2013. Wikimedia Commons

Shipping by sea is typically the cheapest method of transporting goods and materials
Cosco Vancouver. Jeurgen Lehle. 2007. Wikimedia Commons

Canadian log boom operations in Gold River, British Columbia
God River logging. Tim Gage. 2007. Flickr

Women professionals taking part in a panel discussion
Panel discussion. Randstad Canada. 2012. Flickr

Coal abundant regions in Britain that helped sustain industrialization
British coalfields. Notuncurious. 2009. Wikimedia Commons.

At the height of European colonial power in the 1890s, France, Great Britain, the Netherlands, Germany and Russia were part of the primary core
Europe 1890. Hermann Julius Meyer. 1892. Wikimedia Commons.

2007, a Kathmandu street suffering from inadequate garbage collection
Loads of garbage on the streets. Miran Rijavec. 2007. Flickr.

The Global Goals for Sustainable Development
http://www.un.org/sustainabledevelopment/sustainable-development-goals/.

Thai female vendor selling food outside a temple complex
Huay Kaew waterfall grill. Takeaway. 2010. Wikimedia Commons.

Minnesota fast food workers protest for higher wages and other benefits in 2015
Strike and a protest march for a $15 minimum wage in Dinkytown. Fibonacci Blue. 2015. Flickr.

Nations worst affected by the 1998 East Asian Financial Crisis
Asian Financial Crisis. Bluej100. 2009. Wikimedia Commons.

Call center positions have increasingly become outsourced as globalization continues
Contact center two agents. Diana Varisova. 2013. Wikimedia Commons.

Activism against neoliberal economic policy has been growing in many countries
Stop neoliberalism. Davius. 2006. Wikimedia Commons.

Highly-contended elections can influence politicians to focus too heavily on the short-term
Election. Rama. 2007. Wikimedia Commons.

Chapter 7

The ruins of Eridu in Iraq are believed by many to mark the location of the world's oldest city
Eridu. Tais Gilo. 2011. Wikimedia Commons.

Lower Manhattan with its many docks in 1931
Manhattan. U.S. National Archives. 1931. Wikimedia Commons.

The Dharavi area of Mumbai is Asia's second largest slum
Dharavi slum in Mumbai. Kounosu. 2008. Wikimedia Commons.

1648 Nuremberg city layout, areas outside the city walls being considered the hinterlands
Map of Nuremberg. Martin Zeiller. 1656. Wikimedia Commons.

As both the capital and fourth largest city in China, Beijing exerts strong influence well beyond its administrative boundary
Wangfujing Street, Beijing. Nggsc. 2008. Wikimedia Commons.

Detroit in 1942, still a thriving community before job loss, crime and urban decay set in
Detroit skyline. Arthur Siegel. 1942. Wikimedia Commons.

The Brazilian Rocinha slum in Rio de Janeiro (foreground) bordering upscale high-rise buildings just across the highway
Rocinha Brazil slums. Alicia Nijdam. 2008. Wikimedia Commons.

The 2007 collapse of the I-35W Mississippi River bridge in Minneapolis represents catastrophic infrastructure failure and construction negligence.
I35W collapse, day 4, operations & scene. Kevin Rofidal, United States Coast Guard. 2007. Wikimedia Commons.

England's designated green belt areas
The metropolitan green belt among the green belts of England. Hellerick. 2013. Wikimedia Commons.

The 1960s civil rights movement helped open political doors for people of color
1963 March on Washington. Rowland Scherman. 1963. Wikimedia Commons.

Political theorist and author Benjamin Barber
Benjamin R Barber. Erich Habich. 2010. Wikimedia Commons.

Harlem in 1943, a black cultural center
Street scene Harlem. Roger Smith. 1943. Wikimedia Commons.

London community activists resist ongoing gentrification
Broadway market occupation. Targuin Binary. 2006. Wikimedia Commons.

Los Angeles suburban sprawl
South Los Angeles Normandie and Western Avenue aerial view from north. Alfred Twu. 2014. Wikimedia Commons.

Abandoned since 1958, the Packard Automotive Plant still stands undeveloped in Detroit
Abandoned Packard Automotive Factory Detroit. Albert Duce. 2009. Wikimedia Commons.

We want to hear from you

Your feedback is important to us because we strive to provide the highest quality prep materials. Email us any comments or suggestions.

info@sterling–prep.com

Customer Satisfaction Guarantee

Contact us to resolve any issues to your satisfaction.

*We reply to all emails – **check your spam folder***

Thank you for choosing our products to achieve your educational goals!

AP prep books by Sterling Test Prep

- AP Chemistry Practice Questions
- AP Chemistry Review
- AP Physics 1 Practice Questions
- AP Physics 1 Review
- AP Physics 2 Practice Questions
- AP Physics 2 Review
- AP Biology Practice Questions
- AP Biology Review

- AP Psychology
- AP European History
- AP World History
- AP U.S. History
- AP U.S. Government and Politics
- AP Comparative Government and Politics
- AP Environmental Science

SAT Subject Test prep books by Sterling Test Prep

- SAT Chemistry Practice Questions
- SAT Chemistry Review
- SAT Biology Practice Questions
- SAT Biology Review
- SAT Physics Practice Questions
- SAT Physics Review
- SAT U.S. History
- SAT World History

Your purchase helps support global environmental causes

Sterling Test Prep is committed to protecting our planet by supporting environmental organizations for conservation, ecological research, and preservation of vital natural resources. A portion of our profits is donated to help these organizations continue their critical missions.

 The Ocean Conservancy advocates for a healthy ocean with sustainable solutions based on science and cleanup efforts.

 The Rainforest Trust saves critical lands for conservation through land purchases and protected area designations in over 16 countries.

Pacific Whale Foundation saves whales from extinction and protects our oceans through science and advocacy.

AP Biology, Chemistry and Physics 1 & 2 online practice tests at www.Sterling–Prep.com

Our advanced online testing platform allows you to take AP science practice questions on your computer to generate a Diagnostic Report for each test.

By using our online AP tests and Diagnostic Reports, you will:

- Assess your knowledge of topics tested on the AP exam
- Identify your areas of strength and weakness
- Learn important scientific topics and concepts
- Improve your test-taking skills

To access the online AP science tests at a special pricing visit:
http://AP.Sterling–Prep.com/bookowner.htm

Made in United States
Orlando, FL
17 August 2022

21148558R00207